TESTIMONIALS

Having worked with missionaries as a counselor in two mission presidencies and having served as a missionary in South America, I understand that conversion comes from the Holy Ghost, the Book of Mormon and from the testimony of others. However, many times people investigating the Gospel have sincere questions and look for answers from their Bible. Michael Grant has put together a masterful reference book that will enlighten and answer most, if not all of their questions. This is a wonderful tool, and I highly recommend it to our missionaries, those attending mission prep classes, and anyone who has a neighbor, friend or contact that wants to discuss religion.

> John H. Burgon
> First counselor, California Carlsbad Mission

I think the book is amazing! Learning what Bible verses other Christian faiths use to support what they believe and teach, and those Bible verses which are often neglected or ignored that further explain the topic being discussed, has made it so much easier for me to make connections as to what is really being taught. I found it helpful in my understanding of how the Bible and the Book of Mormon complement each other. I think anyone serving a mission or preparing to go on a mission should have access to this book. It will help them be prepared to build on common ground when talking and teaching to people investigating the church. Amazing book, amazing author! Would you please send me another book; I have a friend going on her mission and she wants this book! I want to give it to her as a gift.

> Elder Bret Wilson
> California Carlsbad Mission

Mike, our discussions and your book have made me really think. We as Latter-Day Saints seem to have forgotten the value of the Bible. I want to refocus and gain a better understanding of the value of the Bible: the first witness of Jesus Christ.

> Kevin D. Moffett
> Ordinance worker, San Diego Temple

Michael Grant's book helped me to solidify my understanding of the truths that I already had a testimony of. The book helped me to develop my understanding and appreciation of the Bible as well as increase my ability to teach from it. I recommend it for all LDS missionaries regardless of where they are serving. Thanks for all you did for me Brother Grant!

Elder Shiloh Mangus
California Carlsbad Mission

I didn't realize how poor my Bible knowledge was until I went on my mission. I was struggling at first trying to teach using only the Book of Mormon. My mission was in Texas and the people I was talking with were all Bible-educated Christians. When they would present to me a scripture from the Bible supporting their belief or the teaching of their church, I didn't know a Bible scripture to answer them with. My mission did not begin to take off until I learned to teach from the Bible first and then introduce Book of Mormon scripture. I wish I had this book before I went on my mission.

Chris Morgan
Returned missionary

Brother Grant, I loved this book! I now understand the gospel so much more because I have studied the Bible through this book. I have been able to answer my own questions as well as others'. It has helped my testimony of the Book of Mormon as I have been able to see how they work together and testify of each other. This book is AMAZING! Thank you so much!

Sister Danielle Marie Dean
California Carlsbad Mission

Bible Verses Every Successful LDS Missionary Needs to Know, by Michael Grant, is a very helpful resource for teachers, full-time, and member missionaries. Michael's exhaustive research combined with insightful commentary can help anyone navigate most every gospel topic in the Old and New Testaments. Every member of the church should be well versed in the Bible, and this wonderful book makes that lofty goal more achievable.

Richard Whittier
President, Murrieta California Stake

BIBLE
VERSES

EVERY
SUCCESSFUL
LDS MISSIONARY
NEEDS TO KNOW

MICHAEL GRANT

CFI
An imprint of Cedar Fort, Inc.
Springville, Utah

ISBN 13: 978-1-4621-2209-7

Published by CFI, an imprint of Cedar Fort, Inc.
2373 W. 700 S., Springville, UT 84663
Distributed by Cedar Fort, Inc., www.cedarfort.com

LIBRARY OF CONGRESS CATALOGING-IN-PUBLICATION DATA

Names: Grant, Michael, 1948 June 21 — author.
Title: Bible verses every successful missionary needs to know / Michael Grant.
Description: Springville, Utah : CFI, an imprint of Cedar Fort, Inc., [2018]
  | Includes bibliographical references and index.
Identifiers: LCCN 2018005254 (print) | LCCN 2018007179 (ebook) | ISBN
  9781462129133 (epub, pdf, mobi) | ISBN 9781462122097 (perfect bound : alk.
  paper)
Subjects: LCSH: Church of Jesus Christ of Latter-day Saints--Sacred
  books--Quotations. | Mormon Church--Sacred books--Quotations. |
  Bible--Quotations. | Mormon missionaries--Religious life.
Classification: LCC BX8661 (ebook) | LCC BX8661 .G73 2018 (print) | DDC
  289.3/2--dc23
LC record available at https://lccn.loc.gov/2018005254

Cover design by Shawnda T. Craig
Cover design © 2018 Cedar Fort, Inc.

Printed in the United States of America

10 9 8 7 6 5 4 3 2 1

Printed on acid-free paper

Bible Verses Every Successful LDS Missionary Needs to Know, by Michael Grant, is a collection of scriptures with his own annotations that provides an excellent companion for any scripture study. Although Michael's focus is to help missionaries find connections between the teachings of the Bible and those of the Book of Mormon, I found the collection especially interesting as a general study tool. Michael's commentary is also helpful because he has both the perspective of one who deeply understands LDS teachings and one who derived his initial understanding of Christianity solely from the Bible and traditional interpretations of it. I strongly recommend his work to anyone who enjoys studying scripture.

Matthew Bradford
Bishop, seminary teacher

This is a great book. I have been able to answer my own questions and the questions of those I teach as I've studied the specific topics in the book. Surprisingly, I've been able to connect with those who have great knowledge of the Bible rather than "bashing."

Elder Erik Robert Kapp
California Carlsbad Mission

I wish I had this book before I went on my mission to Ecuador. It didn't take me long to discover that I needed to teach first from the Bible. My first companion asked me, "How's your knowledge of the Bible?" He could tell from the look on my face that the answer was "not very good." He then said to me, "Learn the Bible and teach every lesson from it." Was he ever right. All of us missionaries in Ecuador learned very quickly that we had to teach from the Bible before we could teach from the Book of Mormon. Once we showed them scriptures from the Bible supporting what we were teaching, they were willing to listen to Book of Mormon scripture.

Elder Cason Flygare
Returned missionary

I'm grateful for the opportunity to pen this testimonial. Michael Grant has been able to identify the major topics associated with the differences in Christian doctrine that exists within the thousands of different Christian denominations, and to identify the Bible scriptures that support Book of Mormon doctrine. He has carefully articulated the connection between the scriptures used by non-Mormons to disprove Mormon doctrine, and the Biblical references that prove the Book of Mormon doctrines to be correct.

In this very helpful work, Michael has given some great tools to the full-time missionaries as they meet with members of other denominations and discuss opposite views. He wisely suggests that the book is not designed to assist in "Bible bashing," but instead, to have thoughtful, respectful discussions guided by the Spirit.

Larry Dean
Senior Missionary Coordinator SRS
California San Diego Region

This book is dedicated to the many returned and active missionaries who have contributed their requests, suggestions, experiences, and knowledge; to the missionaries currently serving throughout the world; and to the future missionaries who will be teaching Heavenly Father's children.

Wherefore the Lord said, Forasmuch as this people draw near me with their mouth, and with their lips do honour me, but have removed their heart far from me, and their fear toward me is taught by the precept of men:

Therefore, behold, I will proceed to do a marvellous work among this people, even a marvellous work and a wonder: for the wisdom of their wise men shall perish, and the understanding of their prudent men shall be hid. **(Isaiah 29:13–14)**

CONTENTS

PREFACE

A QUESTION OF FAITH

HOW WOULD YOU FEEL IF PROOF WERE GIVEN THAT WHAT YOU BELIEVE IS WRONG?

This could be about any belief: the Earth is flat, the sun revolves around the Earth, the astronauts never really went to the moon. There really are people who believe these things.

Would you ignore it? Would you fight it? Would you deny it? Would you thoroughly investigate it? Would you allow yourself to learn from it? Would you joyfully grow and benefit from it? Would you accept it?

For example, let's say you were in a car, traveling for the first time to a place you had never been before. A friend you trust has given you directions on how to get to where you are going. You have a road map, but you have not taken the time to check it carefully because you trusted the friend who gave you directions, sincerely believing the way he directed you is correct.

After traveling for a few hours, you stop at a service station for gas. While filling your fuel tank the station attendant asks you where you are from and where you are traveling to. After you tell him, he informs you that you are going in the wrong direction, and that you are hundreds of miles off course.

Now concerned you pull out your map. The station attendant, by referring to your own map, shows you that you are on the wrong road, and going in the wrong direction.

What would you do? Would your pride or stubbornness prevent you from admitting that you are on the wrong road and going in the wrong direction? Would you refuse to further examine the map because it would mean that you would have to make a change in the direction you are traveling to get on the right road? Or would you gladly accept the news and get on the right road?

Well then, if you were to learn from an examination of your Bible that you are traveling on a wrong religious road, that what you have been taught and believe is wrong; would you be willing to let go of what you had been taught and make the change?

A very wise Professor Dumbledore once said to a very troubled Harry Potter: "Harry, sooner or later you are going to have to make a decision between doing what is easy, and what is right."[1]

This is a decision that we all have to make regarding everything we do in life. Because every decision we make, or do not make, comes with either rewards or consequences. If we are happy with the consequences, then we don't need to do anything. But . . . if we want the rewards, then we must thoroughly examine and investigate everything, so that we can make informed and intelligent decisions that will keep us on the correct road.

Each of us, no matter which Christian faith we may belong to, must be willing to take off the blinders of our faith, to research and understand what other Christian faiths believe and teach, and to compare those teachings to the Holy Bible. We must discover for ourselves . . . is my church teaching what Jesus Christ and His Apostles taught? Or is my church teaching the philosophies of men mingled with scripture?

The decision to research, discover, and embrace the truth about God, who He is, who we are, His church, and what the Bible really teaches, is important for a very simple reason: eternity is an awfully long time to be wrong! This is why a true and complete knowledge about God is so critical.

INTRODUCTION

WHO – WHAT – WHEN WHERE – WHY – AND HOW?

I was raised in a family that was Roman Catholic and Presbyterian, educated in Catholic schools, and eventually preparing to become a Catholic priest. Discovering and converting to the Church of Jesus Christ of Latter-Day Saints (more on this later), was a challenge both for me and for those teaching me. My Christian education was entirely based on Biblical scriptures, as is the case for the vast majority of investigators and converts to the LDS Church. What the Mormon missionaries and my LDS friends were teaching me about their faith needed to be substantiated first by the Bible, before I was going to accept any scripture(s) from the Book of Mormon. And I wasn't going to make it easy on them!

Fortunately for me and unfortunately for them, (or so I thought), the missionaries had to scramble to find the Bible scriptures needed to backup their teachings from the Book of Mormon. They knew their Book of Mormon scriptures well, but their knowledge of Biblical scripture . . . needed some help.

Fortunately for them, and not realized by me, they knew someone who did know his Bible, and they brought him along with them for each and every lesson after the first one. Did I mention that I wasn't going to make it easy on them? This guy really knew his Bible! He had a Bible scripture to show me for every one that I presented to him supporting what I had been taught as a Catholic. Fortunately for me, as I was to eventually learn, he wasn't going to make it easy on me either. After having been shown the Bible scriptures supporting LDS doctrines and teachings, the lessons being taught to me began to make sense and were easier to accept. I was on my way to becoming a "Mormon" and I didn't even know it.

Now the big questions that haunted me were "Why isn't my church teaching me these things?" and "Why is my church ignoring these other Bible scriptures?"

I was now on a one-year quest to find, if it existed, the one true church, with priesthood authority, teaching what Jesus Christ and His Apostles taught the early Christians. This meant studying not only what the Mormon missionaries were teaching me but everything I could learn about other Christian faiths, and the history of the Christian Church. Sifting facts and truth from man-made philosophy and doctrine, was a monumental task for an eighteen-year-old aspiring to be a Catholic priest. My entire belief system about God was at risk.

I was, and still very much am, one of those people who does not make decisions based on emotion or good feelings. I wanted all the facts and truth I could find before I was going to make any changes, and I was determined to find them. It wasn't going to be easy giving up that Roman collar.

I studied every mainstream and non-mainstream Christian faith and movement I could find; Baptist, Pentecostal, Presbyterian, Quaker, Methodist, Jehovah's Witness, Christian Science, Amish, Mennonite, Lutheran, Salvation Army, Evangelical and Fundamental churches, just to name a few.

I studied the teachings of the Protestant Reformers; John Wycliff, John Huss, Martin Luther, Huldreich Zwingli, John Calvin, John Knox, and others. I learned about "Sola Scriptura," the belief in the sole authority of Scripture alone; "Sola Fide," the belief that we are saved by faith alone; "Sola Gratia," saved by the grace of God alone; and the "Priesthood of All Believers," the belief that all believers are priests before God, that there is no God-ordained and set-apart priesthood.

When I was done with all this research, along with sore knees and more prayer than I thought any God could listen to . . . there was no longer any doubt in my mind and soul; I knew that I had found the one true church, the church originally established by Jesus Christ.

What my conversion to the LDS faith—later working with missionaries, teaching investigators, and my discussions with other converts to the church—has taught me is that the non-members we may be talking to, need to be shown Bible scriptures supporting LDS teachings and doctrines, before they will accept scripture(s) from the Book of Mormon.

This was also confirmed to me multiple times by returning missionaries when they commented, "My mission success didn't take off until I learned to first teach from the Bible. Once these Bible educated and believing people were shown supporting Biblical scripture, scripture from the Book of Mormon and LDS doctrine were much easier for them to accept."

As any current or return missionary will tell you; quite often when discussing Christian doctrine and teachings with someone not of our faith, the individual not of our faith will often present a scripture from the Bible to substantiate, prove, or defend what they believe. Often, we individually, or our missionaries, don't know of or can't think of an appropriate Bible scripture to present to them that further answers or explains that doctrine or teaching correctly.

Over the years many of our missionaries have come to me asking for a Bible scripture that can be used to answer or clarify a scripture from the Bible presented to them by someone they were talking to. Sometimes the missionaries were approached by someone on a mission to "Bible-Bash" and prove our missionaries and the LDS church wrong. It became all too obvious; our missionaries were

Biblically challenged. Their Biblical knowledge needed to be improved or they were going to continue to lose good potential converts.

This, then, is the purpose of this book, to provide a quick and easy topical reference and study guide with the appropriate Bible scriptures and notes, to help answer those sincere questions and disarm those who are slinging mean-spirited arrows, and allow the spirit to soften hearts.

This book is a supplement to and not a replacement for "Preach My Gospel." As a missionary or teacher, it is first and foremost important that you study, know, and teach from "Preach My Gospel." It is also important to understand that there will be those times when the missionary or member teacher will need to step back, and let the Spirit guide them to fulfill the needs of the individual being taught, and to comfort and change the heart of the slinger of the poison arrows.

My purpose in writing this book is not to prove or disprove any one Christian denomination or faith, as there are literally thousands of them. My purpose is to demonstrate what the Bible really says, what Jesus Christ and His Apostles really did teach the early Christians; and what man has done to change and/or manipulate those teachings. Or in other words, what "philosophies of men" have been "mingled with scripture."[1]

With literally thousands of Christian denominations teaching something different about the same God the Father, His Son Jesus Christ, and the Holy Ghost; they can't all be correct, they can't all be teaching the truth; if they were, they would all be teaching the same thing and there would be only one Church.

These Christian churches all interpret the Holy Bible differently. Yet the Bible they are using tells us that "no prophecy of the scripture is of any private interpretation," (2 Peter 1:20), and that "God is not the author of confusion" (1 Corinthians 14:33), but of order. The Apostle Paul teaches us, "Now this I say, that every one of you saith, I am of Paul; and I of Apollos; and I of Cephas; and I of Christ. Is Christ divided? Was Paul crucified for you? Or were ye baptized in the name of Paul?" (1 Corinthians 1:12–18). The Apostle Paul is teaching the Corinthians that Paul did not start the Church of Paul, that Apollos did not start the Church of Apollos, and that Cephas did not start the Church of Cephas. That "Christ is not divided," that there is only one Christian church: The Church of Jesus Christ. And that all these churches should be teaching the same doctrine. This, too, applies to our day.

An internet search for Christian denominations will reveal that there are over 30,000 different denominations! That's 30,000 different Christian faiths that don't agree with each other, teaching different doctrines and beliefs about the same God. If this isn't confusion . . . what is?

How is anyone who is seeking "knowledge and truth" supposed to find a (the) church that is teaching the teachings and doctrines of Jesus Christ correctly? How is anyone supposed to find the true Christianity as taught by the Savior and His Apostles? This also, is what this book is about.

In each chapter, I will present Bible scriptures used by many Christian churches to substantiate their teachings, when and where I am aware of them. Then we will examine additional scriptures from the Bible that demonstrate that those scriptures being presented by them are, (1) being misinterpreted, (2) being misused, or (3) being purposely ignored for one reason or another, that further explain or clarify the doctrine or teaching. All scripture quotes will be from the King James Version of the Bible unless otherwise noted. The King James Version was chosen because it is the most popular version of the bible in the Christian world.

This book is written primarily for missionaries and teachers of the Church of Jesus Christ of Latter-Day Saints. It is not meant to be a comprehensive work designed to be read by those who are not members of the LDS Church in an attempt to convert them to our faith. Another companion book will be written for this purpose. Therefore, scriptures will be shown along with only short notes, when and where necessary, meant to help missionaries or teachers in their efforts to understand and teach from the Bible.

However, if you are not a member of The Church of Jesus Christ of Latter-Day Saints and are reading this book, and you too have the same questions that I did after talking with the church's missionaries, (i.e. "Why isn't my church teaching me these things? Why is my church ignoring these Bible scriptures"?), please seek out the church's missionaries, listen to what they have to teach you, then pray to our Heavenly Father that His messenger the Holy Ghost, will manifest the truthfulness of these things to you. As the Bible teaches us, *"If any of you lack wisdom, let him ask of God*, that giveth to *all men* liberally, and upbraideth not; and it shall be given him. *But let him ask in faith, nothing wavering.* For he that wavereth is like a wave of the sea driven with the wind and tossed." (James 1:5–6, emphasis added). A pure and honest heart searching for the truth will find it, I promise.

This work is meant for educational and teaching purposes only. Please do not use it for the purpose of "Bible Bashing" or attacking any person's faith, convictions, or church. Use it only for teaching with the Holy Spirit. When an investigator presents you with a Bible scripture, please, don't dispute or attack him or her with another, and by all means, do not argue. No one will learn in a hostile environment, it will only chase away the spirit. Instead, politely acknowledge the scripture and then present another scripture from the Bible and ask, "Have you thought about this scripture"? Hand them your Bible and let them read the scripture out loud to you; then ask them what the scripture means to them. Then if necessary, explain the scripture to them. All discussions should always be with love, compassion, and understanding.

MWG

FOREWORD

HOW THIS BOOK WORKS

Each chapter will begin with the following paragraph below, the first sentence in italicized **bold** type, followed by the appropriate scriptures in normal non-bold type. The scriptures listed will be those that have been presented by members of various faiths while discussing the subject matter, and/or scriptures discovered while researching the beliefs of various Christian faiths.

Scriptures used by some Christian faiths to substantiate their belief and teaching that [the title of the chapter, i.e. ("Baptism for the Dead"), or comments on their belief]:

Followed by a few of the scriptures used by these Christian faiths to promote their beliefs.

Below is an example from the chapter titled "Baptism for the Dead."

Scriptures used by some Christian faiths to substantiate their belief and teaching regarding Baptism for the Dead; that those who did not hear of Christ and His teachings before death, and those who are not baptized, are doomed:

"Now that the dead are raised, even Moses shewed at the bush, when he calleth the Lord the God of Abraham, and the God of Isaac, and the God of Jacob. For he is not a God of the dead, but of the living: for all live unto him." **(Luke 20:37–38)**

"For the living know that they shall die: but the dead know not any thing, neither have they any more a reward; for the memory of them is forgotten." **(Ecclesiastes 9:5)**

The next section is titled **"Now the Rest of the Story . . . ,"** which will show additional Bible scriptures that provide further clarification and understanding on the subject. These scriptures may also be those many Christian faiths choose to ignore, or do not teach in conjunction about he subject in order to promote their teaching or doctrine. This section may also have "***Notes***" following the scripture. The important part or parts of each scripture in this section, as it applies to the topic, will be italicized for emphasis.

Below is an example from the chapter titled "Baptism for the Dead."

Now the Rest of the Story . . . (scriptures that further explain or clarify the topic)

"For to this end Christ both died, and rose, and revived, that he might be *Lord both of the dead and living*." **(Romans 14:9)**

"Else what shall they do which are *baptized for the dead*, if the dead rise not at all? Why are they then baptized for the dead?" **(1 Corinthians 15:29)**

"Verily, verily, I say into the, *Except a man be born of water and of the Spirit, "he cannot enter into the kingdom of God*." **(John 3:5)**

"*For, this cause was a gospel preaching to them that are dead, that they might be judged according to men in the flesh*, but live according to God in the spirit." **(1 Peter 4:6)**

Sometimes you will see a "Note" following a scripture verse. The purpose of this "Note" is to further enhance the understanding of the verse.

Now see a full example for the chapter titled "Baptism for the Dead."

Baptism for the Dead

Scriptures used by some Christian faiths to substantiate their belief and teaching regarding Baptism for the Dead; that those who did not hear of Christ and His teachings before death, and that those who are not baptized are doomed:

"Now that the dead are raised, even Moses shewed at the bush, when he calleth the Lord the God of Abraham, and the God of Isaac, and the God of Jacob. *For he is not a God of the dead, but of the living*: for all live unto him." (**Luke 20:37–38**)

"For the living know that they shall die: but the dead know not any thing, neither have they any more a reward; for the memory of them is forgotten." (**Ecclesiastes 9:5**)

NOW THE REST OF THE STORY . . . (scriptures that further explain or clarify the topic)

"For to this end Christ both died, and rose, and revived, that he might be *Lord both of the dead and living.*" (**Romans 14:9**)

"Else what shall they do which are *baptized for the dead*, if the dead rise not at all? Why are they then baptized for the dead?" (**1 Corinthians 15:29**)

"Verily, verily, I say into the, *Except a man be born of water and of the Spirit, "he cannot enter into the kingdom of God."* (**John 3:5**)

"For, this cause was a gospel preaching to them that are dead, that they might be judged according to men in the flesh, but live according to God in the spirit." (**1 Peter 4:6**)

"For Christ also hath once suffered for sins, the just for the unjust, that he might bring us to God, being put to death in the flesh, but quickened by the Spirit: By which *he went and preached unto the spirits in prison*: Which sometimes are disobedient, when once the long-suffering of God waited in the days of Noah, while the ark was preparing, wherein few, that is, eight souls were saved by water." (**1 Peter 3:18–20**)

> *Note: Why would Christ, during the three days he was dead and before his resurrection, go to the "spirits in prison" and preach to them? Answer: because they cannot be judged for something they knew nothing about. They needed to be given knowledge of Christ and the gospel.*

"Therefore my heart is glad, and my glory rejoices: my flesh also show rest in hope. For thou wilt not leave my soul in hell; neither will thou suffer Thine Holy One to see corruption." (**Psalms 16:9–10**)

"God having provided some better thing for us, that *they [the dead] without us should not be made perfect.*" (**Hebrews 11:40**)

> *Note: The dead cannot be made perfect unless the living perform this required ordinance for them. A better understanding will come from reading the entire chapter (Hebrews 11). Italicized words in brackets [ ] added by the author for clarification and understanding.*

Before You Teach . . .

Before you meet with an investigator to teach a lesson, review the chapters in this book that apply to the lesson you will be teaching. Review the "Preach My Gospel" lesson and determine which Bible scriptures you may want to use for that lesson.

Remember, the person you are teaching is more than likely unfamiliar with the Book of Mormon or may have negative beliefs about it. When you show a scripture or two from the Bible before you use Book of Mormon scriptures, the investigator is more likely to accept or listen to Book of Mormon scripture. You are showing the investigator that the Bible and the Book of Mormon teach the same principles and doctrines.

Review the scriptures listed in the beginning of the chapter that show you the scriptures you may be presented with by the investigator to substantiate the teaching of his or her church regarding the subject to be taught. It is always good to know what scriptures may be presented to you.

Next, review the scriptures in the "**Now the Rest of the Story . . .** (scriptures that further explain or clarify the topic)" section of the chapter to prepare yourself with the scriptures you may need to use demonstrating LDS doctrine from the Bible. You may even want to number them in the order you would like to present them to the person(s) you are teaching. You may even want to list these Bible scriptures in your copy of "Preach My Gospel," in the order you want to use them.

With some investigators, you may only need to show them one scripture from the Bible, for others you will more than likely have to show them multiple Bible scriptures. Showing multiple Bible scriptures helps to strengthen their understanding of the doctrine or principle.

When you show someone a Bible scripture always let them read the scripture out loud to you. Don't read it to them. And then ask them to tell you what their understanding of the scripture is. If they are having difficulty understanding the scripture, explain it to them. Don't move on to another topic until they fully understand the one you are teaching.

When the investigator shows positive excitement and understanding about the scriptures you have been showing them, get excited for them, praise their understanding, encourage them to talk about how they feel.

Always carry this book with you. Refer to it as often as needed. Don't worry about pulling it out to look something up when an investigator asks you a question that you can't remember a Bible scripture for. Eventually, the time will come when your Bible knowledge will be to the point that you won't have to refer to the book anymore.

BEFORE YOU TEACH USING THIS BOOK

1. Read Appendix C: A New Approach to Teaching.
2. If you are preparing to go on a mission;
   - Role Play with a classmate.
   - Role Play with a family member or friend.
3. If you are on your mission Role Play with your companion(s).
4. Remember, as in developing any skill, "practice makes perfect."

HOW TO ROLE PLAY USING THIS BOOK

Choose a chapter subject. Have your companion play the part of the investigator and present you with a Bible verse from the first part of the chapter, "Scriptures used by some Christian faiths to substantiate their belief and teaching." You will then play the part of the missionary, using the Bible verses in the second part of the chapter, "Now the Rest of the Story . . . (scriptures that further explain or clarify the topic)," to respond the Bible verse presented to you.

You can also have your companion present you with a question. You will then locate the chapter for that question or topic and answer the question with the appropriate Bible verse.

Study any notes that may come right after a Bible verse. These notes will help you understand and explain the verse you are using.

This book is meant to be used freely. Write notes in the margins. Highlight parts of the scriptures that will apply to your investigators or to yourself. This is *your* resource to be used in any way that will benefit your study and teaching of the Bible.

Chapter 1

ACCOUNTABILITY

"For we must all appear before the judgment seat of Christ; that every one may receive the things done in his body, according to that he hath done, whether it be good or bad." **(2 Corinthians 5:10)**

What does it mean to be "held accountable"? Webster's Dictionary defines *accountable* as "subject to having to report, explain or justify; being answerable, being responsible." Notice how the definition begins with the words "subject to," implying little choice in the matter. Let's take a look at what the Bible tells us about being accountable.

ACCOUNTABILITY

Scriptures used by some Christian faiths to substantiate their belief and teaching that there will be no "accountability":

"That whosoever believeth in him should not perish, but have eternal life." **(John 3:15)**

"He that believeth and is baptized shall be saved; but he that believeth not shall be damned." **(Mark 16:16)**

"Verily, verily, I say unto you, He that heareth my word, and believeth on him that sent me, hath everlasting life, and shall not come into condemnation; but is passed from death unto life." **(John 5:24)**

"That if thou shalt confess with thy mouth the Lord Jesus, and shalt believe in thine heart that God hath raised him from the dead, thou shalt be saved." **(Romans 10:9)**

"For whosoever shall call upon the name of the Lord shall be saved." **(Romans 10:13)**

"But we believe that through the grace of the Lord Jesus Christ we shall be saved, even as they." **(Acts 15:11)**

NOW THE REST OF THE STORY . . . (scriptures that further explain or clarify the topic)

"So then every one of us shall *give account of himself to God*." **(Romans 14:12)**

"And I saw the dead, small and great, stand before God; and the books were opened: and another book was opened, which is the book of life: and *the dead were judged out of those things which were written in the books, according to their works*. And the sea gave up the dead which were in it; and death and hell delivered up the dead which were in them: and they were judged every man according to their works." **(Revelation 20:12–15)**

"For we must all appear before the judgment seat of Christ; *that every one may receive the things done in his body*, according to that he hath done, *whether it be good or bad*." **(2 Corinthians 5:10)**

"*For if God spared not the angels that sinned, but cast them down to hell*, and delivered them into chains of darkness, to be reserved unto judgment; *And spared not the old world, but saved Noah* the eighth person, a preacher of righteousness, bringing in the flood upon the world of the ungodly; *And turning the cities of Sodom and Gomorrha into ashes condemned them* with an overthrow, making them an ensample unto those that after should live ungodly." **(2 Peter 2:4–6)**

"*For it had been better for them not to have known the way of righteousness*, than, after they have known it, to turn from the holy commandment delivered unto them." **(2 Peter 2:21)**

"The soul that sinneth, it shall die. The son shall not bear the iniquity of the father, neither shall the father bear the iniquity of the son: *the righteousness of the righteous shall be upon him, and the wickedness of the wicked shall be upon him.*" **(Ezekiel 18:20)**

"But *if the wicked will turn from all his sins that he hath committed, and keep all my statutes,* and do that which is lawful and right, *he shall surely live, he shall not die.* All his transgressions that he hath committed, they shall not be mentioned unto him: in his righteousness that he hath done he shall live." **(Ezekiel 18:21–22)**

"A false witness shall not be unpunished, and *he that speaketh lies shall perish.*" **(Proverbs 19:9)**

"But I say unto you, That *every idle word that men shall speak, they shall give account thereof* in the day of judgment." **(Matthew 12:36)**

"But after thy hardness and impenitent heart treasurest up unto thyself wrath against the day of wrath and revelation of the righteous judgment of God; *Who will render to every man according to his deeds.*" **(Romans 2:5–6)**

"Be not deceived; God is not mocked: for *whatsoever a man soweth, that shall he also reap.*" **(Galatians 6:7)**

"For not the hearers of the law are just before God, *but the doers of the law shall be justified.*" **(Romans 2:13)**

"But *be ye doers of the word, and not hearers only,* deceiving your own selves." **(James 1:22)**

"Therefore to him that knoweth to do good, and doeth it not, *to him it is sin.*" **(James 4:17)**

"Because the law worketh wrath: for where no law is, *there is no transgression.*" **(Romans 4:15)**

"Wherefore, as by one man sin entered into the world, and death by sin; and so death passed upon all men, for that all have sinned: For until the law sin was in the world: *but sin is not imputed when there is no law.* Nevertheless death reigned from Adam to Moses, even over them that had not sinned after the similitude of Adam's transgression, who is the figure of him that was to come." **(Romans 5:12–14)**

> Note: Romans 4:15 and Romans 5:12-14 above, help us to understand that man will not be held accountable for God's laws that mankind is not aware of.

See chapter 19: **"Forgiveness"**
See chapter 40: **"Repentance"**
See chapter 29: **"Judgment"**

CHAPTER 2

ANGELS AND VISITATIONS

"And I saw another angel fly in the midst of heaven, having the everlasting gospel to preach unto them that dwell on the earth, and to every nation, and kindred, and tongue, and people." **(Revelation 14:6)**

Modern Christianity teaches that angels no longer minister unto man upon the Earth, that there is no more revelation from God. *If the fullness of the gospel was still on the Earth as taught by modern Christianity, why would God send another angel to preach His gospel unto all that dwell on the earth, to every nation, kindred, tongue, and people, as Revelation 14:6 tells us?* This chapter will help you to explain the mission of angels.

ANGELS AND VISITATIONS

Scriptures used by some Christian faiths to substantiate their belief and teaching that the angel Moroni was not sent to Joseph Smith from God, and that God no longer sends His angels to minister to mankind:

"But though we, or an angel from heaven, preach any other gospel unto you than that which we have preached unto you, let him be accursed." **(Galatians 1:8)**

> *Note: Your response should be, "What did the angel Moroni preach to Joseph Smith that was/is a different gospel than that taught by the Savior and His Apostles?"*

NOW THE REST OF THE STORY . . . (scriptures that further explain or clarify the topic)

"Be not forgetful to entertain strangers: for thereby *some have entertained angels unawares.*" **(Hebrews 13:2)**

"The Revelation of Jesus Christ, which God gave unto him, to shew unto his servants things which must shortly come to pass; and *he sent and signified it by his angel* unto his servant John." **(Revelation 1:1)**

"And I saw another angel fly in the midst of heaven, *having the everlasting gospel to preach unto them that dwell on the earth*, and to every nation, and kindred, and tongue, and people." **(Revelation 14:6)**

> *Note: Many churches will use Galatians 1:8 in their defense against the angel Moroni coming to Joseph Smith, or that there is no more revelation, or that God will not send His angels with revelation to His children on this earth. How can they explain Revelation 1:1 and 14:6?*

Question: *If the fullness of the gospel was still on the Earth, why would God send another angel to preach His gospel unto all that dwell on the earth, to every nation, kindred, tongue, and people?*

"And I fell at his feet [*the angel's*] to worship him. And he [*the angel*] said unto me, See thou do it not: I am thy fellowservant, and of thy brethren that have the testimony of Jesus: worship God: for the testimony of Jesus is the spirit of prophecy." **(Revelation 19:10)**

> *Note: The book of Revelation all came to John by an angel. Does this mean that we now must throw out the book of Revelation because it was delivered to the Apostle John by an angel?*

"Behold, *I will send you Elijah the prophet before the coming of the great and dreadful day of the Lord*: And he shall turn the heart of the fathers to the children, and the heart of the children to their fathers, *lest I come and smite the earth with a curse.*" **(Malachi 4:5–6)**

The *angel Gabriel* came to Zacharias, he then comes to Mary the mother of Jesus. **(Luke 1:11–38)**

> **Two angels testify to the Apostles:** "And when he had spoken these things, while they beheld, he was taken up; and a cloud received him out of their sight. And while they looked steadfastly toward heaven as he went up, behold, two men stood by them in white apparel; Which also said, Ye men of Galilee, why stand ye gazing up into heaven? this same Jesus, which is taken up from you into heaven, shall so come in like manner as ye have seen him go into heaven." **(Acts 1:9–11)**

> **Peter and John are arrested; an angel delivers them from prison:** "And laid their hands on the apostles, and put them in the common prison. But the angel of the Lord by night opened the prison doors, and brought them forth, and said, Go, stand and speak in the temple to the people all the words of this life." **(Acts 5:18–20)**

> "*And the angel of the Lord spake unto Philip,* saying, Arise, and go toward the south unto the way that goeth down from Jerusalem unto Gaza, which is desert." **(Acts 8:26)**

> "And, behold, *the angel of the Lord came upon him,* and a light shined in the prison: and he smote Peter on the side, and raised him up, saying, Arise up quickly. And his chains fell off from his hands. *And the angel said unto him,* Gird thyself, and bind on thy sandals. And so he did. And he saith unto him, Cast thy garment about thee, and follow me. And he went out, and followed him; and wist not that it was true which was done by the angel; but thought he saw a vision." **(Acts 12:7–9)**

> "*For there stood by me this night the angel of God,* whose I am, and whom I serve, Saying, Fear not, Paul; thou must be brought before Cæsar: and, lo, God hath given thee all them that sail with thee." **(Acts 27:23–24)**

> "But while he thought on these things, behold, *the angel of the Lord appeared unto him in a dream,* saying, Joseph, thou son of David, fear not to take unto thee Mary thy wife: for that which is conceived in her is of the Holy Ghost." **(Matthew 1:20–25)**

> "And when Gideon perceived that *he was an angel of the Lord,* Gideon said, Alas, O Lord God! for because I have seen an angel of the Lord face to face." **(Judges 6:22)**

> "And, behold, *the angel that talked with me went forth, and another angel went out to meet him.*" **(Zechariah 2:3)**

> "And *there appeared unto him an angel of the Lord* standing on the right side of the altar of incense." **(Luke 1:11)**

> "And there was war in heaven: Michael and his *angels* fought against the dragon; and the dragon fought and his angels." **(Revelation 12:7)**

See chapter 43: **"Revelation"**

CHAPTER 3

APOSTASY OF THE CHRISTIAN CHURCH

"For I bear them record that they have a zeal of God, but not according to knowledge. For they being ignorant of God's righteousness, and going about to establish their own righteousness, have not submitted themselves unto the righteousness of God. For Christ is the end of the law for righteousness to every one that believeth." **(Romans 10:2–4)**

The Catholic Church declares that priesthood authority has been in place since the Apostle Peter, succeeded through the Popes, that there has been no apostasy of the church. It does acknowledge that the church had its corruption difficulties during the Dark Ages; but it claims the church cleaned up its act and corrected itself. The Protestant churches do not believe in priesthood authority and believe that the Catholic church corrupted the teachings and doctrines of Christ's original church, which then needed to be reformed or taught again. Neither the Catholic or Protestant churches believe in revelation from God that would allow for modern day prophets and a restoration of Christ's church. This chapter will help you to explain the apostasy of the Christian church.

Apostasy of the Christian Church

Scriptures used by some Christian faiths to substantiate their belief and teaching that there has not been an apostasy of the Christian church and that there is no need for a restoration of the church, the priesthood, nor the doctrines taught by the Savior:

"And I say also unto thee, That thou art Peter, and upon this rock I will build my church; and the gates of hell shall not prevail against it." **(Matthew 16:18)**

Now the Rest of the Story . . . (scriptures that further explain or clarify the topic)

Apostasy as It Was Prophesied

"The earth also is defiled under the inhabitants thereof; because *they have transgressed the laws, changed the ordinance, broken the everlasting covenant.*" **(Isaiah 24:2–5)**

"Behold, the days come, *saith the Lord God, that I will send a famine in the land*, not a famine of bread, nor a thirst for water, but *of hearing the words of the Lord*: And they shall wander from sea to sea, and from the north even to the east, they shall run to and fro to seek the word of the Lord, and shall not find it." **(Amos 8:11–12)**

> *Note: Some will say that Isaiah 24:2–5 and Amos 8:11–12 are talking only about the apostasy of Israel. Israel did apostatize multiple times. By reading the scriptures below, you will see that Christianity has not been immune to Apostasy and that Isaiah and Amos could very well be talking about Christianity also.*

"Let no man deceive you by any means: *for that day shall not come, except there come a falling away first*, and that man of sin be revealed, the son of perdition." **(2 Thessalonians 2:3–4)**

"Now the Spirit speaketh expressly, that *in the latter times some shall depart from the faith, giving heed to seducing spirits, and doctrines of devils*; Speaking lies in hypocrisy; having their conscience seared with a hot iron; Forbidding to marry, and commanding to abstain from meats, which God hath created to be received with thanksgiving of them which believe and know the truth." **(1 Timothy 4:1–3)**

"This know also, that in the last days perilous times shall come. For men shall be lovers of their own selves, covetous, boasters, proud, blasphemers, disobedient to parents, unthankful, unholy, Without natural affection, trucebreakers, false accusers, incontinent, fierce, despisers of those that are good, Traitors, heady, high minded, lovers of pleasures more than lovers of God; *Having a form of godliness, but denying the power thereof*: from such turn away. For of this sort are they which creep into houses, and lead captive silly women laden with sins, led away with divers lusts, *Ever learning, and never able to come to the knowledge of the truth.* Now as Jannes and Jambres withstood Moses, so do these also resist the truth: men of corrupt minds, reprobate concerning the faith." **(2 Timothy 3:1–8)**

"For I know this, that *after my departing shall grievous wolves enter in among you,* not sparing the flock. Also of your own selves shall men arise, speaking perverse things, *to draw away disciples after them.*" **(Acts 20:28–30)**

"For *the time will come when they will not endure sound doctrine*; but after their own lusts shall they heap to themselves teachers, having itching ears; And *they shall turn away their ears from the truth,* and shall be turned unto fables." **(2 Timothy 4:3–4)**

"But there were false prophets also among the people, even as *there shall be false teachers among you, who privily shall bring in damnable heresies,* even denying the Lord that bought them, and bring upon themselves swift destruction. And many shall follow their pernicious ways; by reason of whom the way of truth shall be evil spoken of. *And through covetousness shall they with feigned words make merchandise of you.*" **(2 Peter 2:1–3)**

Apostasy Had Already Started
Soon after the Death of Christ

"Beloved, when I gave all diligence to write unto you of the common salvation, it was needful for me to write unto you, and *exhort you that ye should earnestly contend for the faith which was once delivered unto the saints.* For there are certain men crept in unawares, *who were before of old ordained to this condemnation,* ungodly men, turning the grace of our God into lasciviousness, and denying the only Lord God, and our Lord Jesus Christ." **(Jude 1:3–4)**

"I marvel that ye are *so soon removed from him that called you into the grace of Christ unto another gospel*: Which is not another; but there be some that trouble you, *and would pervert the gospel of Christ.* But though we, or an angel from heaven, preach any other gospel unto you than that which we have preached unto you, let him be accursed." **(Galatians 1:6–8)**

"For it hath been declared unto me of you, my brethren, by them which are of the house of Chloe, that there are contentions among you. *Now this I say, that every one of you saith, I am of Paul; and I of Apollos; and I of Cephas; and I of Christ. Is Christ divided? was Paul crucified for you? or were ye baptized in the name of Paul?*" **(1 Corinthians 1:11–13)**

"From which some having swerved have turned aside unto vain jangling; *Desiring to be teachers of the law; understanding neither what they say, nor whereof they affirm.*" **(1 Timothy 1:6–7)**

"For such are *false apostles, deceitful workers,* transforming themselves into the apostles of Christ." **(2 Corinthians 11:13)**

"Ye hypocrites, well did Esaias prophesy of you, saying, This people draweth nigh unto me with their mouth, and honoureth me with their lips; but their heart is far from me. But in vain they do worship me, *teaching for doctrines the commandments of men.*" **(Matthew 15:7–9, Mark 7:7)**

"For I bear them record that they have a zeal of God, *but not according to knowledge. For they being ignorant of God's righteousness, and going about to establish their own righteousness,* have not submitted themselves unto the righteousness of God. For Christ is the end of the law for righteousness to every one that believeth." **(Romans 10:2–4)**

"They profess that they know God; *but in works they deny him,* being abominable, and disobedient, and unto every good work reprobate." **(Titus 1:16)**

"*Woe be unto the pastors that destroy and scatter the sheep of my pasture!* saith the Lord." **(Jeremiah 23:1–4)**

"*I have not sent these prophets,* yet they ran: *I have not spoken to them,* yet they prophesied." **(Jeremiah 23:21)**

"We have also a more sure word of prophecy; whereunto ye do well that ye take heed, as unto a light that shineth in a dark place, until the day dawn, and the day star arise in your hearts: Knowing this first, that *no prophecy of the scripture is of any private interpretation.* For the prophecy came not in old time by the will of man: but holy men of God spake as they were moved by the Holy Ghost." **(2 Peter 1:19–21)**

"Therefore say I unto you, *The kingdom of God shall be taken from you,* and given to a nation bringing forth the fruits thereof." **(Matthew 21:43)**

"For *God is not the author of confusion,* but of peace, as in all the churches of the saints." **(1 Corinthians 14:33)**

"And *he gave some, apostles; and some, prophets*; and some, evangelists; and some, pastors and teachers; For the perfecting of the saints, for the work of the ministry, for the edifying of the body of Christ: *Till we all come in the unity of the faith,* and of the knowledge of the Son of God, unto a perfect man, unto the measure of the stature of the fullness of Christ: *That we henceforth be no more children, tossed to and fro, and carried about with every wind of doctrine,* by the sleight of men, and cunning craftiness, whereby they lie in wait to deceive." **(Ephesians 4:11–14)**

"One Lord, *one faith,* one baptism." **(Ephesians 4:5)**

> *Note: Neither Christ nor His Apostles established different churches teaching different doctrines. When the churches did stray, when they did change the doctrines they were taught, they were chastised and warned that if they did not return to the fold and teach the truth, they would lose their authority and priesthood to act in the name of God and Jesus Christ.*

Only seven churches *still remained that were worthy of mention in the book of Revelation, and the seeds of apostasy were evident even in them.* Revelation 1:11–20 and chapters 2 and 3 show that the church in that day was rapidly going into apostasy.

To the church of Ephesus: "Remember therefore from whence thou art fallen, and repent, and do the first works; or else I will come unto thee quickly, and will remove thy candlestick out of his place, except thou repent." (**Revelation 2:1–5**)

To the church of Laodiceans: "So then because thou art lukewarm, and neither cold nor hot, I will spue thee out of my mouth." (**Revelation 3:16**; see also verses 14–15 and 17–19)

"From that time many of his disciples went back, and walked no more with him. Then said Jesus unto the twelve, Will ye also go away? Then Simon Peter answered him, Lord, to whom shall we go? thou hast the words of eternal life. And we believe and are sure that thou art that Christ, the Son of the living God." (**John 6:66–69**)

---

65 OTHER "APOSTASY" SCRIPTURES YOU MAY WANT TO READ . . .

Isaiah 29:10	2 Corinthians 12:21	James 2:5–6
Isaiah 29:13	1 Timothy 1:20–21	James 4:1
Micah 3:6–7	1 Timothy 4:7	James 4:4
Matthew 24:5	1 Timothy 5:15	1 Peter 5:2
Matthew 24:9–12	2 Timothy 1:15	2 Peter 2:1–2
Matthew 24:24	2 Timothy 2:1–2	2 Peter 2:14
Matthew 27:53	2 Timothy 2:17–18	2 Peter 2:17
Acts 3:19–21	2 Timothy 3:13	2 Peter 3:3
Acts 8:18–21	2 Timothy 4:15–16	2 Peter 3:16–17
Acts 15:1–2	Galatians 2:4	1 John 2:18–19
Acts 15:7	Galatians 3:1	1 John 4:3
Acts 15:25–28	Galatians 4:9	2 John 1:7
Acts 20:29–30	Galatians 4:11	3 John 1:9–10
Acts 21:20	Ephesians 1:10	Jude 1:3–4
Romans 16:17–18	Ephesians 2:19–20	Jude 1:7–8
1 Corinthians 3:3	Philippians 3:2	Jude 1:16–19
1 Corinthians 4:15–16	Colossians 2:8	Revelation 2:20–22
1 Corinthians 4:18–19	2 Thessalonians 2:3	Revelation 3:4
1 Corinthians 5:1	2 Thessalonians 2:7	Revelation 3:8
1 Corinthians 11:18–19	2 Thessalonians 2:9	Revelation 13:7
1 Corinthians 15:12	2 Thessalonians 3:11	Revelation 14:6–7
2 Corinthians 11:3	Titus 1:10–11	

CHAPTER 4

APOSTLES

"And he gave some, apostles; and some, prophets; and some, evangelists; and some, pastors and teachers; For the perfecting of the saints, for the work of the ministry, for the edifying of the body of Christ: Till we all come in the unity of the faith, and of the knowledge of the Son of God, unto a perfect man, unto the measure of the stature of the fullness of Christ: That we henceforth be no more children, tossed to and fro, and carried about with every wind of doctrine, by the sleight of men, and cunning craftiness, whereby they lie in wait to deceive." **(Ephesians 4:11–14)**

Christian churches today teach us that the office of Apostle was not intended to continue after the original Twelve Apostles. That there is no requirement for them. They obviously have not read Ephesians 4:11–14, where we are told that "he gave some apostles . . . *Till we all come in the unity of the faith, . . .* That we *henceforth be no more* children, *tossed to and fro,* and *carried about with every wind of doctrine,* by the *sleight of men,* and cunning craftiness, whereby they *lie in wait to deceive*" (emphasis added). The Apostles kept the churches teaching correct doctrine. This chapter will help you to explain the continuing requirement for Apostles.

Apostles

Scriptures used by Modern-Day Christian faiths to substantiate their belief and teaching that there are no requirements and no need for Apostles in the modern-day church:

There are NONE.

The Original Twelve Apostles (Luke 6:13–16)

1. Simon — a.k.a. "Peter"
2. Andrew — Peter's brother
3. James — son of Zebedee
4. John — the brother of James (the "One Whom Jesus Loved")
5. Philip
6. Bartholomew
7. Matthew — the Tax Collector
8. Thomas — a.k.a. "Didymus"
9. James — son of Alphaeus
10. Simon — the Cananean, aka "Simon the Zealot"
11. Judas — a.k.a. "the brother (or son) of James," a.k.a. "Jude," a.k.a. "Lebbaeus Thaddaeus," not Judas Iscariot
12. Judas Iscariot — a.k.a. "Judas son of Simon Iscariot"

Apostles Called and Ordained after the Original Twelve

1. Matthias — replaced Judas Iscariot (Acts 1:23–26)
2. Saul — a.k.a. "Paul" (Acts 9:1–20, 14:14, 1 Corinthians 1:1)
3. Barnabas (Acts 14:14, 13:1–3)
4. James the brother of Jesus (Galatians 1:19)
5. Timothy is venerated as an Apostle by the Eastern Orthodox Church.[1]

The Deaths of the Apostles

The only two Apostles whose deaths the Bible records are **James the son of Zebedee** (Acts 12:2). King Herod had James "put to death with the sword," and **Judas Iscariot** who betrayed the Savior; but here there is some disagreement in the scriptures. Matthew 27:5–7 tells us that he hanged himself. Acts 1:18 says he purchased the "Potters Field," falling headlong, and his bowels gushed out.

The circumstances of the deaths of the other Apostles are related through church tradition without any reliable historical or traditional support, so we should not put too much weight on any of the accounts.

The most commonly accepted church tradition regarding the death of an Apostle is that the Apostle Peter was crucified upside-down in Rome in fulfillment of Jesus's prophecy (John 21:18).

The following are the most popular "traditions" concerning the deaths of the other Apostles:

Matthew suffered martyrdom in Ethiopia, killed by a sword wound.

John faced martyrdom when he was thrown in a huge basin of boiling oil during a wave of persecution in Rome. He was miraculously unharmed and delivered from death. He was then exiled and sentenced to the mines on the prison island of Patmos. He wrote his prophetic book of Revelation on Patmos. John was later freed and returned to what is now modern-day Turkey. He died as an old man, the only Apostle to die peacefully. Or did he die?

James, the brother of Jesus, a.k.a. "James the Just," was the leader of the church in Jerusalem. He was thrown from the southeast pinnacle of the temple (over a hundred feet down) when he refused to deny his faith in Christ. When they discovered that he survived the fall, his enemies beat him to death with a club.

James, the son of Alpheus, is one of at least three James referred to in the New Testament. There is some confusion as to which is which, but this James is reckoned to have ministered in Syria. The Jewish historian Josephus reported that he was stoned and then clubbed to death.

Bartholomew, a.k.a. "Nathanael," was a missionary to Asia. He witnessed in present-day Turkey and was martyred for his preaching in Armenia, being flayed to death by a whip, possibly beheaded or even crucified head down.

Andrew, the brother of Peter, was severely scourged and crucified on an x-shaped cross in Greece.

Thomas, a.k.a. "Didymus," was stabbed with a spear in India during one of his missionary trips to establish the church there and possibly burned up in an oven.

Matthias was the Apostle chosen to replace the traitor Judas Iscariot. Tradition states that he was either burned to death in Syria or he was stoned and then beheaded.

Paul was tortured and then beheaded by the evil Emperor Nero in Rome in AD 67.

Mark, although not an Apostle, died after being dragged through the streets of Alexandria.

Luke, although not an Apostle, was hanged from an olive tree in Greece.

Jude, a.k.a. "Judas," aka "the brother (or son) of James," aka "Thaddaeus" was shot to death with arrows.

Philip was crucified or hung upside down by hooks through his ankles.

Simon Zelotes, a.k.a. "Simon the Zealot," was crucified in Britain.

There are traditions regarding the other Apostles as well, but none with any reliable historical or traditional support. It is not so important how the Apostles died. What is important is the fact that they were all willing to die for their faith. If Jesus had not been resurrected, the disciples would have known it. People will not die for something they know to be a lie. *The fact that all of the Apostles were willing to die horrible deaths, refusing to renounce their faith in Christ, is tremendous evidence that they had truly witnessed the Resurrection of Jesus Christ.*

NOW THE REST OF THE STORY . . . (scriptures that further explain or clarify the topic)

"And when it was day, he called unto him his disciples: and *of them he chose twelve*, whom also *he named apostles*; Simon, (whom he also named Peter,) and Andrew his brother, James and John, Philip and Bartholomew, Matthew and Thomas, James the son of Alphæus, and Simon called Zelotes, And Judas the brother of James, and Judas Iscariot, which also was the traitor." **(Luke 6:13–16**; see also **Matthew 10:1–4)**

"Ye have not chosen me, but *I have chosen you, and ordained you*, that ye should go and bring forth fruit, and that your fruit should remain: that whatsoever ye shall ask of the Father in my name, he may give it you." **(John 15:16)**

"And *he ordained twelve*, that they should be with him, and *that he might send them forth to preach*, And to have power to heal sicknesses, and to cast out devils." **(Mark 3:14–15)**

> *Note: Note the wording "he ordained" and "he might send." No one but Christ had the power or the authority to ordain or send themselves or anyone else, until Christ gave this authority to His Apostles.*

"And *I will give unto thee the keys of the kingdom of heaven*: and whatsoever thou shalt bind on earth shall be bound in heaven: and whatsoever thou shalt loose on earth shall be loosed in heaven." **(Matthew 16:19)**

> *Note: This is where Peter received the keys to the Kingdom of Heaven, and powers of the priesthood.*

NOW SEE . . .

"Verily I say unto you, *Whatsoever ye shall bind on earth shall be bound in heaven*: and whatsoever ye shall loose on earth shall be loosed in heaven." **(Matthew 18:18)**

> *Note: This is where the Apostles received the keys to the Kingdom of Heaven and powers of the priesthood.*

"*Then said Jesus* to them again, Peace be unto you: *as my Father hath sent me, even so send I you*. And when he had said this, he breathed on them, and saith unto them, Receive ye the Holy Ghost: Whose so ever sins ye remit, they are remitted unto them; and whose so ever sins ye retain, they are retained." **(John 20:21–23)**

"Wherefore of these men which have companied with us all the time that the Lord Jesus went in and out among us, Beginning from the baptism of John, unto that same day that he was taken up from us, *must one be ordained* to be a witness with us of his resurrection. And they appointed two, Joseph called Barsabas, who was surnamed Justus, and Matthias. And they prayed, and said, *Thou, Lord, which knowest the hearts of all men, shew whether of these two thou hast chosen,* That he may take part of this ministry and apostleship, from which Judas by transgression fell, that he might go to his own place. And they gave forth their lots; and *the lot fell upon Matthias*; and he was numbered with the eleven apostles." **(Acts 1:21–26)**

> *Note: The eleven remaining Apostles knew that with the death of Judas Iscariot, or any Apostle, another must be chosen to take his place among them. Matthias is chosen, called and ordained an Apostle to replace Judas Iscariot.*

"Now there were in the church that was at Antioch certain prophets and teachers; as Barnabas, and Simeon that was called Niger, and Lucius of Cyrene, and Manaen, which had been brought up with Herod the tetrarch, and Saul. As they ministered to the Lord, and fasted, *the Holy Ghost said, Separate me Barnabas and Saul* for the work whereunto *I have called them.* And when they had fasted and prayed, and *laid their hands on them,* they sent them away. **(Acts 13:1–3)**

> *Note: Saul (Paul) and Barnabas are called and ordained Apostles.*

"*Paul,* a servant of Jesus Christ, *called to be an apostle,* separated unto the gospel of God." **(Romans 1:1)**

"*Paul, called to be an apostle* of Jesus Christ *through the will of God,* and Sosthenes our brother." **(1 Corinthians 1:1)**

"Now therefore ye are no more strangers and foreigners, but fellow citizens with the saints, and of the household of God; and are *built upon the foundation of apostles and prophets,* Jesus Christ himself being the chief corner stone; in whom all the building fitly framed together groweth unto an holy temple in the Lord: in whom ye also are builded together for an habitation of God through the Spirit." **(Ephesians 2:19–22)**

"And *he gave* some, *apostles*; and some, *prophets*; and some, *evangelists*; and some, *pastors* and *teachers*; For the perfecting of the saints, for the work of the ministry, for the edifying of the body of Christ: *Till we all come in the unity of the faith,* and of the knowledge of the Son of God, unto a perfect man, unto the measure of the stature of the fullness of Christ: *That we henceforth be no more children, tossed to and fro, and carried about with every wind of doctrine,* by the sleight of men, and cunning craftiness, whereby they lie in wait to deceive." **(Ephesians 4:11–14)**

> *Note: "Till we all come in the unity of the faith," nowhere in the New Testament is it stated or indicated, or even hinted at, that the requirement for Apostles was temporary. Quite to the contrary. And why? So the people would not be "carried about with every wind of doctrine."*
>
> *Ephesians 4:11–14 is very clear; Prophets, Apostles, and the priesthood will be the leaders of Christ's church UNTIL we all come in the unity of the*

faith. With all the different Christian denominations teaching different doctrines and beliefs there is no unity of the faith yet.

"Therefore also said the wisdom of God, *I will send them* prophets and *apostles*, and *some of them they shall slay and persecute.*" **(Luke 11:49)**

> *Note: The scriptures and history show that mankind has persecuted and killed the prophets and apostles of God throughout the Old Testament, the New Testament, and since.*

See chapter 38: **"Priesthood of God"**
See chapter 39: **"Prophets"**

CHAPTER 5

ATONEMENT OF JESUS CHRIST

"For God sent not his Son into the world to condemn the world; but that the world through him might be saved." (**John 3:17**)

What is the "Atonement of Jesus Christ"? It is the ransom paid by Jesus Christ, through His suffering in Gethsemane and His death on the cross, which nullifies the effects of sin. Christ's Atonement allows everyone to be resurrected. For those who repent of their sins, it also opens the way to continued growth and progression through the eternities. Most Christians believe that the Atonement began and finished with the crucifixion of Jesus Christ, whereas Latter-day Saints believe that the Atonement began in the Garden of Gethsemane. Most but not all Christian faiths accept, agree, and teach the Atonement of Jesus Christ. Among them there is much controversy, with the main difference being what is required for Christ's Atonement to manifest itself in our lives.

ATONEMENT OF JESUS CHRIST

Scriptures used by some Christian faiths to substantiate their belief and teaching about the Atonement of Jesus Christ:

"In whom we have redemption through his blood, the forgiveness of sins, according to the riches of his grace." (**Ephesians 1:7**; see also **Colossians 1:14**)

"But if we walk in the light, as he is in the light, we have fellowship one with another, and the Blood of Jesus Christ his Son cleanseth us from all sin." (**1 John 1:7**)

"And from Jesus Christ, who is the faithful witness, and the first begotten of the dead, and the prince of the kings of the earth. Unto him that loved us, and washed us from our sins in his own blood." (**Revelation 1:5**)

"That whosoever believeth in him should not perish, but have eternal life." (**John 3:15**)

"For whosoever shall call upon the name of the Lord shall be saved." (**Romans 10:13**)

> *Note: Because of the blood that was shed on the cross, all one must do is believe in Jesus Christ and they will attain salvation. No repentance by mankind is required. No good works of Christian charity are required.*

NOW THE REST OF THE STORY . . . (scriptures that further explain or clarify the topic)

"I, even I, am the Lord; and *beside me there is no saviour.*" (**Isaiah 43:11**)

"But he was wounded for our transgressions, he was bruised for our iniquities: the chastisement of our peace was upon him; and *with his stripes we are healed.*" (**Isaiah 53:5**)

"And she shall bring forth a son, and thou shalt call his name Jesus: for *he shall save his people from their sins.*" (**Matthew 1:21**)

"For the Son of man is come *to save that which was lost.*" (**Matthew 18:11**)

"Even as *the Son of man came* not to be ministered unto, but to minister, and *to give his life a ransom for many.*" (**Matthew 20:28**)

"For this is my blood of the new testament, *which is shed for many for the remission of sins.*" (**Matthew 26:28**)

"The next day John seeth Jesus coming unto him, and saith, Behold the Lamb of God, *which taketh away the sin of the world.*" (**John 1:29**)

"For God sent not his Son into the world to condemn the world; but *that the world through him might be saved.*" (**John 3:17**)

"*I am the living bread which came down from heaven:* if any man eat of this bread, he shall live for ever: and the bread that I will give is my flesh, which I will give for the life of the world." (**John 6:51**)

"Jesus said unto her, *I am the resurrection*, and the life: *he that believeth in me, though he were dead, yet shall he live.*" **(John 11:25)**

"Jesus saith unto him, I am the way, the truth, and the life: *no man cometh unto the Father, but by me.*" **(John 14:6)**

"For I delivered unto you first of all that which I also received, how that *Christ died for our sins* according to the scriptures." **(1 Corinthians 15:3)**

"For as in Adam all die, even so *in Christ shall all be made alive.*" **(1 Corinthians 15:22)**

"And being made perfect, *he became the author of eternal salvation* unto all them that obey him." **(Hebrews 5:9)**

"And for this cause *he is the mediator of the new testament*, that by means of death, for the redemption of the transgressions that were under the first testament, they which are called might receive the promise of eternal inheritance." **(Hebrews 9:15)**

"Neither is there salvation in any other: for *there is none other name under heaven* given among men, *whereby we must be saved.*" **(Acts 4:12)**

"*Whom God hath set forth to be a propitiation through faith in his blood*, to declare his righteousness for the remission of sins that are past, *through the forbearance of God.*" **(Romans 3:25)**

"Much more then, being now justified by his blood, *we shall be saved from wrath through him.*" **(Romans 5:9)**

"And not only so, but we also joy in God through our Lord Jesus Christ, *by whom we have now received the atonement.*" **(Romans 5:11)**

"*Who his own self bare our sins* in his own body on the tree, *that we*, being dead to sins, *should live unto righteousness*: by whose stripes ye were healed." **(1 Peter 2:24)**

"But if we walk in the light, as he is in the light, we have fellowship one with another, and *the blood of Jesus Christ his Son cleanseth us from all sin.*" **(1 John 1:7)**

"*Who gave himself for our sins*, that he might deliver us from this present evil world, *according to the will of God and our Father.*" **(Galatians 1:4)**

"Who gave himself for us, *that he might redeem us from all iniquity*, and purify unto himself a peculiar people, zealous of good works." **(Titus 2:14)**

"And he came out, and went, as he was wont, to the mount of Olives (Gethsemane); and his disciples also followed him. And when he was at the place, he said unto them, Pray that ye enter not into temptation. And he was withdrawn from them about a stone's cast, and kneeled down, and prayed, Saying, *Father, if thou be willing, remove this cup from me: nevertheless not my will, but thine, be done.* And there appeared an angel unto him from heaven, strengthening him. And being in an agony he prayed more earnestly: and *his sweat was as it were great drops of blood falling down to the ground.*" **(Luke 22:39–44)**

See chapter 6: "**Baptism**"
See chapter 18: "**Faith, Grace & Works — Sincere Belief Is Not Enough**"
See chapter 40: "**Repentance**"

CHAPTER 6

BAPTISM

"Go ye therefore, and teach all nations, baptizing them the name of the Father, and of the Son, and of the Holy Ghost: Teaching them to observe all things whatsoever I have commanded you: and, lo, I am with you always, even unto the end of the world. Amen." (**Matthew 28:19–20**)

Baptism by immersion is a requirement for salvation and must be performed by the authority of God, by someone holding the priesthood. This chapter will help you to explain the requirement for, and the proper ordinance of baptism.

BAPTISM

Scriptures used by some Christian faiths to substantiate their belief and teaching that baptism is not a requirement:

"In whom we have redemption through his blood, the forgiveness of sins, according to the riches of his grace." **(Ephesians 1:7**; see also **Colossians 1:14)**

"But if we walk in the light, as he is in the light, we have fellowship one with another, and the Blood of Jesus Christ his Son cleanseth us from all sin." **(1 John 1:7)**

"And from Jesus Christ, who is the faithful witness, and the first begotten of the dead, and the prince of the kings of the earth. Unto him that loved us, and washed us from our sins in his own blood." **(Revelation 1:5)**

"That whosoever believeth in him should not perish, but have eternal life." **(John 3:15)**

"That if thou shalt confess with thy mouth the Lord Jesus, and shalt believe in thine heart that God hath raised him from the dead, thou shalt be saved." **(Romans 10:9)**

"For whosoever shall call upon the name of the Lord shall be saved." **(Romans 10:13)**

"For the grace of God that bringeth salvation hath appeared to all men." **(Titus 2:11)**

> *Note: Should one make a change from one Christian faith to another, many churches that do require baptism, will also require rebaptism into that faith.*

NOW THE REST OF THE STORY . . . (scriptures that further explain or clarify the topic)

"Verily, verily, I say unto thee, *Except a man be born of water and of the Spirit, he cannot enter into the kingdom of God.*" **(John 3:5)**

"And he said unto them, Go ye onto the world, and preach the gospel to every creature. *He that believeth and is baptized shall be saved*; but he that believeth not shall be damned." **(Mark 16:15–16)**

"Go ye therefore, and teach all nations, *baptizing them the name of the Father, and of the Son, and of the Holy Ghost*: Teaching them to observe all things whatsoever I have commanded you: and, lo, I am with you always, even unto the end of the world. Amen." **(Matthew 28:19–20)**

"Therefore we are buried with him by *baptism into death*: that like as Christ was raised up from the dead by the glory of the Father, even so we also should walk in newness of life. For if we have been planted together in the likeness of His death, we shall be also in the likeness of His resurrection." **(Romans 6:4–5** [read verses 3–6]; see also **Colossians 2:12)**

"And all the people that heard him, and the publicans, justified God, being baptized with the baptism of John. But the Pharisees and lawyers *rejected the counsel of God* against themselves, *being not baptized of him*." **(Luke 7:29–30)**

"Of the *doctrine of baptisms, and of laying on of hands*, and of resurrection of the dead, and of eternal judgment." **(Hebrews 6:2)**

"One Lord, one faith, *one baptism*." **(Ephesians 4:5)**

Baptism by Immersion

Note: There are no examples nor scriptures in the Bible of baptism by sprinkling or pouring of water, every example of baptism in the Bible is of baptism by immersion.

"And Jesus, when he was baptized, *went up straightway out of the water*: and, lo, the heavens were opened unto him, and he saw the Spirit of God descending like a dove, and lighting upon him: And lo a voice from heaven, saying, This is my beloved Son, in whom I am well pleased." **(Matthew 3:16–17)**

> *Note: Jesus was baptized by John the Baptist in the Jordan River, by immersion.*

"Then went out to him Jerusalem, and all Judæa, and all the region round about Jordan, And were baptized of him *in Jordan*, confessing their sins." **(Mathew 3:5–6)**

> *Note: "In Jordan" is translated "near the Jordan River" in many Bible translations. John the Baptist baptized wherever there was a river because the only accepted form of baptism at that time was by immersion.*

"And John also was baptizing in Ænon near to Salim, *because there was much water there*: and they came, and were baptized." **(John 3:23)**

"And he commanded the chariot to stand still: *and they went down both into the water*, both Philip and the eunuch; and he baptized him." **(Acts 8:38)**

"Know ye not, that so many of us as were baptized into Jesus Christ were baptized into his death? Therefore *we are buried with him by baptism* into death: that like as Christ was raised up from the dead by the glory of the Father, even so we also should walk in newness of life. *For if we have been planted together in the likeness of his death, we shall be also in the likeness of his resurrection*." **(Romans 6:3–5)**

> *Note: Paul explains here that baptism is symbolic of the death, burial, and resurrection of Jesus Christ, which can only be accomplished by immersion baptism and not by sprinkling or pouring of water baptism.*

Baptism of Infants or Little Children

"*Repent*, and *be baptized* every one of you in the name of Jesus Christ, *for the remission of sins*, and you shall receive the gift of the Holy Ghost." **(Acts 2:38**; see also verses 37 and 39**)**

> *Note: An infant or child who has not yet reached the age of knowledge or accountability cannot sin, nor can such child confess or be apologetic and thus are incapable of repentance for their supposed sins. There is not*

one account of an infant baptism occurring anywhere in the entire New Testament.

"Verily I say unto you, Whosoever shall not receive the kingdom of God as a little child, he shall not enter therein. And he took them up in his arms, put his hands upon them, *and blessed them.*" **(Mark 10:15–16)**

"But Jesus said, Suffer little children, and forbid them not, to come unto me: for of such is the kingdom of heaven. And *he laid his hands on them,* and departed thence." **(Matthew 19:14)**

"But Jesus said, Let the *little children* come to me and do not hinder them, *for to such belongs the kingdom of heaven.*" **(Matthew 19:14 ESV)**

> *Note: Reread the ESV rendition of this scripture: "for to such belongs the kingdom of heaven." Little children are innocent and do not need to be baptized as infants.*

"I write unto you, little children, *because your sins are forgiven you for his name's sake.* I write unto you, fathers, because ye have known him that is from the beginning. I write unto you, young men, because ye have overcome the wicked one. I write unto you, *little children, because ye have known the Father.*" **(1 John 2:12–13)**

"**The Decree for the Armenians**," in the Bull "Exultate Deo" of Pope Eugene IV, is often referred to as a decree of the Council of Florence AD 1439. While it is not necessary to hold this decree to be a dogmatic definition of the matter and form and minister of the sacraments, it is undoubtedly a practical instruction, emanating from the Holy See, and as such, has full authenticity in a canonical sense. That is, it is authoritative. The decree speaks thus of Baptism:

"The minister of this sacrament is the priest, to whom it belongs to baptize, by reason of his office. In case of necessity, however, not only a priest or deacon, but even a layman or women, nay, even a pagan or heretic can baptize, provided he observes the form used by the Church, and intends to perform what the Church performs. The effect of this sacrament is the remission of all sin, original and actual; likewise of all punishment which is due for sin."[1]

Note: We see here where the Catholic Church has changed the requirement of baptism to be performed by a duly ordained holder of the priesthood. Allowing baptism to be performed by anyone, even a pagan, or a heretic. Some other Christian churches allow this also. This further demonstrates how important the requirement of baptism is to most Christian churches.

See chapter 7: "**Baptism for the Dead**"

CHAPTER 7

BAPTISM FOR THE DEAD

"Else what shall they do which are baptized for the dead, if the dead rise not at all? Why are they then baptized for the dead?" **(1 Corinthians 15:29)**

Baptism for the Dead was practiced by the early Christian Church until it was condemned by the Roman Church at the Council of Hippo in AD 393 and then ratified at the Council of Carthage in AD 419, Canon 18 (GK. Canon XX.). This was done through the wisdom of man, and not by revelation or direction from Heaven. Where did the Roman Church get the authority to condemn and discontinue the early Christian Church's practice of Baptism for the Dead?

Baptism for the Dead

Scriptures used by some Christian faiths to substantiate their belief and teaching that those who did not hear of Christ and His teachings before death, and those who are not baptized, are doomed, and some Christian churches teach that baptism is not necessary at all:

"Now that the dead are raised, even Moses shewed at the bush, when he calleth the Lord the God of Abraham, and the God of Isaac, and the God of Jacob. For he is not a God of the dead, but of the living: for all live unto him." **(Luke 20:37–38)**

"For the living know that they shall die: but the dead know not any thing, neither have they any more a reward; for the memory of them is forgotten." **(Ecclesiastes 9:5)**

Now the Rest of the Story . . . (scriptures that further explain or clarify the topic)

"For to this end Christ both died, and rose, and revived, that he might be *Lord both of the dead and living.*" **(Romans 14:9)**

"Else what shall they do which are *baptized for the dead*, if the dead rise not at all? Why are they then baptized for the dead?" **(1 Corinthians 15:29)**

"Verily, verily, I say unto thee, *Except a man be born of water and of the Spirit, he cannot enter into the kingdom of God.*" **(John 3:5)**

"For this cause was the gospel preached also to them that are dead, that they might be judged according to men in the flesh, but live according to God in the spirit." **(1 Peter 4:6)**

"For Christ also hath once suffered for sins, the just for the unjust, that he might bring us to God, being put to death in the flesh, but quickened by the Spirit: By which *he went and preached unto the spirits in prison*: Which sometimes are disobedient, when once the long-suffering of God waited in the days of Noah, while the ark was preparing, wherein few, that is, 8 souls were saved by water." **(1 Peter 3:18–20)**

> *Note: Why would Christ during the three days he was dead and before his resurrection, go to the "spirits in prison" and preach to them? Answer: because they cannot be judged for something they knew nothing about. They needed to be given knowledge of Christ and the Gospel.*

"Therefore my heart is glad, and my glory rejoices: my flesh also show rest in hope. For *thou wilt not leave my soul in hell*; neither will thou suffer Thine Holy One to see corruption." **(Psalms 16:9–10)**

"For David speaketh concerning him, I foresaw the Lord always before my face, for he is on my right hand, that I should not be moved: Therefore did my heart rejoice, and my tongue was glad; moreover also my flesh shall rest in hope: *Because thou wilt not leave my soul in hell*, neither wilt thou suffer thine Holy One to see corruption. Thou hast made known to me the ways of life; thou shalt make me full of joy with thy countenance. Men and brethren, let me freely speak unto you of the patriarch David, that he is both dead and buried, and his sepulchre is with us unto this day. Therefore being a prophet, and knowing that God had sworn with an oath to him, that of the fruit of his loins, according to the flesh, he would raise up Christ to sit on his throne; He seeing this before spake of the resurrection of Christ, *that his soul was not left in hell*, neither his flesh did see corruption." (**Acts 2:25–31**)

> *Note: God manifest it to David that he would someday leave hell and return to the Father in Heaven.*

"Jesus said unto her, I am the resurrection, and the life: *he that believeth in me, though he were dead, yet shall he live*: And whosoever liveth and believeth in me shall never die. Believest thou this?" (**John 11:25–26**)

"Behold, I will send you Elijah the prophet before the coming of the great and dreadful day of the Lord: And *he shall turn the heart of the fathers to the children, and the heart of the children to their fathers*, lest I come and smite the earth with a curse." (**Malachi 4:5–6**)

"God having provided some better thing for us, that *they [the dead] without us should not be made perfect*." (**Hebrews 11:40**)

> *Note: The dead cannot be made perfect unless the living perform this required ordinance for them. A better understanding will come from reading the entire chapter (Hebrews 11). Italicized words in brackets [ ] added by the author for clarification and understanding.*

Baptism for the dead was practiced by the early Christian Church until it was condemned by the Roman Church at the Council of Hippo in AD 393 and then ratified at the Council of Carthage in AD 419, Canon 18 (GK. Canon XX.).

Where did the Roman Church get the authority to condemn and discontinue the early Christian Church's practice of baptism for the dead?

CHAPTER 8

BIBLE – ADD TO OR TAKE AWAY FROM

"I have yet many things to say unto you, but ye cannot bear them now. Howbeit when he, the Spirit of truth, is come, he will guide you into all truth: for he shall not speak of himself; but whatsoever he shall hear, that shall he speak: and he will shew you things to come." (**John 16:12–13**)

Catholic and Protestant Christian churches believe and teach that the Bible is complete and inerrant, that there is no more holy writ to be provided in any form. This chapter will help you to explain this misunderstanding.

Bible — Add To
or Take Away From

Scriptures used by some Christian faiths to substantiate their belief and teaching that the Bible is complete and that there are no other and will be no other scriptures:

"For I testify unto every man that heareth the words of the prophecy of this book, If any man shall add unto these things, God shall add unto him the plagues that are written in this book: And if any man shall take away from the words of the book of this prophecy, God shall take away his part out of the book of life, and out of the holy city, and from the things which are written in this book."
(Revelation 22:18–19)

> *Note: This scripture is referring to the book of Revelation and ONLY the book of Revelation.*

> *Note: The Bible as we know it did not exist until, (in his Easter letter), Athanasius Bishop of Alexandria, produced a list of books that would become the books of the New Testament in AD 367. Then in AD 397, at the Synod of Carthage, the church architects decided on an "official" collection of books, which is the current Bible that we have today.*

> *Note: John wrote the book of Revelation BEFORE he wrote his Epistles and his gospel. Revelation was written about AD 96, John's Epistles and gospel were written about AD 98 to 100.*

Now See . . .

"Ye shall not add unto the word which I command you, neither shall ye diminish ought from it, that ye may keep the commandments of the Lord your God which I command you." (**Deuteronomy 4:2**)

And . . .

"Every word of God is pure: he is a shield unto them that put their trust in him. Add thou not unto his words, lest he reprove thee, and thou be found a liar."
(Proverbs 30:5–6)

> *Note: Does this mean that EVERYTHING written since Deuteronomy 4:2 and Proverbs 30:5–6 is adding unto the word of God and are invalid? Or that Revelation 22:18–19 is talking ONLY about the book of Revelation?*

"What thing soever I command you, observe to do it: thou shalt not add thereto, nor diminish from it." (**Deuteronomy 12:32**)

"But though we, or an angel from heaven, preach any other gospel unto you than that which we have preached unto you, let him be accursed. As we said before, so say I now again, If any man preach any other gospel unto you than that ye have received, let him be accursed." **(Galatians 1:8–9)**

> *Note: We of The Church of Jesus Christ of Latter-Day Saints and the Book of Mormon are not adding to or taking away from the word of God. We are not "teaching any other gospel." We are teaching exactly what the Apostles and the early Christian Church taught, as true doctrine has been restored through revelation from our Heavenly Father. It is the thousands of Christian Sects today that have changed the doctrine and teachings of the Savior.*

NOW THE REST OF THE STORY . . . (scriptures that further explain or clarify the topic)

Scriptures testifying that the Bible is NOT complete and that there are other scriptures:

"Behold, the former things are come to pass, and *new things do I declare*: before they spring forth I tell you of them." **(Isaiah 42:9)**

"*I have yet many things to say unto you, but ye cannot bear them now.* Howbeit when he, the Spirit of truth, is come, he will guide you into all truth: for he shall not speak of himself; but whatsoever he shall hear, that shall he speak: and he will shew you things to come." **(John 16:12–13)**

"Surely the Lord God will do nothing, *but he revealeth his secret unto his servants the prophets.*" **(Amos 3:7)**

> *Note: If there are no prophets, who will God reveal these things to?*

"The word of the Lord came again unto me, saying, Moreover, thou son of man, take thee one stick, and *write upon it, For Judah,* and for the children of Israel his companions: then take another stick, and *write upon it, For Joseph,* the stick of Ephraim, and for all the house of Israel his companions: *And join them one to another into one stick*; and they shall become one in thine hand. And when the children of thy people shall speak unto thee, saying, Wilt thou not shew us what thou meanest by these? Say unto them, Thus saith the Lord God; Behold, I will take the stick of Joseph, which is in the hand of Ephraim, and the tribes of Israel his fellows, and will put them with him, even with the stick of Judah, and make them one stick, and they shall be one in mine hand. *And the sticks whereon thou writest shall be in thine hand before their eyes.*" **(Ezekiel 37:15–20)**

> *Note: What is the Stick (Book) of Judah? Where is it? What is the Stick (Book) of Joseph? Where is it?*

WHERE ARE THESE BOOKS (SCRIPTURES) MENTIONED IN THE BIBLE THAT WE DON'T HAVE?

Book of the Covenant **(Exodus 24:4)**
Book of the Wars of the Lord **(Numbers 21:14)**

Book of Jasher (**Joshua 10:13**)
Book of the Acts of Solomon (**1 Kings 11:14**)
The Book of Gad the Seer (**1 Chronicles 29:29**)
Nathan the Prophet (**1 Chronicles 29:29**, and **2 Chronicles 9:29**)
Prophecy of Ahijah (**2 Chronicles 9:29**)
Visions of Iddo (**2 Chronicles 9:29**)
Book of Shemaiah (**2 Chronicles 12:15**)
Book of Jehu (**2 Chronicles 20:34**)
Acts of Uzziah (**2 Chronicles 26:22**)
Saying of the Seers (**2 Chronicles 33:19**)
Paul's Epistle to the Saints of Laodicea (**Colossians 4:16**)
Paul's First Epistle to the Corinthians (**1 Corinthians 5:9**)
Former Epistle of Jude (**Jude 1:3**)
Prophecies of Enoch (**Jude 1:14**)

> Note: *All the Books of the New Testament were written by ONLY 6 Apostles, of which only four were among the original twelve, they are Matthew, John, Peter, and Jude; Paul, and James (the brother of Jesus) are not of the original 12.*

WHERE ARE THE WRITINGS OF THE OTHER EIGHT ORIGINAL APOSTLES?

Are we to believe that they NEVER wrote anything? If their writings are someday discovered, are they to be REJECTED because they are not in our present-day Bible? Are their writings not to be accepted as the word of God, valid and holy, as the 27 books we currently have? And where are the writings of the other four Apostles mentioned in the Bible, Matthias (Acts 1:21–26), who was the replacement for Judas Iscariot, and Barnabas and Saul (Paul) (Acts 13:1–4), and James the Lord's brother? Are we to believe that they never wrote anything either?

It wasn't long after the death of the Apostles and Prophets, that uninspired zealots equipped with the philosophies of men wasted no time in changing the pure teachings of Jesus Christ in order to establish a church of their own liking. Complicated doctrines such as that of the "Trinity" gave these men power over the believers.

We have the collection of books that we call the Holy Bible because of the efforts of the Catholic Church. Yet since the time of the King James Version of the Bible, Protestant Christianity has rejected the fourteen books of the Apocrypha as contained in the earlier Catholic Bible. Because of the Protestant rejection of these books, does it make them invalid, and not the word of God? Or does it mean as per **Revelation 22:18–19**, that these Protestants who removed the word of God from the Bible, will suffer "the plagues that are written in this book" and lose their "part out of the book of life"?

What about all the different translations or versions of the Bible? There are over fifty different English versions of the Bible alone. Some try to claim that although the exact choice of words or sentence structure is different in each translation, the meaning is identical. Unfortunately this is not always true.

EXAMPLE #1: MARK 16:16

King James Version: "He *that believeth* and is baptized shall be saved."

New American Standard Version: "He who *has believed* and has been baptized shall be saved."

Different words and sentences, and the meaning is NOT identical. Did you catch the difference? The NASV says "He who *HAS believed*," past tense; while the King James says "He that *believeth*," present tense. Just because you may have believed and now no longer believe, does not assure you salvation. If you once believed in God and later you turn against God, do you think He will welcome you with open arms? The NASV leads you to believe so.

Unfortunately many Christians believe from Bible translations such as the NASV that all you have to do is believe at one time in your life, and you can live the rest of your life however you choose.

EXAMPLE #2: JOHN 19:17

King James Version: "And he *bearing his cross* went forth into a place called the place of a skull, which is called in the Hebrew Golgotha: Where they crucified him."

The New World Translation: *"Bearing the torture stake* for himself, he went out to the so-called Skull Place, which is Golgotha in Hebrew. There they nailed him to the stake."

The New World Translation (1950, the Jehovah's Witness Bible) should be avoided because its considered by all biblical scholars, other than those who belong to the Jehovah's Witnesses Church, to be corrupt, being a sectarian paraphrase rather than a true translation of the Holy Scriptures.

And let's not forget the translation and copy errors made by the early Christian scribes and copyists. We must remember that the printing press and the computer were not available to these men and women when they made copies of the scriptures. Many of them wrote notes in the margins and when someone else continued with their work, these margin notes often made their way into the body of the texts. Some of these changes were made accidently, and others were made intentionally by those who were determined to make the scriptures agree with their personal or churches' beliefs, teachings and doctrine. Some of these changes were made in modern times; the Jehovah's Witnesses New World Translation (1950), is a glaring example of this.

There are those who claim that God will not allow his "word" to be corrupted by man. Even though every educated and honest biblical scholar worth his salt will not only tell you that this view is ignorant, wrong, and not based on scientific fact;

they will actually show you these changes. Yet in spite of this there are those who refuse to accept proven scientific fact.

If God would allow His covenant people (the Jews) to crucify His Son, and allow man to murder His ordained Apostles, how in the world could we ever justify thinking that He would not allow man to modify, corrupt or delete His word from the Holy Bible?

Here is something else to think about: There are not just hundreds, but thousands of Christian denominations (faiths), and they can't even agree with each other when it comes to scripture interpretation and doctrine.

They all teach something different about the same God the Father and Jesus Christ! If they did agree with each other on these things, there would be only one Christian church. No Catholics, no Baptists (dozens of different sects there), no Presbyterians, no Methodists, no Pentecostals, no Quakers, no Amish, no Episcopalians, no Fundamentalists, no Christian Science, no Jehovah's Witness, no Seventh Day Adventists; just one Christian church with the same name, all believing the same doctrine and teaching the same truths.

If God will allow all these different Christian denominations (faiths) to teach something different about Him, His Son, and His church; what would ever convince you that God wouldn't allow the same corruption to happen to the book we call the Bible?

Paul the Apostle spoke about the existence of *one true church* when he preached that there is "one Lord, *one faith*, one baptism." (**Ephesians 4:5**).

Paul then asked, "Now this I say, that every one of you saith, I am of Paul; and I of Apollos; and I of Cephas; and I of Christ. *Is Christ divided?* was Paul crucified for you? or were ye baptized in the name of Paul?" (**1 Corinthians 1:12–18**)

Paul taught that "*God is not the author of confusion*" "but of "order." (**1 Corinthians 14:33, 40**)

Does all this sound like anything other than "confusion," and the lack of "order"?

And what about the Christian creeds; the Nicene Creed, the Apostles Creed, the Athanasian, etc.? These man-made creeds, comprised of the philosophies of men mingled with scripture, were composed, added, and made doctrine after the 27 books of the New Testament were written. Nowhere are they mentioned in the Bible. And there are many different versions of these creeds, changed by the different Christian denominations to present "their" beliefs.

Aren't these man-made creeds just another way that man had added to the Bible and to the doctrines and teachings of Jesus Christ and his Apostles?

Isn't this . . . **Man making God into what man wants God to be?**

See chapter 9: **"Bible Errors — Contradictions — Inerrancy"**
See chapter 10: **"Bible Incomplete — Missing Scripture"**

CHAPTER 9

BIBLE ERRORS
CONTRADICTIONS
INERRANCY

"And about the ninth hour Jesus cried with a loud voice, saying, 'Eli, eli, lama sabachthani?' that is to say, 'My God, my God, why hast thou forsaken me?' . . . Jesus, when he cried again with a loud voice, yielded up the ghost." **(Matthew 27:46, 50)**

"And when Jesus had cried with a loud voice, he said, 'Father, unto thy hands I commend my spirit:' and having said thus, he gave up the ghost." **(Luke 23:46)**

"When Jesus therefore had received the vinegar, he said, 'It is finished:' and he bowed his head, and gave up the ghost." **(John 19:30)**

If as Catholic and Protestant Christian churches believe and teach, that the Bible is complete and inerrant; why then do these three scriptures quoting the Savior's last and final words on the cross, not agree with each other? This chapter will help you to demonstrate the Bible's errors, contradictions, and inerrancy; and why more than the Bible should be welcomed by truth seeking peoples.

BIBLE ERRORS
CONTRADICTIONS — INERRANCY

(These are just a few . . . There are many more.)

Scriptures used by some Christian faiths to substantiate their belief and teaching that the Bible is the complete word of God and without errors or contradictions:

Sola scriptura **is the Christian doctrine that Biblical Scripture alone is the supreme authority** in all matters of doctrine and practice for the Christian faith. **The Bible is complete, authoritative, inerrant and true.** *(See the chapter "Bible — Supreme Authority — Sola Scriptura" in this book.)*

"All Scripture is breathed out by God and profitable for teaching, for reproof, for correction, and for training in righteousness." **(2 Timothy 3:16 ESV, NIV)**

> *Note: Evangelical and Fundamentalist Protestant Christians teach that the Bible is 100% the inerrant word of God and that He spoke His word directly to the biblical writers as they wrote it down.*

NOW THE REST OF THE STORY . . . (scriptures that further explain or clarify the topic)

THE DEATH OF JESUS CHRIST

"The God of our fathers raised up Jesus, whom ye slew and *hanged on a tree*." **(Acts 5:30)**

"For Christ dispatched me, not to go baptizing, but to go declaring the good news, not with wisdom of speech, that *the torture stake* [cross] of the Christ should not be made useless. For the speech about *the torture stake* [cross] is foolishness to those who are perishing, but to us who are being saved it is God's power." **(1 Corinthians 1:17–18 NWT**; see also **Matthew 10:38 NWT)**

"And saying, Thou that destroyest the temple, and buildest it in three days, save thyself. If thou be the Son of God, *come down from the cross*." **(Matthew 27:40)**

"And they compel one Simon a Cyrenian, who passed by, coming out of the country, the father of Alexander and Rufus, *to bear his cross*." **(Mark 15:21)** (Simon carried His cross.)

"And he *bearing his cross* went forth into a place called the place of a skull, which is called in the Hebrew Golgotha: Where they *crucified him*, and two other with him, on either side one, and Jesus in the midst." **(John 19:17)**

> *Note: Was Christ crucified on a cross, hanged on a tree, or died on a torture stake?*

Jesus's Last Words

"And about the ninth hour Jesus cried with a loud voice, saying, 'Eli, eli, lama sabachthani?' that is to say, *'My God, my God, why hast thou forsaken me?'* . . . Jesus, when he cried again with a loud voice, yielded up the ghost." **(Matthew 27:46, 50)**

"And when Jesus had cried with a loud voice, he said, *'Father, unto thy hands I commend my spirit:'* and having said thus, he gave up the ghost." **(Luke 23:46)**

"When Jesus therefore had received the vinegar, he said, *'It is finished:'* and he bowed his head, and gave up the ghost." **(John 19:30)**

> *Note: Which one of these did Jesus really say? Matthew, Luke, and John ALL disagree as to what Jesus actually said.*

What Did Pilate Write on the Title above Jesus's Head?

"And Pilate wrote a title, and put it on the cross. And the writing was, *Jesus of Nazareth the King of the Jews.* This title then read many of the Jews: for the place where Jesus was crucified was nigh to the city: and it was written in Hebrew, and Greek, and Latin." **(John 19:19–20)**

"And set up over his head his accusation written, *THIS IS JESUS THE KING OF THE JEWS.*" **(Matthew 27:37)**

"And the superscription of his accusation was written over, *THE KING OF THE JEWS.*" **(Mark 15:26)**

"And a superscription also was written over him in letters of Greek, and Latin, and Hebrew, *THIS IS THE KING OF THE JEWS.*" **(Luke 23:38)**

> *Note: Matthew, Mark, Luke, and John ALL differ. Which one is correct?*

Who Is the Lord God the God Of?

"Now that the dead are raised, even Moses shewed at the bush, when he calleth the Lord the God of Abraham, and the God of Isaac, and the God of Jacob. *For he is not a God of the dead,* but of the living: for all live unto him." **(Luke 20:37–38)**

"For to this end Christ both died, and rose, and revived, that he might be *Lord both of the dead and living.*" **(Romans 14:9)**

> *Note: Is God the God only of the living, or is He the God of both the living and the dead? The answer: He is the God of both the living and the dead.*

Who Is the Father of Jesus?

"Therefore being a prophet, and knowing that God had sworn with an oath to him, *that of the fruit of his loins, according to the flesh, he would raise up Christ* to sit on his throne." **(Acts 2:30)**

"Blessed be *God,* even *the Father* of our Lord Jesus Christ, the Father of mercies, and the God of all comfort." **(2 Corinthians 1:3)**

"Now the birth of Jesus Christ was on this wise: When as his mother Mary was espoused to Joseph, before they came together, she was found with *child of the Holy Ghost*." **(Matthew 1:18)**

Note: Who is the father of Jesus Christ, God the Father or the Holy Ghost?

WHO IS THE FATHER OF JOSEPH?

"And *Jacob* begat Joseph the husband of Mary, of whom was born Jesus, who is called Christ." **(Matthew 1:16)**

"And Jesus himself began to be about thirty years of age, being (as was supposed) the son of Joseph, which was the son of *Heli*." **(Luke 3:23)**

WHO JUDGES MANKIND — GOD THE FATHER, JESUS, OR THE APOSTLES?

"*Our God shall come*, and shall not keep silence: a fire shall devour before him, and it shall be very tempestuous round about him. He shall call to the heavens from above, and to the earth, *that he may judge his people*. Gather my saints together unto me; those that have made a covenant with me by sacrifice. And the heavens shall declare his righteousness: *for God is judge himself*. Selah." **(Psalms 50:3–6)**

"And if ye call on *the Father*, who without respect of persons *judgeth* according to every man's work, pass the time of your sojourning here in fear." **(1 Peter 1:17)**

"For *the Father judgeth no man, but hath committed all judgment unto the Son*." **(John 5:22)**

"Then answered Peter and said unto him, Behold, we have forsaken all, and followed thee; what shall we have therefore? And Jesus said unto them, Verily I say unto you, *That ye which have followed me*, in the regeneration when the Son of man shall sit in the throne of his glory, *ye also shall sit upon twelve thrones, judging the twelve tribes of Israel*." **(Matthew 19:27–28**; see also **Luke 22:29–30)**

THE DEATH OF JUDAS ISCARIOT

"Now this man (Judas) purchased a field with the reward of iniquity; and *falling headlong*, he *burst asunder in the midst, and all his bowels gushed out*." **(Acts 1:18)**

"And he (Judas) cast down the pieces of silver in the temple, and departed, and went and *hanged himself*. And the chief priests . . . bought with them the potter's field." **(Matthew 27:5–7)**

WHO BOUGHT THE POTTER'S FIELD?

"Now *this man purchased a field with the reward of iniquity*; and falling headlong, he burst asunder in the midst, and all his bowels gushed out. And it was known unto all the dwellers at Jerusalem; insomuch as that field is called in their proper tongue, Aceldama, that is to say, The field of blood." **(Acts 1:18–19)**

"*And the chief priests took the silver pieces*, and said, It is not lawful for to put them into the treasury, because it is the price of blood. And they took counsel, *and bought with them the potter's field*, to bury strangers in. Wherefore that field was called, The field of blood, unto this day." **(Matthew 27:6–8)**

> *Note: Did Judas jump off a cliff or hang himself? Did Judas or the chief priests buy the potters field?*

Just How Many Beasts Were on the Ark?

"Of *every clean beast thou shalt take to thee by sevens*, the male and his female: and of *beasts that are not clean by two*, the male and his female." **(Genesis 7:2)**

"Of *clean beasts, and of beasts that are not clean*, and of fowls, and of every thing that creepeth upon the earth, There went *in two and two* unto Noah into the ark, the male and the female, as God had commanded Noah." **(Genesis 7:8–9)**

> *Note: These two scriptures are only six verses apart and yet they disagree.*

Which Did God Create First: Beasts or Man?

"And *God made the beast of the earth* after his kind, and cattle after their kind, and every thing that creepeth upon the earth after his kind: and God saw that it was good. *And God said, Let us make man* in our image, after our likeness: and let them have dominion over the fish of the sea, and over the fowl of the air, and over the cattle, and over all the earth, and over every creeping thing that creepeth upon the earth." **(Genesis 1:25–26)**

> *Note: In Genesis 1:25 God makes <u>the beasts first</u>, next in Genesis 1:26 God makes man.*

"And the Lord God said, *It is not good that the man should be alone*; I will make him an help meet for him. *And out of the ground the Lord God formed every beast* of the field, and every fowl of the air; *and brought them unto Adam to see what he would call them*: and whatsoever Adam called every living creature, that was the name thereof." **(Genesis 2:18–19)**

> *Note: In Genesis 2:18, God makes <u>man first</u>, next in Genesis 2:19 God makes the beasts.*

Paul's Vision

"And the men which journeyed with him stood speechless, *hearing a voice*, but seeing no man." **(Acts 9:7)**

"And they that were with me saw indeed the light, and were afraid; *but they heard not the voice* of him that spake to me." **(Acts 22:9)**

> *Note: Did they or did they not hear a voice?*

How Many Years of Famine Were There?

"So Gad came to David, and told him, and said unto him, Shall *seven years of famine* come unto thee in thy land? or wilt thou flee three months before thine enemies, while they pursue thee?" **(2 Samuel 24:13)**

"So Gad came to David, and said unto him, Thus saith the Lord, Choose thee. Either *three years of famine* or three months to be destroyed before thy foes, while that the sword of thine enemies overtaketh thee." **(1 Chronicles 21:11)**

Who Moved David to Number Israel?

"And again *the anger of the Lord* was kindled against Israel, and he moved David against them to say, Go, number Israel and Judah." **(2 Samuel 24:1)**

"And *Satan* stood up against Israel, and provoked David to number Israel." **(1 Chronicles 21:1)**

> *Note: Who moved David to number Israel: the Lord or Satan?*

Does God Tempt Mankind?

"And it came to pass after these things, that *God did tempt Abraham*: and he said, Behold, here I am." **(Genesis 22:1)**

"Let no man say when he is tempted, I am tempted of God; for *God cannot be tempted with evil, neither tempteth he any man*." **(James 1:13)**

How Many Children Did Michal, the Daughter of Saul, Have?

"Therefore *Michal the daughter of Saul had no child* unto the day of her death." **(2 Samuel 6:23)**

"But the king took the two sons of Rizpah the daughter of Aiah, whom she bare unto Saul, Armoni and Mephibosheth; and *the five sons of Michal the daughter of Saul*, whom she brought up for Adriel the son of Barzillai the Meholathite." **(2 Samuel 21:8)**

How Old Was Jehoiachin When He Began to Reign?

"Jehoiachin was *eighteen years old* when he began to reign, and he reigned in Jerusalem three months. And his mother's name was Nehushta, the daughter of Elnathan of Jerusalem." **(2 Kings 24:8)**

"Jehoiachin was *eight years old* when he began to reign, and he reigned three months and ten days in Jerusalem: and he did that which was evil in the sight of the Lord." **(2 Chronicles 36:9)**

BELIEVE IN CHRIST AND YOU WILL NEVER DIE?

"*And whosoever liveth and believeth in me shall never die.* Believest thou this?" **(John 11:26)**

"*For as in Adam all die*, even so in Christ shall all be made alive." **(1 Corinthians 15:22)**

DOES GOD DWELL IN TEMPLES OR NOT?

"God that made the world and all things therein, seeing that he is Lord of heaven and earth, *dwelleth not in temples made with hands*." **(Acts 17:24**; see also **Acts 7:48–49)**

"Go and tell my servant David, Thus saith the Lord, *Shalt thou build me an house for me to dwell in?*" **(2 Samuel 7:5**; see also **Exodus 25:8)**

"And whoso shall swear by the temple, sweareth by it, *and by him that dwelleth therein*." **(Matthew 23:21)**

WILL THE SINS OF MAN BE FORGIVEN OR NOT?

"Verily I say unto you, *All sins shall be forgiven unto the sons of men*, and blasphemies wherewith soever they shall blaspheme: But he that shall blaspheme against the Holy Ghost hath never forgiveness, but is in danger of eternal damnation." **(Mark 3:28–29)**

"*Envyings, murders, drunkenness, revellings, and such like*: of the which I tell you before, as I have also told you in time past, that *they which do such things shall not inherit the kingdom of God*." **(Galatians 5:21)**

HOW MANY ANGELS GREETED MARY MAGDALENE AT THE TOMB?

"In the end of the Sabbath . . . came Mary Magdalene and the other Mary to see the sepulcher . . . for *the angel of the Lord descended from heaven*, and came and rolled back the stone from the door, and sat upon it." **(Matthew 28:1–7**; see also **Mark 16:1–7)**

> *Note: Per Matthew and Mark, there was one angel.*

"And they found the stone rolled away from the sepulchre. . . . And it came to pass, as they were much perplexed thereabout, behold, *two men stood by them in shining garments*." **(Luke 24:2, 4**; see also verses 1, 3, 5 & 6; see also **John 20:11–12)**

> *Note: Per Luke and John there were two angels.*

JUST WHAT DID JESUS CHRIST SAY TO CAIAPHAS?

"Jesus saith unto him, *Thou hast said*: nevertheless I say unto you, Hereafter shall ye see the Son of man sitting on the right hand of power, and coming in the clouds of heaven." **(Matthew 26:64)**

"And Jesus said, *I am*: and ye shall see the Son of man sitting on the right hand of power, and coming in the clouds of heaven." **(Mark 14:62)**

"Art thou the Christ? tell us. And he said unto them, *If I tell you, ye will not believe*: And if I also ask you, *ye will not answer me, nor let me go*. Hereafter shall the Son of man sit on the right hand of the power of God. Then said they all, Art thou then the Son of God? And he said unto them, *Ye say that I am*." **(Luke 22:67–70)**

> *Note: Either the Savior answered directly or He did not. These gospel passages disagree as to what exactly He did say.*

Does God Send Evil Spirits upon Man?

"*And the evil spirit from the Lord was upon Saul*, as he sat in his house with his javelin in his hand: and David played with his hand. And *Saul sought to smite David* even to the wall with the javelin; but he slipped away out of Saul's presence, and he smote the javelin into the wall: and David fled, and escaped that night." **(1 Samuel 19:9–10)**

"Let no man say when he is tempted, I am tempted of God; for *God cannot be tempted with evil, neither tempteth he any man*." **(James 1:13)**

> *Note: 1 Samuel 18:9–10 tells us there was an "evil spirit from the Lord," yet James 1:13 tells us that God does NOT tempt man nor send evil spirits to do so for Him.*

Will the Earth Remain Forever?

"Who laid the foundations of *the earth, that it should not be removed for ever*." **(Psalms 104:5)**

"One generation passeth away, and another generation cometh: *but the earth abideth for ever*." **(Ecclesiastes 1:4)**

"And I saw *a new heaven and a new earth: for the first heaven and the first earth were passed away*; and there was no more sea." **(Revelation 21:1)**

> *Note: Psalms 104:5 and Ecclesiastes 1:4, tell us the earth will remain forever. However, Revelation 21:1, tells us first earth is to be replaced with a new earth.*

Is Wisdom Good or Not?

"Wisdom is the principal thing; *therefore get wisdom*: and with all thy getting get understanding." **(Proverbs 4:7)**

"*For it is written, I will destroy the wisdom of the wise*, and will bring to nothing the understanding of the prudent." **(1 Corinthians 1:19)**

The Lord's Prayer— What Did Jesus Really Say?

"After this manner therefore pray ye: Our Father which art in heaven, Hallowed be thy name. Thy kingdom come. Thy will be done *in earth, as it is in heaven*. Give us this day our daily bread. And *forgive us our debts*, as we forgive our debtors. And lead us not into temptation, but deliver us from evil: *For thine is the kingdom, and the power, and the glory, for ever*. Amen." **(Matthew 6:9–13)**

"And he said unto them, When ye pray, say, Our Father which art in heaven, Hallowed be thy name. Thy kingdom come. Thy will be done, *as in heaven, so in earth*. Give us day by day our daily bread. And *forgive us our sins*; for we also forgive every one that is indebted to us. And lead us not into temptation; but deliver us from evil." **(Luke 11:2–4)**

> *Note: If God spoke the words of the Bible, why don't Matthew and Luke agree as to the wording of the Lord's Prayer? Would He not have spoken the same words to Matthew and Luke as His Son Jesus had spoken them?*

And There Are Many, Many More!

The Sins of the Fathers (Isaiah 14:21 vs. Deuteronomy 24:16)
Moses Personality (Numbers 12:3 vs. Numbers 31:14, 17–18)
Who Shall Bear Burdens? (Galatians 6:2 vs. 6:5)
Who Has Ascended to Heaven? (2 Kings 2:11 vs. John 3:13)
Can God Be Seen? (1 Timothy 6:16 vs. Genesis 32:30)
God of War or of Peace? (Exodus 15:3 vs. Romans 15:33)
Did Jesus Baptize or Not? (John 3:22, 26 vs. John 4:2)

See chapter 8: **"Bible — Add to or Take Away From"**
See chapter 10: **"Bible Incomplete — Missing Scripture"**

CHAPTER 10

BIBLE INCOMPLETE MISSING SCRIPTURE

All the Books of the New Testament were written by ONLY six Apostles, of which only four were among the original twelve Apostles: Matthew, John, Peter, and Jude; Paul and James the brother of Jesus are not of the original twelve.

Where are the writings of the other eight original Apostles?

Are we to believe that they NEVER wrote anything? If their writings are someday discovered, are they to be REJECTED because they are not in our present day Bible? Are their writings not to be accepted as the word of God, valid and holy, as the twenty-seven books we currently have? And where are the writings of the other two Apostles mentioned in the Bible, Matthias (Acts 1:21–26), who was the replacement for Judas Iscariot, and Barnabas (Acts 13:1–4). Are we to believe that they never wrote anything either?

BIBLE INCOMPLETE
MISSING SCRIPTURE

Scriptures used by some Christian faiths to substantiate their belief and teaching that the Bible is the full, complete, and final word of God:

"All Scripture is breathed out by God and profitable for teaching, for reproof, for correction, and for training in righteousness." **(2 Timothy 3:16 ESV)**

> *Note: This scripture is often used by Protestant, Evangelical and Fundamentalist Christians to validate their claim that God personally dictated to the biblical writers exactly what they were to write; that God Himself wrote the Bible.*

"For I testify unto every man that heareth the words of the prophecy of this book, If any man shall add unto these things, God shall add unto him the plagues that are written in this book: And if any man shall take away from the words of the book of this prophecy, God shall take away his part out of the book of life, and out of the holy city, and from the things which are written in this book." **(Revelation 22:18–19)**

> *Note: This scripture talks about the book of Revelation and ONLY the book of Revelation.*

> *Note: John wrote the book of Revelation BEFORE he wrote his Epistles. Revelation written about AD 90 to 95, John's Epistles written about AD 95 to 110.*

Now See . . .

"Ye shall not add unto the word which I command you, neither shall ye diminish ought from it, that ye may keep the commandments of the Lord your God which I command you." **(Deuteronomy 4:2)**

"Every word of God is pure: he is a shield unto them that put their trust in him. Add thou not unto his words, lest he reprove thee, and thou be found a liar." **(Proverbs 30:5–6)**

> *Note: Does this mean that EVERYTHING written since Deuteronomy 4:2 and Proverbs 30:5–6 is adding unto the word of God and invalid? Or further proof that Revelation 22:18–19 is talking only about the book of Revelation?*

"According as his divine power hath given unto us all things that pertain unto life and godliness, through the knowledge of him that hath called us to glory and virtue." **(2 Peter 1:3)**

"Henceforth I call you not servants; for the servant knoweth not what his lord doeth: but I have called you friends; for all things that I have heard of my Father I have made known unto you." **(John 15:15)**

Now the Rest of the Story . . . (scriptures that further explain or clarify the topic)

"*I have yet many things to say unto you, but ye cannot bear them now.* Howbeit when he, the Spirit of truth, is come, he will guide you into all truth: for he shall not speak of himself; but whatsoever he shall hear, that shall he speak: and he will shew you things to come." (**John 16:12–13**)

> *Note: See John 16:1–11, Jesus is telling the Apostles of His death and resurrection, that He must now go to His Father, and that the Holy Ghost will come. In verse 12 above, He tells His Apostles that He has much more to tell them, to teach them, but they are not ready to receive them yet, and that the Holy Ghost will bring these things to them later. If the Holy Ghost is to give "many things" that the Apostles "[could not] bear" at that time, then Christ did not "make known unto them" all things that He had heard of His Father" as John 15:15 so says.*

"But the Comforter, *which is the Holy Ghost*, whom the Father will send in my name, *he shall teach you all things*, and bring all things to your remembrance, whatsoever I have said unto you." (**John 14:26**)

> *Note: If the Bible is the "full and complete word of God" as so claimed by Protestant Christianity, why would Jesus Christ say to His disciples and Apostles that, "the Holy Ghost . . . he shall teach you all things"?*

Where Are These Books (Scriptures) Mentioned in the Bible That We Don't Have?

1. Book of the Covenant (**Exodus 24:4**)
2. Book of the Wars of the Lord (**Numbers 21:14**)
3. Book of Jasher (**Joshua 10:13**)
4. Book of the Acts of Solomon (**1 Kings 11:14**)
5. The Book of Gad the Seer (**1 Chronicles 29:29**)
6. Nathan the Prophet (**1 Chronicles 29:29**, and **2 Chronicles 9:29**)
7. Prophecy of Ahijah (**2 Chronicles 9:29**)
8. Visions of Iddo (**2 Chronicles 9:29**)
9. Book of Shemaiah (**2 Chronicles 12:15**)
10. Book of Jehu (**2 Chronicles 20:34**)
11. Acts of Uzziah (**2 Chronicles 26:22**)
12. Saying of the Seers (**2 Chronicles 33:19**)
13. Paul's Epistle to the Saints of Laodicea (**Colossians 4:16**)
14. Paul's First Epistle to the Corinthians (**1 Corinthians 5:9**)
15. Former Epistle of Jude (**Jude 1:3**)
16. Prophecies of Enoch (**Jude 1:14**)

> *Note: All the Books of the New Testament were written by ONLY six Apostles, of which only four were among the original twelve Apostles;*

Matthew, John, Peter and Jude; Paul and James the brother of Jesus are not of the original twelve Apostles.

WHERE ARE THE WRITINGS OF THE OTHER EIGHT ORIGINAL APOSTLES?

Are we to believe that they NEVER wrote anything? If there writings are someday discovered, are they to be REJECTED because they are not in our present day Bible? Are their writings not to be accepted as the word of God, valid and holy, as the twenty-seven books we currently have? And where are the writings of the other two Apostles mentioned in the Bible, Matthias (Acts 1:21–26), who was the replacement for Judas Iscariot, and Barnabas (Acts 13:1–4). Are we to believe that they never wrote anything either?

"The word of the Lord came again unto me, saying, Moreover, thou son of man, take thee one stick, and *write upon it, For Judah,* and for the children of Israel his companions: then take another stick, and *write upon it, For Joseph,* the stick of Ephraim, and for all the house of Israel his companions: *And join them one to another into one stick*; and they shall become one in thine hand. And when the children of thy people shall speak unto thee, saying, Wilt thou not shew us what thou meanest by these? Say unto them, Thus saith the Lord God; Behold, I will take the stick of Joseph, which is in the hand of Ephraim, and the tribes of Israel his fellows, and will put them with him, even with the stick of Judah, and make them one stick, and they shall be one in mine hand. *And the sticks whereon thou writest shall be in thine hand before their eyes.*" **(Ezekiel 37:15–20)**

> *Note: What is the Stick (Book) of Judah? Where is it? What is the Stick (Book) of Joseph? Where is it?*

"Therefore, brethren, stand fast, and hold the traditions which ye have been taught, whether by *word, or our epistle.*" **(2 Thessalonians 2:15)**

> *Note: Much of what the Apostles taught was by word of mouth only and never written down.*

"And there are also many other things which Jesus did, the which, if they should be written every one, I suppose that even *the world itself could not contain the books that should be written.* Amen." **(John 21:25)**

"And many other signs truly did Jesus in the presence of his disciples, *which are not written in this book.*" **(John 20:30)**

The Bible as we know it did not exist until in his Easter letter, Athanasius, Bishop of Alexandria, produced a list of books that would become the books of the New Testament in AD 367. Then in AD 397, at the Synod of Carthage, the church architects decided on an "official" collection of books, which is the current Bible that we have today.[1]

Ironically, 2,000 years has not settled the argument as to which books should be determined canonical. The Roman Catholic Church has its selection of books it has determined to be canonical, the Orthodox Catholic churches have their selection of books and to this day have not decreed them to be canonical. And then the Protestant churches had to have their own determination as to which books were indeed the word of God; so they discarded the 14 Apocrypha books from the Roman Catholic Bible. But then this is still not the end of the Protestant controversy, as some of their churches do use and accept the Apocrypha books as the word of God.

The church could not make a decision on which of the Old Testament books to accept and canonize until the seventeenth century. And the book of Revelation was disputed and not finally accepted until the fifteenth century.

And of course the question must be asked . . . If the writings of the other seven original Apostles (Judas Iscariot excluded) whose writings are not in our current Bible and the writings of the other two Apostles who were selected and ordained later are discovered, will they be accepted as divine scripture and allowed to be added to our current Bible? Or will those books have to be discarded because of **Revelation 22:18–19?**

Nowhere within its inspired pages does the Bible make the claim that it is the only word of God.

See chapter 8: **"Bible — Add To or Take Away From"**
See chapter 9: **"Bible Errors — Contradictions — Inerrancy"**

CHAPTER 11

BIBLE
SUPREME AUTHORITY
SOLA SCRIPTURA

Sola scriptura is the Christian doctrine that **Biblical Scripture alone is the supreme authority** in all matters of doctrine and practice for the Christian faith. **The Bible is complete, authoritative, inerrant, and true.**

Bible — Supreme Authority
Sola Scriptura

Sola scriptura is the Christian doctrine that Biblical Scripture alone is the supreme authority in all matters of doctrine and practice for the Christian faith. **The Bible is complete, authoritative, inerrant and true.**

The phrase *"sola scriptura"* is from the Latin: *sola* having the idea of "alone," "ground," "base," and the word *scriptura* meaning "writings"—referring to the Scriptures.

Sola scriptura was the rallying cry of the Protestant Reformation. For centuries the Roman Catholic Church had made its traditions superior in authority to the Bible. This resulted in many practices that were in fact contradictory to the Bible. Some examples are prayer to saints and/or Mary, the Immaculate Conception, transubstantiation, infant baptism, indulgences, and papal authority.

The primary Catholic argument against *sola scriptura* is that the Bible does not explicitly teach *sola scriptura*. Catholics argue that the Bible nowhere states that it is the only authoritative guide for faith and practice. While this is true, the Bible itself may not explicitly argue for *sola scriptura*, it most definitely does not allow for traditions that contradict its message.

Sola scriptura is not as much of an argument against tradition as it is an argument against unbiblical, extra-biblical and/or anti-biblical doctrines. *Sola scriptura* does not nullify the concept of church traditions. Rather, *sola scriptura* gives a solid foundation on which to base church traditions. There are many practices, in both Catholic and Protestant churches, that are the result of traditions, not the explicit teaching of Scripture.

Some Evangelical and Baptist denominations state the doctrine of *sola scriptura* more strongly: Scripture is self-authenticating, clear (perspicuous) to the rational reader, its own interpreter ("Scripture interprets Scripture"), and sufficient of itself to be the final authority of Christian doctrine.

Sola scriptura rejects any original infallible authority other than the Bible. In this view, all secondary authority is derived from the authority of the Scriptures and is therefore subject to reform when compared to the teaching of the Bible. Church councils, preachers, biblical commentators, private revelation, or even a message allegedly from an angel or an apostle are not an original authority alongside the Bible in the *sola scriptura* approach.[1]

Scriptures used by some Christian faiths to substantiate their belief and teaching regarding Sola Scriptura:

"All Scripture is God-breathed and is useful for teaching, rebuking, correcting and training in righteousness." (**2 Timothy 3:16 NIV**)

"All Scripture is breathed out by God and profitable for teaching, for reproof, for correction, and for training in righteousness." **(2 Timothy 3:16 ESV)**

Now the Rest of the Story . . . (scriptures that further explain or clarify the topic)

"All scripture is *given by inspiration of God*, and is profitable for doctrine, for reproof, for correction, for instruction in righteousness." **(2 Timothy 3:16 KJV, ASV, NASB, NLT, RSV, NRSV, Douay-Rheims, NWT, Wycliffe)**

> *Note: The KJV and others state that scripture is "inspired" by God, while the NIV and ESV state that God actually "spoke or dictated" the words of scripture. God Himself did not speak or dictate one word of the Holy Scriptures.*

"For the prophecy came not in old time by the will of man: but holy men of God spake *as they were moved by the Holy Ghost*." **(2 Peter 1:21)**

See chapter 38: **"Priesthood of God — Authority"**
See chapter 4: **"Apostles"**
See chapter 39: **"Prophets"**
See chapter 43: **"Revelation"**
See chapter 31: **"Man-Made Churches"**

CHAPTER 12

THE BOOK OF MORMON

"And other sheep I have, which are not of this fold: them also I must bring, and they shall hear my voice; and there shall be one fold, and one shepherd." **(John 10:16)**

Modern Christianity believes and teaches that God's chosen people, His prophets, and Jesus Christ were only in the Holy Lands of the Middle East. That all scripture came from this area, and there is no other holy scripture other than the Bible. This chapter will help you discuss the Book of Mormon.

THE BOOK OF MORMON

Scriptures used by some Christian faiths to substantiate their belief and teaching that the Book of Mormon is not the word of God:

"For I testify unto every man that heareth the words of the prophecy of this book, If any man shall add unto these things, God shall add unto him the plagues that are written in this book: And if any man shall take away from the words of the book of this prophecy, God shall take away his part out of the book of life, and out of the holy city, and from the things which are written in this book." **(Revelation 22:18–19)**

> *Note: This scripture is referring to the book of Revelation and ONLY the book of Revelation.*

> *Note: The Bible as we know it did not exist until (in his Easter letter) Athanasius Bishop of Alexandria, produced a list of books that would become the books of the New Testament in AD 367. Then in AD 397, at the Synod of Carthage, the church architects decided on an "official" collection of books, which is the current Bible that we have today.*

> *Note: John wrote the book of Revelation BEFORE he wrote his Epistles and his gospel. Revelation was written about AD 96, John's Epistles and gospel were written about AD 98 to 100.*

NOW SEE . . .

"Ye shall not add unto the word which I command you, neither shall ye diminish ought from it, that ye may keep the commandments of the Lord your God which I command you." **(Deuteronomy 4:2)**

AND . . .

"Every word of God is pure: he is a shield unto them that put their trust in him. Add thou not unto his words, lest he reprove thee, and thou be found a liar." **(Proverbs 30:5–6)**

> *Note: Does this mean that EVERYTHING written since Deuteronomy 4:2 and Proverbs 30:5–6 is adding unto the word of God and are invalid? Or that Revelation 22:18–19 is talking ONLY about the book of Revelation?*

"What thing soever I command you, observe to do it: thou shalt not add thereto, nor diminish from it." **(Deuteronomy 12:32)**

"But though we, or an angel from heaven, preach any other gospel unto you than that which we have preached unto you, let him be accursed. As we said before, so say I now again, If any man preach any other gospel unto you than that ye have received, let him be accursed." **(Galatians 1:8–9)**

> *Note: We of the Church of Jesus Christ of Latter-Day Saints and the Book of Mormon are not adding to or taking away from the word of God. We*

are not *"teaching any other gospel." We are teaching exactly what the Apostles and the early Christian Church taught, as true doctrine has been restored through revelation from our Heavenly Father. It is the thousands of Christian Sects today that have changed the doctrine and teachings of the Savior.*

Now the Rest of the Story . . . (scriptures that further explain or clarify the topic)

"And other sheep I have, which are not of this fold: them also I must bring, and they shall hear my voice; and there shall be one fold, and one shepherd." **(John 10:16)**

"The word of the Lord came again unto me, saying, Moreover, thou son of man, take thee one stick, and *write upon it, For Judah,* and for the children of Israel his companions: then take another stick, and *write upon it, For Joseph,* the stick of Ephraim, and for all the house of Israel his companions: *And join them one to another into one stick*; and they shall become one in thine hand. And when the children of thy people shall speak unto thee, saying, Wilt thou not shew us what thou meanest by these? Say unto them, Thus saith the Lord GOD; Behold, I will take the stick of Joseph, which is in the hand of Ephraim, and the tribes of Israel his fellows, and will put them with him, even with the stick of Judah, and make them one stick, and they shall be one in mine hand. *And the sticks whereon thou writest shall be in thine hand before their eyes."* **(Ezekiel 37:15–20)**

> *Note: What is the Stick (Book) of Judah? Where is it? What is the (Stick) Book of Joseph? Where is it?*

"For the Lord hath poured out upon you the spirit of deep sleep, and hath closed your eyes: the prophets and your rulers, the seers hath he covered. And the vision of all is become unto you as *the words of a book that is sealed*, which men deliver to one that is learned, saying, Read this, I pray thee: and he saith, I cannot; for it is sealed: And the book is delivered to him that is not learned, saying, Read this, I pray thee: and he saith, I am not learned. Wherefore the Lord said, Forasmuch as this people draw near me with their mouth, and with their lips do honour me, but have removed their heart far from me, and their fear toward me is taught by the precept of men: Therefore, behold, I will proceed to do a marvellous work among this people, even a marvellous work and a wonder: for the wisdom of their wise men shall perish, and the understanding of their prudent men shall be hid." **(Isaiah 29:10–14)**

Urim and Thummim

"Hebrew term that means 'Lights and Perfections.' An instrument prepared of God to assist man in obtaining revelation from the Lord and in translating languages" (Bible Dictionary, "Urim and Thummim"). The following Bible scriptures support Urim and Thummim, but unfortunately do not explain their usage.

"And thou shalt put in the breastplate of judgment the *Urim and the Thummim*; and they shall be upon Aaron's heart, when he goeth in before the Lord: and Aaron shall bear the judgment of the children of Israel upon his heart before the Lord continually." (**Exodus 28:30**; see also **Leviticus 8:7–8**)

"And he shall stand before Eleazar the priest, who shall ask counsel for him after the judgment of *Urim* before the Lord: at his word shall they go out, and at his word they shall come in, both he, and all the children of Israel with him, even all the congregation." (**Numbers 27:21**)

"And of Levi he said, Let *thy Thummim and thy Urim* be with thy holy one, whom thou didst prove at Massah, and with whom thou didst strive at the waters of Meribah." (**Deuteronomy 33:8**)

"And when Saul inquired of the Lord, the Lord answered him not, neither by dreams, nor by *Urim*, nor by prophets." (**1 Samuel 28:6**)

"And the Tirshatha said unto them, that they should not eat of the most holy things, till there stood up a priest with *Urim and with Thummim*." (**Ezra 2:63**; see also **Nehemiah 4:65**)

See chapter 8: **"Bible — Add To or Take Away From"**
See chapter 9: **"Bible Errors — Contradictions — Inerrancy"**
See chapter 10: **"Bible — Incomplete — Missing Scripture"**
See chapter 11: **"Bible — Supreme Authority — Sola Scriptura"**

CHAPTER 13

CHRIST'S CHURCH

"And he gave some, apostles; and some, prophets; and some, evangelists; and some, pastors and teachers; For the perfecting of the saints, for the work of the ministry, for the edifying of the body of Christ: Till we all come in the unity of the faith, and of the knowledge of the Son of God, unto a perfect man, unto the measure of the stature of the fullness of Christ: That we henceforth be no more children, tossed to and fro, and carried about with every wind of doctrine, by the sleight of men, and cunning craftiness, whereby they lie in wait to deceive." **(Ephesians 4:11–14)**

A Google search will show that there are over 30,000 different Christian faiths! 30,000! Let's assume that this is a little high and estimate that there are only 300 different Christian faiths. That's still 300 different churches teaching 300 different beliefs about the same God and Jesus Christ! Did the Savior and his Apostles establish multiple churches with instructions to each to teach different doctrines? This chapter will help you to explain why Jesus Christ established only one true church.

CHRIST'S CHURCH

If we desired to find Christ's true Church today, we would want to match the spiritual blueprint found in the New Testament against every Christian church in the world until we discovered a church that matched that blueprint—organization for organization, teaching for teaching, ordinance for ordinance, fruit for fruit, and revelation for revelation.

In our search, we would find some churches that had some similarities—a teaching here a teaching there, and some may even agree on multiple teachings, an ordinance that is the same, some offices that bear common names, but our search is not for a church that teaches a few similarities, our search is for the one church that matches the blueprint in every material aspect.

While most churches have some truths and render much good, there can only be one church that has the full truth and power to act for God. Why would God establish multiple churches and authorize His servants to teach conflicting messages when the scriptures clearly declare that "God is not the author of confusion" (1 Corinthians 14:33)?

NOW THE REST OF THE STORY . . . (scriptures that further explain or clarify the topic)

"For *God is not the author of confusion*, but of peace, as in all churches of the saints." **(1 Corinthians 14:33, 40)**

"Let all things be done *decently and in order*." **(1 Corinthians 14:40)**

Paul the Apostle spoke the truth about the existence of one true church when he preached that there is "one Lord, *one faith*, one baptism" **(Ephesians 4:5).**

"Now this I say, that every one of you saith, I am of Paul; and I of Apollos; and I of Cephas; and I of Christ. *Is Christ divided?* was Paul crucified for you? or were ye baptized in the name of Paul?" **(1 Corinthians 1:12–13)**

"Now I beseech you, brethren, by the name of our Lord Jesus Christ, *that ye all speak the same thing*, and *that there be no divisions among you*; but *that ye be perfectly joined together in the same mind and in the same judgment*." **(1 Corinthians 1:10)**

"Now therefore ye are no more strangers and foreigners, but fellow citizens with the saints, and of the household of God; and are *built upon the foundation of apostles and prophets*, Jesus Christ himself being the chief corner stone; *in whom all the building fitly framed together groweth unto an holy temple in the Lord*: in whom ye also are builded together for an habitation of God through the Spirit." **(Ephesians 2:19–22)**

"And he gave some, apostles; and some, prophets; and some, evangelists; and some, pastors and teachers; *For the perfecting of the saints*, for the work of the ministry, for the edifying of the body of Christ: *Till we all come in the unity of the faith*, and of *the knowledge of the Son of God*, unto a perfect man, unto the measure of the stature of the fullness of Christ: *That we henceforth be no more children, tossed to and fro, and carried about with every wind of doctrine*, by the sleight of men, and cunning craftiness, whereby they lie in wait to deceive." **(Ephesians 4:11–14)**

> *Note: Other priesthood officers of Christ's church: "Bishops" (1 Timothy 3, Titus 1:7); "Elders" (Acts 14:23, Titus 1:5); "Deacons" (Philippians 1:1).*

Neither Christ nor his Apostles established different churches teaching different doctrines. When the churches did stray, when they did change the doctrines they were taught, they were chastised and warned that if they did not return to the fold and teach the truth, that they would lose their authority and priesthood to act in the name of God and Jesus Christ.

If all Christian churches were God's "true church," they would ALL be teaching the same gospel doctrines, principles and truths. They would all have and hold the same priesthood.

The question is . . . Why don't they?

Only seven churches still remained that were worthy of mention in the book of Revelation, and the seeds of apostasy were evident even in them. **(Revelation 1:11–20 and Revelation 2, 3)**

To the church of Ephesus: "Remember therefore from whence thou art fallen, and repent, and do the first works; or else I will come unto thee quickly, and *will remove thy candlestick [priesthood authority to act in the name of God]* out of his place, except thou repent." **(Revelation 2:5**; see also verses 1–4)

To the church of Laodiceans: "So then because thou art lukewarm, and neither cold nor hot, I will *spue thee out of my mouth*." **(Revelation 3:19**; see also verses 14–18)

"And Simon Peter answered and said, Thou art the Christ, the Son of the living God. And Jesus answered and said unto him, Blessed art thou, Simon Bar-jona: *for flesh and blood hath not revealed it unto thee, but my Father which is in heaven*." **(Matthew 16:16–17)**

Now See . . .

"And I say also unto thee, That thou art Peter, *and upon this rock I will build my church*; and the gates of hell shall not prevail against it." **(Matthew 16:18)**

Now See . . .

"Moreover, brethren, I would not that ye should be ignorant, how that all our fathers were under the cloud, and all passed through the sea; And were all baptized unto Moses in the cloud and in the sea; And did all eat the same spiritual meat; And did all drink the same spiritual drink: for they drank of that *spiritual Rock* that followed them: *and that Rock was Christ.*" (**1 Corinthians 10:1–4**)

> *Note: Matthew 16:16–18 and 1 Corinthians 10:1–4, help us to understand that when the Savior was talking to Peter, He was NOT telling Peter that he Peter was the "ROCK" upon which Christ will build His church, but that the "REVELATION" Peter had received from the Savior's Father, and continued REVELATION from GOD, was the "ROCK" Christ will build His church upon, and that Christ was that "Rock."*

> *Note: The word translated as "Peter" in the original Greek version of the Bible is "Petros," which means "small rock or pebble"; whereas the Greek word for "rock" is "petra," which means bedrock. Many often misinterpret Matthew 16:18 as Peter being the "rock" because they misinterpret "Petros" and "petra." Now see Matthew 16:23 and Mark 8:33, "But he turned, and said unto Peter, Get thee behind me, Satan: thou art an offence unto me." Jesus rebuked Peter and called him Satan. Would the Savior build his church on someone that he just called Satan?*

"And they continued *steadfastly in the apostles' doctrine* and fellowship, and in breaking of bread, and in prayers." (**Acts 2:42**)

"To the general assembly and *church of the firstborn*, which are written in heaven, and to God the Judge of all, and to the spirits of just men made perfect." (**Hebrews 12:23**)

See the Following Chapters Also

1. Apostles
2. Baptism
3. Baptism for the Dead
4. Bible — Add To or Take Away From
5. Bible Incomplete — Missing Scripture
6. Commandments — Not Just 10!
7. Creation — Who Created the Heavens and the Earth?
8. Death
9. Faith, Grace & Works — Sincere Belief Is Not Enough
10. Forgiveness
11. Godhead — Trinity — Three Separate Beings
12. God — Who Is He?
13. Holy Ghost
14. How Can I Know the Truth? Testimony
15. Heaven — Hell — Degrees of Glory

CHAPTER 14

THE COMMANDMENTS
NOT JUST TEN!

"Teaching them to observe all things whatsoever I have commanded you: and, lo, I am with you always, even unto the end of the world. Amen." **(Matthew 28:20)**

When we talk about commandments, many Christians think only of the Ten Commandments and assume that is all there are. And if they are keeping those 10, they are doing all that is required of them. This chapter will help you to explain the rest of the commandments.

The Commandments — Not Just Ten!

"And God spake all these words, saying, I am the Lord thy God, which have brought thee out of the land of Egypt, out of the house of bondage.

1. **Thou shalt have no other gods before me.**
2. **Thou shalt not make unto thee any graven image, or any likeness of any thing that is in heaven above, or that is in the earth beneath, or that is in the water under the earth.** Thou shalt not bow down thyself to them, nor serve them: for I the Lord thy God am a jealous God, visiting the iniquity of the fathers upon the children unto the third and fourth generation of them that hate me; And shewing mercy unto thousands of them that love me, and keep my commandments.
3. **Thou shalt not take the name of the Lord thy God in vain;** for the Lord will not hold him guiltless that taketh his name in vain.
4. **Remember the sabbath day, to keep it holy.** Six days shalt thou labour, and do all thy work: But the seventh day is the sabbath of the Lord thy God: in it thou shalt not do any work, thou, nor thy son, nor thy daughter, thy manservant, nor thy maidservant, nor thy cattle, nor thy stranger that is within thy gates: For in six days the Lord made heaven and earth, the sea, and all that in them is, and rested the seventh day: wherefore the Lord blessed the sabbath day, and hallowed it.
5. **Honour thy father and thy mother:** that thy days may be long upon the land which the Lord thy God giveth thee.
6. **Thou shalt not kill.**
7. **Thou shalt not commit adultery.**
8. **Thou shalt not steal.**
9. **Thou shalt not bear false witness against thy neighbour.**
10. **Thou shalt not covet** thy neighbour's house, thou shalt not covet thy neighbour's wife, nor his manservant, nor his maidservant, nor his ox, nor his ass, nor any thing that is thy neighbour's."

(Exodus 20:1–17; see also **Deuteronomy 5:6–21)**

The Two GREATEST Commandments

"Master, which is the great commandment in the law? Jesus said unto him, *Thou shalt love the Lord thy God with all thy heart*, and with all thy soul, and with all thy mind. This is the first and great commandment. And the second is like unto it, *Thou shalt love thy neighbour as thyself.* On these two commandments hang all the law and the prophets." **(Matthew 22:36–40)**

DID THE TEN COMMANDMENTS EXIST BEFORE MOSES RECEIVED THEM ON MOUNT SINAI?

The Bible doesn't tell us. Or does it? **Romans 4:15** tells us, *"Because the law worketh wrath: for where no law is, there is no transgression."* Does this mean that Cain was unduly punished for the murder of his brother Abel? Would God punish someone for a transgression when there was no law regarding such? Of course not. God's laws and commandments were given to man in the Garden of Eden, when they partook of the fruit of the Tree of Knowledge of Good and Evil . . . "And the Lord God said, Behold, the man is become as one of us, to know good and evil" **(Genesis 3:22)**, and man has been held accountable to them ever since.

THE COMMANDMENTS OF CHRIST

In which are included the commandments of his apostles, concerning which he said, *"He that heareth you, heareth me"* (**Luke 10:16**), and Paul, *"The things that I write are the commandments of the Lord"* (**1 Corinthians 14:37**).

---

1. ADULTERY

"Ye have heard that it was said by them of old time, Thou shalt not commit adultery: But I say unto you, *That whosoever looketh on a woman to lust after her hath committed adultery with her already in his heart.*" (**Matthew 5:27–28**)

"But I say unto you, That *whosoever shall put away his wife, saving for the cause of fornication, causeth her to commit adultery*: and whosoever shall marry her that is divorced committeth adultery." (**Matthew 5:32**)

> *Note: "whosoever shall marry her that is divorced committeth adultery" applies only to someone marrying another who was divorced for committing adultery or fornication.*

2. AWAIT MY RETURN — LIVE YOUR LIFE RIGHTEOUSLY

"Watch therefore: for ye know not what hour your Lord doth come. . . ." Therefore be ye also ready: for in such an hour as ye think not the Son of man cometh." (**Matthew 24:42–44**)

"But he that shall endure unto the end, *the same shall be saved.*" (**Matthew 24:13**)

3. Be Born Again

"Jesus answered and said unto him, Verily, verily, I say unto thee, *Except a man be born again, he cannot see the kingdom of God.*" (**John 3:3**)

"Marvel not that I said unto thee, *Ye must be born again.*" (**John 3:7**)

"Jesus answered, Verily, verily, I say unto thee, *Except a man be born of water and of the Spirit, he cannot enter into the kingdom of God.*" (**John 3:5**)

4. Be Converted and Become as Little Children

"And said, Verily I say unto you, *Except ye be converted, and become as little children, ye shall not enter into the kingdom of heaven.*" (**Matthew 18:3**)

5. Be of One Mind

"Now I beseech you, brethren, by the name of our Lord Jesus Christ, that ye all speak the same thing, and that there be no divisions among you; but *that ye be perfectly joined together in the same mind and in the same judgment.*" (**1 Corinthians 1:10**)

6. Be Subject to Rulers

"Put them in mind to *be subject to principalities and powers, to obey magistrates,* to be ready to every good work." (**Titus 3:1**)

"*Submit yourselves to every ordinance of man for the Lord's sake*: whether it be to the king, as supreme." (**1 Peter 2:13–17**)

7. Bear One Another's Burdens

"Put on therefore, as the elect of God, holy and beloved, bowels of *mercies, kindness, humbleness of mind, meekness, longsuffering.*" (**Colossians 3:12**)

"*Distributing to the necessity of saints*; given to hospitality." (**Romans 12:13**)

"Rejoice with them that do rejoice, and *weep with them that weep.*" (**Romans 12:15**)

"We then that are strong ought to *bear the infirmities of the weak,* and not to please ourselves. Let every one of us please his neighbour for his good to edification." (**Romans 15:1–2**)

"Pure religion and undefiled before God and the Father is this, To *visit the fatherless and widows in their affliction,* and to keep himself unspotted from the world." (**James 1:27**)

8. Beware of Covetousness

"And he said unto them, Take heed, and *beware of covetousness*: for a man's life consisteth not in the abundance of the things which he possesseth." (**Luke 12:15**)

9. Beware of False Prophets

"*Beware of false prophets, which come to you in sheep's clothing*, but inwardly they are ravening wolves." (**Matthew 7:15**)

"Beloved, believe not every spirit, but try the spirits whether they are of God: because *many false prophets are gone out into the world.*" (**1 John 4:1**)

10. Bring in the Poor

"Then said he also to him that bade him, When thou makest a dinner or a supper, call not thy friends, nor thy brethren, neither thy kinsmen, nor thy rich neighbours; lest they also bid thee again, and a recompence be made thee. But *when thou makest a feast, call the poor, the maimed, the lame, the blind: And thou shalt be blessed*; for they cannot recompense thee: for thou shalt be recompensed at the resurrection of the just." (**Luke 14:12–14**)

"But whoso hath this world's good, and seeth his brother have need, and shutteth up his bowels of compassion from him, how dwelleth the love of God in him? My little children *let us not love in word, neither in tongue; but in deed and in truth.*" (**1 John 3:17–18**)

11. Charity

"And *above all things have fervent charity among yourselves*: for charity shall cover the multitude of sins. Use hospitality one to another without grudging. As every man hath received the gift, even so *minister the same one to another*, as good stewards of the manifold grace of God." (**1 Peter 4:8–10**)

"I have shewed you all things, how that so *labouring ye ought to support the weak*, and to remember the words of the Lord Jesus, how he said, *It is more blessed to give than to receive.*" (**Acts 20:35**)

"And *above all these things put on charity*, which is the bond of perfectness. And *let the peace of God rule in your hearts*, to the which also ye are called in one body; and be ye thankful. *Let the word of Christ dwell in you richly in all wisdom.*" (**Colossians 3:14–16**)

12. Control Your Anger — Be Reconciled

"But now ye also *put off all these; anger, wrath, malice, blasphemy, filthy communication out of your mouth*. Lie not one to another, seeing that ye have put off the old man with his deeds." (**Colossians 3:8–9**)

"*Let no corrupt communication proceed out of your mouth*, but that which is good to the use of edifying, that it may minister grace unto the hearers." (**Ephesians 4:29**)

"But I say unto you, That *whosoever is angry with his brother without a cause shall be in danger of the judgment*: and whosoever shall say to his brother, Raca, shall be in danger of the council: but *whosoever shall say, Thou fool, shall be in danger of hell fire.*" **(Matthew 5:22–24)**

"Be ye angry, and sin not: *let not the sun go down upon your wrath.*" **(Ephesians 4:26)**

"Wherefore, my beloved brethren, *let every man be swift to hear, slow to speak, slow to wrath.*" **(James 1:19)**

"*Sound speech, that cannot be condemned*; that he that is of the contrary part may be ashamed, having no evil thing to say of you." **(Titus 2:8)**

13. Choose the Narrow Way

"Enter ye in at the strait gate: for wide is the gate, and broad is the way, that leadeth to destruction, and many there be which go in thereat: Because *strait is the gate, and narrow is the way, which leadeth unto life, and few there be that find it.*" **(Matthew 7:13–14)**

14. Confess

"*Confess your faults one to another*, and pray one for another, *that ye may be healed.* The effectual fervent prayer of a righteous man availeth much." **(James 5:16)**

15. Deny Yourself and Take Up HIS Cross

"And he said to them all, If any man will come after me, let him deny himself, and take up his cross daily, and follow me. *For whosoever will save his life shall lose it: but whosoever will lose his life for my sake, the same shall save it.*" **(Luke 9:23)**

16. Despise Not the Little Ones

"Take heed that ye *despise not one of these little ones*; for I say unto you, That in heaven their angels do always behold the face of my Father which is in heaven." **(Matthew 18:10)**

17. Do Not Be a Busybody in Other Men's Matters

"But *let none of you suffer* as a murderer, or as a thief, or as an evildoer, or *as a busybody in other men's matters.*" **(1 Peter 4:15)**

18. Do Not Cast Pearls

"Give not that which is holy unto the dogs, *neither cast ye your pearls before swine*, lest they trample them under their feet, and turn again and rend you." **(Matthew 7:6)**

19. Do Not Murmur

"*Do all things without murmurings and disputings*: That ye may be blameless and harmless, the sons of God, without rebuke, in the midst of a crooked and perverse nation, among whom ye shine as lights in the world." **(Philippians 2:14–15)**

20. Do unto Others

"Therefore *all things whatsoever ye would that men should do to you, do ye even so to them*: for this is the law and the prophets." **(Matthew 7:12; Luke 6:31)** (The Golden Rule)

"Recompense to no man evil for evil. *Provide things honest in the sight of all men*." **(Romans 12:17**; see also **1 Thessalonians 5:15)**

"Wherefore putting away lying, *speak every man truth with his neighbour*: for we are members one of another." **(Ephesians 4:25)**

"*Not rendering evil for evil, or railing for railing*: but contrariwise blessing; knowing that ye are thereunto called, that ye should inherit a blessing." **(1 Peter 3:9)**

21. Forgive Others — Forgiveness to the Utmost Extent

"Then came Peter to him, and said, Lord, *how oft shall my brother sin against me, and I forgive him?* till seven times? *Jesus saith unto him*, I say not unto thee, Until seven times: but, *Until seventy times seven*." **(Matthew 18:21–22**; see also verses 23–35)

"Then his lord, after that he had called him, said unto him, O thou wicked servant, *I forgave thee all that debt*, because thou desiredst me: *Shouldest not thou also have had compassion on thy fellow servant*, even as I had pity on thee?" **(Matthew 18:32–33)**

"Forbearing one another, and *forgiving one another*, if any man have a quarrel against any: *even as Christ forgave you, so also do ye*." **(Colossians 3:13)**

"And be ye kind one to another, tenderhearted, *forgiving one another, even as God for Christ's sake hath forgiven you*." **(Ephesians 4:32)**

"For if ye forgive men their trespasses, your heavenly Father will also forgive you: *But if ye forgive not men their trespasses, neither will your Father forgive your trespasses*." **(Matthew 6:14–15)**

22. Go to Offenders

"Moreover *if thy brother shall trespass against thee, go and tell him his fault between thee and him alone*: if he shall hear thee, thou hast gained thy brother. But if he will not hear thee, then take with thee one or two more, that in the mouth of two or three witnesses every word may be established. And if he shall neglect to hear them, tell it unto the church: but if he neglect to hear the church, let him be unto thee as an heathen man and a publican." **(Matthew 18:15–17)**

23. Honor Marriage — See the chapter on "Marriage" in this book.

24. Honor Your Parents

"For God commanded, saying, *Honour thy father and mother*: and, He that curseth father or mother, let him die the death." **(Matthew 15:4)**

"Children, obey your parents in the Lord: for this is right. *Honour thy father and mother*; (which is the first commandment with promise;) That it may be well with thee, and thou mayest live long on the earth. " **(Ephesians 6:1–3)**

"Children, *obey your parents in all things*: for this is well pleasing unto the Lord." **(Colossians 3:20)**

25. Humility

"*Let nothing be done through strife or vainglory*; but in lowliness of mind let each esteem other better than themselves." **(Philippians 2:3)**

"Likewise, ye younger, submit yourselves unto the elder. Yea, all of you be subject one to another, and *be clothed with humility*: for God resisteth the proud, and giveth grace to the humble. Humble yourselves therefore under the mighty hand of God, that he may exalt you in due time." **(1 Peter 5:5–6)**

26. Judge Not, That Ye Be Not Judged

"*Judge not, that ye be not judged*. For with *what judgment ye judge, ye shall be judged*: and with what measure ye mete, it shall be measured to you again." **(Matthew 7:1–2**; see also **Romans 14)**

27. Keep My Commandments

"If ye love me, *keep my commandments*." **(John 14:15)**

28. Lay Up Treasures

"*Lay not up for yourselves treasures upon earth*, where moth and rust doth corrupt, and where thieves break through and steal: *But lay up for yourselves treasures in heaven*, where neither moth nor rust doth corrupt, and where thieves do not break through nor steal: *For where your treasure is, there will your heart be also*." **(Matthew 6:19–21)**

"*Labour not for the meat which perisheth, but for that meat which endureth unto everlasting life*, which the Son of man shall give unto you: for him hath God the Father sealed." **(John 6:27)**

"*For the love of money is the root of all evil*: which while some coveted after, they have erred from the faith, and pierced themselves through with many sorrows." **(1 Timothy 6:10)**

"And he said unto them, Take heed, and beware of covetousness: for *a man's life consisteth not in the abundance of the things which he possesseth.*" (**Luke 12:15**)

"So is *he that layeth up treasure for himself,* and *is not rich toward God.*" (**Luke 12:18–21**)

"No servant can serve two masters: for either he will hate the one, and love the other; or else he will hold to the one, and despise the other. *Ye cannot serve God and mammon.*" (**Luke 16:13**; see also **Matthew 6:24**)

29. LET YOUR LIGHT SHINE

"*Let your light so shine before men, that they may see your good works,* and glorify your Father which is in heaven." (**Matthew 5:16**; see also verses 14–15)

"Whosoever therefore shall confess me before men, *him will I confess also before my Father which is in heaven.*" (**Matthew 10:32–33**)

"That ye may be blameless and harmless, the sons of God, without rebuke, in the midst of a crooked and perverse nation, *among whom ye shine as lights in the world.*" (**Philippians 2:15**)

30. LOVE NOT THE WORLD

"*Love not the world,* neither the things that are in the world. If any man love the world, the love of the Father is not in him. *For all that is in the world, the lust of the flesh, and the lust of the eyes, and the pride of life, is not of the Father,* but is of the world. And the world passeth away, and the lust thereof: but he that doeth the will of God abideth for ever." (**1 John 2:15–17**)

31. LOVE THE LORD

"Jesus said unto him, *Thou shalt love the Lord thy God with all thy heart, and with all thy soul, and with all thy mind.* This is the first and great commandment." (**Matthew 22:37–38**)

"For I am come to set a man at variance against his father, and the daughter against her mother, and the daughter in law against her mother in law. And a man's foes shall be they of his own household. *He that loveth father or mother more than me is not worthy of me*: and *he that loveth son or daughter more than me is not worthy of me.*" (**Matthew 10:35–37**)

32. LOVE YOUR ENEMIES — DO GOOD UNTO ALL MEN

"But I say unto you, *Love your enemies, bless them that curse you, do good to them that hate you, and pray for them which despitefully use you, and persecute you.*" (**Matthew 5:44**; see also **Luke 6:27–28**, and **Romans 12:14**)

"Therefore *if thine enemy hunger, feed him; if he thirst, give him drink*: for in so doing thou shalt heap coals of fire on his head." (**Romans 12:20**)

"As we have therefore opportunity, *let us do good unto all men*, especially unto them who are of the household of faith." **(Galatians 6:10)**

33. LOVE YOUR NEIGHBOR — LOVE ONE ANOTHER

"And the second is like unto it, *Thou shalt love thy neighbour as thyself.*" **(Matthew 22:39)**

"A new commandment I give unto you, That ye *love one another; as I have loved you*, that ye also love one another." **(John 13:34)**

"*Be kindly affectioned one to another with brotherly love*; in honour preferring one another." **(Romans 12:10)**

34. PARTAKE OF THE SACRAMENT — HOLY COMMUNION

"That the Lord Jesus the same night in which he was betrayed took bread: And when he had given thanks, he brake it, and said, Take, eat: this is my body, which is broken for you: this do in remembrance of me. After the same manner also he took the cup, when he had supped, saying, This cup is the new testament in my blood: this do ye, as oft as ye drink it, in remembrance of me. *For as often as ye eat this bread, and drink this cup, ye do shew the Lord's death till he come.*" **(1 Corinthians 11:23–26)**

"And as they were eating, Jesus took bread, and blessed it, and brake it, and gave it to the disciples, and said, Take, *eat; this is my body.* And he took the cup, and gave thanks, and gave it to them, saying, *Drink ye all of it; For this is my blood of the new testament, which is shed for many for the remission of sins.*" **(Matthew 26:26–28)**

"And they continued steadfastly in the apostles' doctrine and fellowship, and *in breaking of bread, and in prayers.*" **(Acts 2:42; Acts 20:7)**

35. PRACTICE SECRET DISCIPLINES — see Matthew 6:1–18

36. PRAYER

"*Pray without ceasing. In every thing give thanks*: for this is the will of God in Christ Jesus concerning you." **(1 Thessalonians 5:17–18)**

"*And when thou prayest, thou shalt not be as the hypocrites are*: for they love to pray standing in the synagogues and in the corners of the streets, that they may be seen of men. Verily I say unto you, They have their reward. But thou, when thou prayest, enter into thy closet, and when thou hast shut thy door, pray to thy Father which is in secret; and thy Father which seeth in secret shall reward thee openly. But when ye pray, use not vain repetitions, as the heathen do: for they think that they shall be heard for their much speaking." **(Matthew 6:5–7)**

37. Render to Caesar — Pay Your Debts

"They say unto him, Cæsar's. Then saith he unto them, *Render therefore unto Cæsar the things which are Cæsar's; and unto God the things that are God's.*" (**Matthew 22:21**; see also verses 19–20)

"*Render therefore to all their dues: tribute to whom tribute is due*; custom to whom custom; fear to whom fear; honour to whom honour. *Owe no man any thing*, but to love one another: for he that loveth another hath fulfilled the law." (**Romans 13:7–8**)

38. Repent

"I tell you, Nay: but, *except ye repent, ye shall all likewise perish.*" (**Luke 13:5**)

"And the times of this ignorance *God* winked at; but now *commandeth all men every where to repent.*" (**Acts 17:30**)

"*Repent ye therefore*, and be converted, *that your sins may be blotted out*, when the times of refreshing shall come from the presence of the Lord." (**Acts 3:19**; see also **Matthew 4:17; 2 Peter 3:9**)

39. Seek God's Kingdom

"But *seek ye first the kingdom of God*, and his righteousness; *and all these things shall be added unto you.*" (**Matthew 6:33**)

40. Speak Not Evil of One Another

"*Speak not evil one of another*, brethren." (**James 4:11; Titus 3:2**)

"Wherefore *laying aside* all malice, and all guile, and hypocrisies, and envies, and *all evil speakings.*" (**1 Peter 2:1**)

41. Strive to Be Godlike

"*Be ye therefore perfect*, even as your Father which is in heaven is perfect." (**Matthew 5:48**)

"*Follow peace with all men, and holiness*, without which no man shall see the Lord." (**Hebrews 12:14**)

"But as he which hath called you is holy, so be ye holy in all manner of conversation; Because it is written, *Be ye holy; for I am holy.*" (**1 Peter 1:15–16**)

"Finally, brethren, whatsoever things are *true*, whatsoever things are *honest*, whatsoever things are *just*, whatsoever things are *pure*, whatsoever things are *lovely*, whatsoever things are of *good report*; if there be any *virtue*, and if there be any *praise*, think on these things." (**Philippians 4:8**)

"But thou, O man of God, flee these things; and *follow after righteousness, godliness, faith, love, patience, meekness.*" (**1 Timothy 6:11**)

"Let the word of Christ dwell in you richly in all wisdom; teaching and admonishing one another in psalms and hymns and spiritual songs, singing with grace in your hearts to the Lord." **(Colossians 3:16)**

42. TAKE MY YOKE

"Come unto me, all ye that labour and are heavy laden, and I will give you rest. *Take my yoke upon you, and learn of me*; for I am meek and lowly in heart: *and ye shall find rest unto your souls.* For my yoke is easy, and my burden is light." **(Matthew 11:29)**

43. THE DISOBEDIENT AND THE LAZY

"But if any provide not for his own, and specially for those of his own house, he hath denied the faith, and is worse than an infidel." **(1 Timothy 5:8)**

"For even when we were with you, this we commanded you, that *if any would not work, neither should he eat.*" **(2 Thessalonians 3:10)**

44. TITHING

"Will a man rob God? *Yet ye have robbed me.* But ye say, Wherein have we robbed thee? *In tithes and offerings.* Ye are cursed with a curse: for ye have robbed me, even this whole nation. Bring ye all the tithes into the storehouse, that there may be meat in mine house, and prove me now herewith, saith the Lord of hosts, *if I will not open you the windows of heaven, and pour you out a blessing, that there shall not be room enough to receive it.*" **(Malachi 3:8–10)**

45. WATCH AND PRAY

"Watch and pray, that ye enter not into temptation: the spirit indeed is willing, but the flesh is weak." **(Matthew 26:41)**

46. TO HIM THAT KNOWETH AND DOETH NOT

"Therefore *to him that knoweth to do good, and doeth it not, to him it is sin.*" **(James 4:17)**

"For whosoever shall keep the whole law, and yet offend in one point, he is guilty of all." (James 2:10)

Many have believed, and some even taught, that there are only Ten Commandments; follow them and that is all we need to do. Some have even gone so far as to label them the Ten Suggestions; picking and choosing those they wish to comply with. But as we can easily see above, there are a lot more than just Ten Command-ments and not one of them is a Suggestion.

CHAPTER 15

CREATION – WHO CREATED THE HEAVENS AND THE EARTH?

"And to make all men see what is the fellowship of the mystery, which from the beginning of the world hath been hid in God, who created all things by Jesus Christ." **(Ephesians 3:9)**

Although most Christian faiths believe that Jesus Christ was the Creator of the Heavens and the Earth, there are some faiths who believe that God the Father was the Creator.

CREATION — WHO CREATED THE HEAVENS AND THE EARTH?

Scriptures used by some Christian faiths to substantiate their belief and teaching that God the Father created the Heavens and the Earth:

"In the beginning God created the heaven and the earth." **(Genesis 1:1)**

"And the Lord God formed man of the dust of the ground, and breathed into his nostrils the breath of life; and man became a living soul." **(Genesis 2:7)**

"The great God that formed all things both rewardeth the fool, and rewardeth transgressors." **(Proverbs 26:10)**

"God that made the world and all things therein, seeing that he is Lord of heaven and earth, dwelleth not in temples made with hands." **(Acts 17:24)**

"Through faith we understand that the worlds were framed by the word of God, so that things which are seen were not made of things which do appear." **(Hebrews 11:3)**

"And unto the angel of the church of the Laodiceans write; These things saith the Amen, the faithful and true witness, the beginning of the creation of God." **(Revelation 3:14)**

"Saying with a loud voice, Fear God, and give glory to him; for the hour of his judgment is come: and worship him that made heaven, and earth, and the sea, and the fountains of waters." **(Revelation 14:7)**

NOW THE REST OF THE STORY . . . (scriptures that further explain or clarify the topic)

"And to make all men see what is the fellowship of the mystery, which from the beginning of the world hath been hid in God, *who created all things by Jesus Christ.*" **(Ephesians 3:9)**

"Hath in these last days spoken unto us by *his Son*, whom he hath appointed heir of all things, by whom also he made the worlds." **(Hebrews 1:2)**

"In the beginning *was the Word*, and the Word was with God, and the Word was God. The same was in the beginning with God. *All things were made by him; and without him was not any thing made that was made.*" **(John 1:1–3)**

"He was in the world, *and the world was made by him*, and the world knew him not. . . . And the Word was made flesh, and dwelt among us, (and we beheld his glory, the glory as of the only begotten of the Father,) full of grace and truth." **(John 1:10–14)**

"Who hath delivered us from the power of darkness, and hath translated us into the kingdom of his dear Son: In whom we have redemption through his blood, even the forgiveness of sins: Who is the image of the invisible God, the firstborn of every creature: *For by him were all things created, that are in heaven, and that are in earth*, visible and invisible, whether they be thrones, or dominions, or principalities, or powers: all things were created by him, and for him: And he is before all things, and by him all things consist. And he is the head of the body, the church: who is the beginning, the firstborn from the dead; that in all things he might have the preeminence. For it pleased the Father that in him should all fullness dwell." **(Colossians 1:13–19)**

"That they may see, and know, and consider, and understand together, that the hand of the Lord hath done this, and *the Holy One of Israel hath created it*." **(Isaiah 41:20)**

"Thus saith the Lord, *thy redeemer*, and he that formed thee from the womb, I am the Lord *that maketh all things*; that stretcheth forth the heavens alone; that spreadeth abroad the earth by myself." **(Isaiah 44:24)**

CONCLUSION

Jesus Christ is the creator of the heavens, the Earth, and all things.

CHAPTER 16

DEATH

"For, this cause was the gospel preached also to them that are dead, that they might be judged according to men in the flesh, but live according to God in the spirit." **(1 Peter 4:6)**

Christianity today teaches that once you die, your opportunity to hear the gospel of Jesus Christ is over. If you lived in a country where Christianity was banned, well that is just too bad, you don't get a second chance, or in this case, a first chance. Let's see what the Bible really says about this.

DEATH

Scriptures used by some Christian faiths to substantiate their belief and teachings about death:

"His breath goeth forth, he returneth to his earth; in that very day his thoughts perish." **(Psalm 146:4)**

"For the living know that they shall die: but the dead know not any thing, neither have they any more a reward; for the memory of them is forgotten." **(Ecclesiastes 9:5)**

"Whatsoever thy hand findeth to do, do it with thy might; for there is no work, nor device, nor knowledge, nor wisdom, in the grave, whither thou goest." **(Ecclesiastes 9:10)**

NOW THE REST OF THE STORY . . . (scriptures that further explain or clarify the topic)

"For, this cause was the gospel preached also to them that are dead, that they might be judged according to men in the flesh, but live according to God in the spirit." **(1 Peter 4:6)**

"For Christ also hath once suffered for sins, the just for the unjust, that he might bring us to God, being put to death in the flesh, but quickened by the Spirit: By which also *he went and preached unto the spirits in prison*; Which sometime were disobedient, when once the longsuffering of God waited in the days of Noah, while the ark was a preparing, wherein few, that is, eight souls were saved by water." **(1 Peter 3:18–20)**

> *Note: Why would Christ during the three days he was dead and before his resurrection, go to the "spirits in prison" and preach to them? Answer: because they cannot be judged for something they knew nothing about. They needed to be given knowledge of Christ and the Gospel. How could they be spoken to and receive this knowledge unless they had a living conscience spirit body?*

"Then shall the dust return to the earth as it was: and *the spirit shall return unto God who gave it.*" **(Ecclesiastes 12:7)**

"For to this end Christ both died, and rose, and revived, that he might be *Lord both of the dead and living.*" **(Romans 14:9)**

"Therefore my heart is glad, and my glory rejoices: my flesh also show rest in hope. For *thou wilt not leave my soul in hell*; neither will thou suffer Thine Holy One to see corruption." **(Psalms 16:9–10)**

"For great is thy mercy toward me: and *thou hast delivered my soul from the lowest hell.*" **(Psalms 86:13)**

> *Note: In Psalms 16:9–10 and 86:13, David is rejoicing because God will not leave his soul in hell.*

"Jesus said unto her, I am the resurrection, and the life: *he that believeth in me, though he were dead, yet shall he live*: And whosoever liveth and believeth in me shall never die. Believest thou this?" **(John 11:25–26)**

"For David speaketh concerning him, I foresaw the Lord always before my face, for he is on my right hand, that I should not be moved: Therefore did my heart rejoice, and my tongue was glad; moreover also my flesh shall rest in hope: Because *thou wilt not leave my soul in hell*, neither wilt thou suffer thine Holy One to see corruption." **(Acts 2:25–27)**

"Men and brethren, let me freely speak unto you of the patriarch David, that he is both dead and buried, and his sepulchre is with us unto this day. Therefore being a prophet, and knowing that God had sworn with an oath to him, that of the fruit of his loins, according to the flesh, he would raise up Christ to sit on his throne; He seeing this before spake of the resurrection of Christ, that *his soul was not left in hell*, neither his flesh did see corruption." **(Acts 2:29–31)**

"*Not every one that saith unto me, Lord, Lord, shall enter into the kingdom of heaven*; but he that doeth the will of my Father which is in heaven. Many will say to me in that day, Lord, Lord, have we not prophesied in thy name? and in thy name have cast out devils? and in thy name done many wonderful works? *And then will I profess unto them, I never knew you: depart from me, ye that work iniquity.*" **(Matthew 7:21–23)**

"But the children of the murderers he slew not: according unto that which is written in the book of the law of Moses, wherein the LORD commanded, saying, The fathers shall not be put to death for the children, nor the children be put to death for the fathers; but *every man shall be put to death for his own sin*." **(2 Kings 14:6**; see also **2 Chronicles 25:4)**

> **Note: No one, man, woman, nor child, shall be punished for the sins of another.**

"For the wages of sin is death; but *the gift of God is eternal life through Jesus Christ our Lord*." **(Romans 6:23)**

WHAT HAPPENS AFTER WE DIE?

Watch this LDS video: https://www.youtube.com/watch?v=rUPdxHT6Qo8

See chapter 24: **"Heaven — Hell — Degrees of Glory"**
See chapter 42: **"Resurrection of the Physical Body"**
See chapter 45: **"Salvation for All Mankind"**
See chapter 46: **"Salvation for the Dead"**

CHAPTER 17

DO NOT OPPOSE OTHER CHRISTIAN GROUPS

"For where two or three are gathered together in my name, there am I in the midst of them." **(Matthew 18:20)**

Unfortunately, there are those individuals and churches that make it their "ministry" to attack and malign those Christian faiths that they do not agree with. This practice is in total disagreement with Bible teachings. This chapter will help you to explain this when you are confronted by someone who is not of our faith or any faith, and wants to "Bible bash."

Do Not Oppose Other
Christian Groups

Scriptures used by some Christian faiths to substantiate their belief and teaching to malign, discredit, demean, or slander other Christian faiths:

There aren't any scriptures justifying this practice.

"Bible Bashing," the practice of using scripture to attack other Christian denominations and their beliefs is unfortunately a popular past-time of many individuals and "not-so-Christian" groups.

The following scriptures are for the education of those individuals and organizations that make it their mission or ministry to discredit, demean, or otherwise slander other Christian faiths.

NOW THE REST OF THE STORY . . . (scriptures that further explain or clarify the topic)

"And John answered him, saying, Master, we saw one casting out devils in thy name, and he followeth not us: and we forbad him, because he followeth not us. But Jesus said, *Forbid him not*: for there is no man which shall do a miracle in my name, that can lightly speak evil of me. *For he that is not against us is on our part.*" **(Mark 9:38–40 KJV)**

"'Teacher,' said John, 'we saw a man driving out demons in your name and we told him to stop, because he was not one of us.' *'Do not stop him,'* Jesus said. *'No one who does a miracle in my name can in the next moment say anything bad about me, for whoever is not against us is for us.'*" **(Mark 9:38–40 NIV)**

"John said to him, 'Teacher, we saw someone casting out demons in your name, and we tried to stop him, because he was not following us.' But Jesus said, *'Do not stop him, for no one who does a mighty work in my name will be able soon afterward to speak evil of me. For the one who is not against us is for us.'*" **(Mark 9:38–40 ESV & NRSV)**

"John said to Him, 'Teacher, we saw someone casting out demons in Your name, and we tried to prevent him because he was not following us.' But Jesus said, *'Do not hinder him, for there is no one who will perform a miracle in My name, and be able soon afterward to speak evil of Me. For he who is not against us is for us.'*" **(Mark 9:38–40 NASV)**

> *Note: Mark 9:38–40, in all five of the English translations of the Bible listed above, teaches the same doctrine.*

"And John answered and said, Master, we saw one casting out devils in thy name; and we forbad him, because he followeth not with us. And Jesus said unto him, *Forbid him not: for he that is not against us is for us.*" (**Luke 9:49–50**)

"Whosoever therefore shall confess me before men, *him will I confess also before my Father which is in heaven.*" (**Matthew 10:32**)

"For where two or three are gathered together in my name, there am *I in the midst of them.*" (**Matthew 18:20**)

"And Jesus said, Are ye also yet without understanding? Do not ye yet understand, that whatsoever entereth in at the mouth goeth into the belly, and is cast out into the draught? But those things which proceed out of the mouth come forth from the heart; and they defile the man. *For out of the heart proceed evil thoughts*, murders, adulteries, fornications, thefts, *false witness*, blasphemies." (**Matthew 15:16–19**)

CHAPTER 18

FAITH, GRACE & WORKS SINCERE BELIEF IS NOT ENOUGH

"And I saw the dead, small and great, stand before God; and the books were opened: and another book was opened, which is the book of life: and the dead were judged out of those things which were written in the books, according to their works. And the sea gave up the dead which were in it; and death and hell delivered up the dead which were in them: and they were judged every man according to their works." **(Revelation 20:12–15)**

Some Churches teach that all one must do to obtain salvation is to believe in Jesus Christ—just believe and have faith. They mock and attack those who believe also in doing good works, saying that "you are trying to work your way into Heaven." Let's take a look at what the Bible has to say . . .

FAITH, GRACE & WORKS —
SINCERE BELIEF IS NOT ENOUGH

Scriptures used by some Christian faiths to substantiate their belief and teaching that "Belief and Faith" in Jesus Christ and "The Grace of God" is all that is required for Salvation:

"That whosoever believeth in him should not perish, but have eternal life." **(John 3:15)**

"He that believeth and is baptized shall be saved; but he that believeth not shall be damned." **(Mark 16:16)**

"Verily, verily, I say unto you, He that heareth my word, and believeth on him that sent me, hath everlasting life, and shall not come into condemnation; but is passed from death unto life." **(John 5:24)**

"For by grace are ye saved through faith; and that not of yourselves: it is the gift of God: Not of works, lest any man should boast." **(Ephesians 2:8–9)**

"That if thou shalt confess with thy mouth the Lord Jesus, and shalt believe in thine heart that God hath raised him from the dead, thou shalt be saved." **(Romans 10:9)**

"For whosoever shall call upon the name of the Lord shall be saved." **(Romans 10:13)**

"But we believe that through the grace of the Lord Jesus Christ we shall be saved, even as they." **(Acts 15:11)**

"For the grace of God that bringeth salvation hath appeared to all men." **(Titus 2:11)**

"And if by grace, then is it no more of works: otherwise grace is no more grace. But if it be of works, then is it no more grace: otherwise work is no more work." **(Romans 11:6)**

"Knowing that a man is not justified by the works of the law, but by the faith of Jesus Christ, even we have believed in Jesus Christ, that we might be justified by the faith of Christ, and not by the works of the law: for by the works of the law shall no flesh be justified. . . . I do not frustrate the grace of God: for if righteousness come by the law, then Christ is dead in vain." **(Galatians 2:16, 21)**

> *Note: Works and "the works of the law" spoken of in these verses are the law of Moses. Paul is explaining that the Atonement of Christ and the grace of God replaces the law of Moses. When Paul speaks of the "works of the law," he refers to what we know as the six hundred and thirteen precepts of the Torah, such as Jewish prohibitions against eating pork, the mandate of circumcision, and the observance of Passover. Paul's epistles to the Romans and to the Galatians are particularly concerned with some baptized Jewish Christians who wrongly believed that the observance*

of circumcision and the other ceremonial precepts were necessary for salvation. Some Roman and Galatian Christians had wrongly concluded that a Christian must believe in Jesus and obey the ceremonial precepts of Moses in order to be saved.

Now See for Further Understanding . . .

"What shall we say then? That the Gentiles, which followed not after righteousness, have attained to righteousness, even the righteousness which is of faith. But Israel, which followed after the law of righteousness, hath not attained to the law of righteousness. Wherefore? Because they sought it not by faith, but as it were by the works of the law. For they stumbled at that stumblingstone." **(Romans 9:30–32)**

Sola Fide (*by faith alone*) was the other watchword of the Reformation. This doctrine maintains that we are justified before God (and thus saved) by faith alone, not by anything we do, not by anything the church does for us, and not by faith plus anything else. It was also recognized by the early Reformers that Sola Fide is not rightly understood until it is seen as anchored in the broader principle of **Sola Gratia**, by grace alone. Hence the Reformers were calling the church back to the basic teaching of Scripture where the apostle Paul states that we are "saved by grace through faith and that not of ourselves, it is the gift of God," **(Ephesians 2:8)**.[1]

Now the Rest of the Story . . . (scriptures that further explain or clarify the topic)

"All scripture is given by inspiration of God, and is profitable for doctrine, for reproof, for correction, for instruction in righteousness: That the man of God may be perfect, *throughly furnished unto all good works.*" **(2 Timothy 3:16–17)**

> *Note: Verse 16 is often used by modern-day Christians in their claim that God actually dictated the Bible verbiage unto those who wrote it down, (see the KJV, ESV, NIV verses in chapter Faith, Grace & Works — Sincere Belief is Not Enough). Verse 17 is a great example of God instructing man to do good works.*

"Also unto thee, O Lord, belongeth mercy: for *thou renderest to every man according to his work.*" **(Psalms 62:12)**

"Let your light so shine before men, *that they may see your good works*, and glorify your Father which is in heaven." **(Matthew 5:16)**

"In all things shewing thyself *a pattern of good works*: in doctrine shewing uncorruptness, gravity, sincerity." **(Titus 2:7)**

"What doth it profit, my brethren, though a man say he hath faith, *and have not works?* Can faith save him?" **(James 2:14)**

"Even so *faith, if it hath not works, is dead*, being alone. Yea, a man may say, Thou hast faith, and I have works: *shew me thy faith without thy works*, and *I will shew thee my faith by my works*." (**James 2:17–18**)

"Thou believest that there is one God; thou doest well: *the devils also believe*, and tremble. But wilt thou know, O vain man, that *faith without works is dead*?" (**James 2:19–20**)

"Seest thou how faith wrought with his works, and *by works was faith made perfect*?" (**James 2:22**)

"Ye see then how that *by works a man is justified*, and not by faith only." (**James 2:24**)

"For as the body without the spirit is dead, so *faith without works is dead* also." (**James 2:26**)

"Therefore to him that knoweth to do good, and doeth it not, to him it is sin." (**James 4:17**)

"They profess that they know God; *but in works they deny him*, being abominable, and disobedient, and unto every good work reprobate." (**Titus 1:16**)

"For the Son of man shall come in the glory of his Father with his angels; and *then he shall reward every man according to his works*." (**Matthew 16:27**)

"*For God shall bring every work into judgment*, with every secret thing, whether it be good, or whether it be evil." (**Ecclesiastes 12:14**)

"Who will render to every man *according to his deeds*." (**Romans 2:6**)

"And if ye call on *the Father*, who without respect of persons *judgeth according to every man's work*, pass the time of your sojourning here in fear." (**1 Peter 1:17**)

"And I saw the dead, small and great, stand before God; and the books were opened: and another book was opened, which is the book of life: and *the dead were judged* out of those things which were written in the books, *according to their works*. And the sea gave up the dead which were in it; and death and hell delivered up the dead which were in them: and *they were judged every man according to their works*." (**Revelation 20:12–13**)

"And God is able to make all *grace abound toward you*; that ye, always having all sufficiency in all things, may abound *to every good work*." (**2 Corinthians 9:8**)

"Who gave himself for us, that he might redeem us from all iniquity, and purify unto himself a peculiar people, *zealous of good works*." (**Titus 2:14**)

"But he that shall endure unto the end, the same *shall be saved*." (**Matthew 24:13**)

SINCERE BELIEF IS NOT ENOUGH

"Wherefore by their fruits ye shall know them. *Not everyone that saith unto me, Lord, Lord, shall enter into the kingdom of heaven*; but he that doeth the will of my

Father which is in heaven. Many will say to me in that day, Lord, Lord, have we not prophesied in thy name? and in thy name have cast out devils? and in thy name done many wonderful works? And then will I profess unto them, I never knew you: depart from me, ye that work iniquity." (Matthew 7:20–23)

"Ye hypocrites, well did Esaias prophesy of you, saying, This people draweth nigh unto me with their mouth, and honoureth me with their lips; but their heart is far from me. But in vain they do worship me, *teaching for doctrines the commandments of men.*" (Matthew 15:7–9)

"For I bear them record that they have a zeal of God, *but not according to knowledge.* For they being *ignorant of God's righteousness*, and going about *to establish their own righteousness*, have not submitted themselves unto the righteousness of God. For Christ is the end of the law for righteousness to every one that believeth." (Romans 10:2–4)

"*But they have not all obeyed the gospel.* For Esaias saith, Lord, who hath believed our report?" (Romans 10:16)

Here are the definitions of "Faith," "Grace," and "Salvations"; *as defined in the LDS Bible Dictionary.*

Faith: Faith is the substance of things hoped for, the evidence of things not seen, but which are true (**Hebrews 11:1**), and must be centered in Jesus Christ in order to produce salvation. To have faith is to have confidence in something or someone. The Lord has revealed Himself and His perfect character, possessing in their fullness all the attributes of love, knowledge, justice, mercy, unchangeableness, power, and every other needful thing, so as to enable the mind of man to place confidence in Him without reservation. Faith is kindled by hearing the testimony of those who have faith (**Romans 10:14–17**). Miracles do not produce faith, but strong faith is developed by obedience to the gospel of Jesus Christ; in other words, faith comes by righteousness, although miracles often confirm one's faith.

Faith is a principle of action and of power, and by it one can command the elements, heal the sick, and influence any number of circumstances when occasion warrants (**Jacob 4:4–7**). Even more important, by faith one obtains a remission of sins and eventually can stand in the presence of God.

All true faith must be based upon correct knowledge or it cannot produce the desired results. Faith in Jesus Christ is the first principle of the gospel and is more than belief, since true faith always moves its possessor to some kind of physical and mental action; it carries an assurance of the fulfillment of the things hoped for. A lack of faith leads one to despair, which comes because of iniquity.

Although faith is a gift, it must be cultured and sought after until it grows from a tiny seed to a great tree. The effects of true faith in Jesus Christ include (1) an actual knowledge that the course of life one is pursuing is acceptable to the Lord (see **Hebrews 11:4**); (2) a reception of the blessings of the Lord that are available to man in this life; and (3) an assurance of personal salvation in the world to come. These things involve individual and personal testimony, guidance, revelation, and spiritual knowledge. Where there is true faith there are miracles, visions, dreams, healings, and all the gifts of God that He gives to His saints. Jesus pointed out some obstacles to faith in **John 5:44** and **12:39–42** (see also **James 1:6–8**).

Other references to faith include **2 Corinthians 5:7; Ephesians 2:8–9; Hebrews 11; James 2:14–26; 1 Peter 1:8–9.**

Grace: The enabling power from God that allows men and women to obtain blessings in this life and to gain eternal life and exaltation after they have exercised faith, repented, and given their best effort to keep the commandments. Such divine help or strength is given through the mercy and love of God. Every mortal person needs divine grace because of Adam's fall and also because of man's weaknesses. However, grace cannot suffice without total effort on the part of the recipient.

It is through the grace of the Lord Jesus, made possible by His atoning sacrifice, that mankind will be raised in immortality, every person receiving his body from the grave in a condition of everlasting life. It is likewise through the grace of the Lord that individuals, through faith in the Atonement of Jesus Christ and repentance of their sins, receive strength and assistance to do good works that they otherwise would not be able to maintain if left to their own means. This grace is an enabling power that allows men and women to lay hold on eternal life and exaltation after they have expended their own best efforts.

Salvation: To be saved from both physical and spiritual death. All people will be saved from physical death by the grace of God, through the death and resurrection of Jesus Christ. Each individual can also be saved from spiritual death as well by the grace of God, through faith in Jesus Christ. This faith is manifested in a life of obedience to the laws and ordinances of the gospel and service to Christ.

Martin Luther was the originator of "justification by faith alone." He characterized the Epistle of James as "an epistle of straw"—largely because it seemed to disagree with his teaching of "justification by faith alone."

The Eastern Orthodox churches also do not accept *solafidianism*, the doctrine of salvation by faith alone. "Eastern Orthodox Christians emphasize a unity of faith and works. For the Orthodox, being conformed to the image of Christ . . . includes a response of our faith and works."[2]

Some Modern Protestant writers, sensing the danger that a "grace alone" position could become "cheap grace" (to borrow an expression from the theologian Dietrich Bonhoeffer) or "a theologically thin, no-sweat Christianity," some modern

Protestant writers have adopted a similar position, recognizing that works also play a vital role in salvation.[3]

Catholic theology: The doctrine that salvation depends both on God's grace and man's good works is very old in Catholic theology. One of the canons at the Council of Trent specifically repudiates the notion of grace alone: "If anyone saith that justifying faith is nothing else but confidence in the divine mercy which remits sin for Christ's sake alone; or, that this confidence alone is that whereby we are justified, let him be anathema." Are we to say, then, that Roman Catholicism is not Christian because it does not subscribe to the doctrine of salvation by grace alone?[4]

The generations immediately following the New Testament period also recognized the need for both grace and works for salvation. The famous Didache, "The Teaching of the Twelve Apostles," which dates back to before AD 70, is conspicuous for its moralism and legalism. It is also significant that the oldest datable literary document of the Christian religion soon after the time of the Apostles, the letter of Clement of Rome to the Corinthians, written in the last decade of the first century, emphasizes "good works, as it is in the Epistle of James."[5]

CHAPTER 19

FORGIVENESS

"For if ye forgive men their trespasses, your heavenly Father will also forgive you: But if ye forgive not men their trespasses, neither will your Father forgive your trespasses." **(Matthew 6:14–15)**

Many Christians mistakenly believe that only God must forgive mankind for their sins and trespasses. The Bible teaches us that we too must forgive all who sin and trespass against us, or we will not be forgiven for our trespasses and sins.

FORGIVENESS

Some Christian faiths teach that all one must do is believe in Jesus Christ and your sins will be forgiven. Yet the Scriptures clearly demonstrate and teach that unless we also forgive those who have trespassed against us, our sins and trespasses will not be forgiven us.

"That whosoever believeth in him should not perish, but have eternal life." **(John 3:15)**

"Verily, verily, I say unto you, He that heareth my word, and believeth on him that sent me, hath everlasting life, and shall not come into condemnation; but is passed from death unto life." **(John 5:24)**

"That if thou shalt confess with thy mouth the Lord Jesus, and shalt believe in thine heart that God hath raised him from the dead, thou shalt be saved." **(Romans 10:9)**

"But we believe that through the grace of the Lord Jesus Christ we shall be saved, even as they." **(Acts 15:11)**

NOW THE REST OF THE STORY . . . (scriptures that further explain or clarify the topic)

"For if ye forgive men their trespasses, your heavenly Father will also forgive you: *But if ye forgive not men their trespasses, neither will your Father forgive your trespasses.*" **(Matthew 6:14–15)**

"But I say unto you, That every idle word that men shall speak, they shall give account thereof in the day of judgment. For by thy words thou shalt be justified, and *by thy words thou shalt be condemned.*" **(Matthew 12:36–37)**

"Then his lord, after that he had called him, said unto him, *O thou wicked servant,* I forgave thee all that debt, because thou desiredst me: *Shouldest not thou also have had compassion on thy fellowservant,* even as I had pity on thee? And his lord was wroth, and delivered him to the tormentors, till he should pay all that was due unto him. *So likewise shall my heavenly Father do also unto you, if ye from your hearts forgive not every one his brother their trespasses.*" **(Matthew 18:32–35)**

> *Note: See (Matthew 18:23–35) for the complete story.*

"Then came Peter to him, and said, Lord, how oft shall my brother sin against me, and I forgive him? till seven times? *Jesus saith unto him,* I say not unto thee, Until seven times: but, Until *seventy times seven.*" **(Matthew 18:21–22)**

"Judge not, and ye shall not be judged: condemn not, and ye shall not be condemned: *forgive, and ye shall be forgiven.*" **(Luke 6:37)**

"And *be ye kind one to another,* tenderhearted, *forgiving one another,* even as God for Christ's sake hath forgiven you." **(Ephesians 4:32)**

"If we confess our sins, he is faithful and just to forgive us our sins, and to cleanse us from all unrighteousness." **(1 John 1:9)**

"For with the heart man believeth unto righteousness; and with the mouth confession is made unto salvation." **(Romans 10:10)**

See chapter 1: "**Accountability**"
See chapter 18: "**Faith, Grace & Works — Sincere Belief Is Not Enough**"
See chapter 40: "**Repentance**"

CHAPTER 20

GOD HAS A PHYSICAL BODY

MAN CREATED IN GOD'S PHYSICAL IMAGE

"Behold, what manner of love the Father hath bestowed upon us, that we should be called the sons of God: therefore the world knoweth us not, because it knew him not. Beloved, now are we the sons of God, and it doth not yet appear what we shall be: but we know that, when he shall appear, we shall be like him; for we shall see him as he is." **(1 John 3:2–3)**

Trinitarian Christianity teaches that God does not have a physical body or any form whatsoever. Why do they ignore the scriptures of the Bible which says He does?

GOD HAS A PHYSICAL BODY

MAN CREATED IN GOD'S PHYSICAL IMAGE

Scriptures used by some Christian faiths to substantiate their belief and teaching that God the Father is a spirit only, that He does not have a physical body or parts. Some biblical scriptures have been taken out of context and or misinterpreted to promote the belief in an intangible God:

"God is a Spirit: and they that worship him must worship him in spirit and in truth." **(John 4:24)**

> *Note: Does this mean that when man worships God man's spirit must depart from his physical body in order to worship God?*

> *Note: John 4:24 is the ONLY scripture in the entire Bible that says God is a spirit.*

> *Note: See the chapter "Man has both a Physical & Spiritual Body" in this book.*

"Who is the image of the invisible God, the firstborn of every creature." **(Colossians 1:15)**

"Now unto the King eternal, immortal, invisible, the only wise God, be honour and glory for ever and ever. Amen." **(1 Timothy 1:17)**

> *Note: Colossians 1:15, 1 Timothy 1:17, and Hebrews 11:27 are the only three places in the Bible that use the word "invisible" to describe God. (See Hebrews 11:27 below.)*

"Can any hide himself in secret places that I shall not see him? saith the Lord. Do not I fill heaven and earth? saith the Lord." **(Jeremiah 23:24)**

> *Note: God is not talking about His essence filling the heavens and the earth. He is proclaiming His almighty power, His majesty, His glory, His influence, which "fills the heavens and earth" not His person.*

"And he said, Thou canst not see my face: for there shall no man see me, and live." **(Exodus 33:20)**

"No man hath seen God at any time; the only begotten Son, which is in the bosom of the Father, he hath declared him." **(John 1:18, 1 John 4:12)**

> *Note: Now see John 6:46 and 3 John 1:11 below for the explanation.*

"Not that any man hath seen the Father, *save he which is of God, he hath seen the Father.*" **(John 6:46)**

> *Note: Now see 3 John 1:11 for the explanation for who or "which is of God."*

"Beloved, follow not that which is evil, but that which is good. *He that doeth good is of God*: but *he that doeth evil hath not seen God.*" (**3 John 1:11**)

> *Note: Only those that God has chosen as worthy and righteous men of faith such as Moses, Jeremiah, Stephen, and other prophets, have seen Him.*

> *Note: "Theophany": The term used by modern-day Christians to explain those scriptures stating that mankind has seen God. "God is taking on a form other than His natural state of being (a spirit), so that mankind, His creation, can see Him. They are not really seeing God, only a form He allows them to see."*

NOW THE REST OF THE STORY . . . (scriptures that further explain or clarify the topic)

"And God said, Let us make man *in our image, after our likeness*: and let them have dominion over the fish of the sea, and over the fowl of the air, and over the cattle, and over all the earth, and over every creeping thing that creepeth upon the earth. So God created man in his own image, *in the image of God created he him; male and female created he them.*" (**Genesis 1:26–27**)

> *Note: The operative word in this verse is the Hebrew verb "tsalam," "to create in one's own image." Tsalam in modern Hebrew is used to mean "photocopy," or to create an exact duplicate of something.*

"This is the book of the generations of Adam. *In the day that God created man, in the likeness of God made he him; Male and female* created he them; and blessed them, and called their name Adam, in the day when they were created." (**Genesis 5:1–2**)

NOW SEE . . .

"And *Adam* lived an hundred and thirty years, and *begat a son in his own likeness, after his image*; and called his name Seth." (**Genesis 5:3**)

> *Note: Adam begat Seth in Adam's likeness and image, just as God created man in His likeness and image. Man is created both "physically" and "spiritually" in God's image.*

"Then went up Moses, and Aaron, Nadab, and Abihu, and seventy of the elders of Israel: *And they saw the God of Israel*: and there was *under his feet* as it were a paved work of a sapphire stone, and as it were the body of heaven in his clearness. And upon the nobles of the children of Israel he laid not *his hand*: also *they saw God*, and did eat and drink." (**Exodus 24:9–11**)

"And Jacob was left alone; *and there wrestled a man with him until the breaking of the day*. And when he saw that he prevailed not against him, he touched the hollow of his thigh; and the hollow of Jacob's thigh was out of joint, as he wrestled with him. And he said, Let me go, for the day breaketh. And he said, I will not let thee go, except thou bless me. And he said unto him, What is thy name? And he said, Jacob. And he said, Thy name shall be called no more Jacob, but Israel: for as a prince hast thou power with God and with men, and hast prevailed. And Jacob asked him, and said, Tell me, I pray thee, thy name. And he said, Wherefore is it that thou dost ask after my name? And he blessed him there. And Jacob called the name of the place Peniel: *for I have seen God face to face*, and my life is preserved." **(Genesis 32:24–30)**

"And *God appeared unto Jacob again*, when he came out of Padan-aram, and blessed him. And God said unto him, Thy name is Jacob: thy name shall not be called any more Jacob, but Israel shall be thy name: and he called his name Israel." **(Genesis 35:9–10)**

"*And the Lord spake unto Moses face to face*, as a man speaketh unto his friend." **(Exodus 33:11)**

"By faith he forsook Egypt, not fearing the wrath of the king: for he endured, as *seeing him who is invisible*." **(Hebrews 11:27)**

"And the Lord said, Behold, there is a place by me, and thou shalt stand upon a rock: And it shall come to pass, while my glory passeth by, that I will put thee in a clift of the rock, and *will cover thee with my hand* while I pass by: And I will take away mine hand, *and thou shalt see my back parts*: but my face shall not be seen." **(Exodus 33:21–23)**

"And the Lord spake suddenly unto Moses, and unto Aaron, and unto Miriam, . . . *My servant Moses* is not so, who is faithful in all mine house. *With him will I speak mouth to mouth*." **(Numbers 12:4–8)**

"And the Lord delivered unto me two tables of stone written with the *finger of God*." **(Deuteronomy 9:10**; see also **Exodus 31:18)**

"Therewith bless we God, even the Father; and therewith curse we *men, which are made after the similitude of God*." **(James 3:9)**

"For a *man* indeed ought not to cover his head, forasmuch as *he is the image and glory of God*." **(1 Corinthians 11:7)**

Now See . . .

"In whom the god of this world hath blinded the minds of them which believe not, lest the light of the glorious gospel of *Christ, who is the image of God*, should shine unto them." **(2 Corinthians 4:4)**

> *Note: Many Christians claim that "the image of God" means His goodness, purity, sinlessness. 1 Corinthians 11:7 tells us that "man" is the "image of God" and 2 Corinthians 4:4 tells us that Christ "is the image of God." Does this mean that both "man" and "Christ" are "good, pure, and sinless"? No. So obviously this is teaching us that both man and Christ are in the physical image of God.*

"Let this mind be in you, which was also in *Christ Jesus*: Who, *being in the form of God*, thought it not robbery to be equal with God." **(Philippians 2:5–6)**

"God, who at sundry times and in divers manners spake in time past unto the fathers by the prophets, Hath in these last days spoken unto us by *his Son*, whom he hath appointed heir of all things, by whom also he made the worlds; Who being the brightness of his glory, and *the express image of his person*, and upholding all things by the word of his power, when he had by himself purged our sins, sat down on the right hand of the Majesty on high." **(Hebrews 1:1–3)**

"For our conversation is in heaven; from whence also we look for the Saviour, the Lord Jesus Christ: *Who shall change our vile body, that it may be fashioned like unto his glorious body*, according to the working whereby he is able even to subdue all things unto himself." **(Philippians 3:20–21)**

> Note: *If Jesus Christ is going to "change our vile body, that it may be fashioned like unto his glorious body," AND if as the scriptures teach that Jesus Christ is in the "image and form" of God the Father, then God the Father must also have a body.*

"But he, being full of the Holy Ghost, looked up steadfastly into heaven, and saw the glory of God, and *Jesus standing on the right hand of God*." **(Acts 7:55–56)**

"Behold, what manner of love the Father hath bestowed upon us, that we should be called the sons of God: therefore the world knoweth us not, because it knew him not. Beloved, now are we the sons of God, and it doth not yet appear what we shall be: but we know that, *when he shall appear, we shall be like him; for we shall see him as he is.*" **(1 John 3:2–3)**

"And they shall see *his face*; and his name shall be in their foreheads." **(Revelation 22:4**; see also verses 1–3**)**

"Take heed that ye despise not one of these little ones; for I say unto you, That in heaven their *angels do always behold the face of my Father* which is in heaven." **(Matthew 18:10)**

"For what man knoweth the things of a man, save *the spirit of man which is in him*? even so the things of God knoweth no man, but the Spirit of God." **(1 Corinthians 2:11)**

"To the general assembly and church of the firstborn, which are written in heaven, and to God the Judge of all, and *to the spirits of just men* made perfect." **(Hebrews 12:23)**

"Furthermore we have had fathers of our flesh which corrected us, and we gave them reverence: shall we not much rather be in subjection unto the *Father of spirits*, and live?" **(Hebrews 12:9)**

"For in him we live, and move, and have our being; as certain also of your own poets have said, *For we are also his offspring*. Forasmuch then as we are *the offspring of God*, we ought not to think that the Godhead is like unto gold, or silver, or stone, graven by art and man's device." **(Acts 17:28–29)**

"For ye are bought with a price: therefore glorify *God in your body, and in your spirit*, which are God's." **(1 Corinthians 6:20)**

"For, this cause was a gospel preaching to them that are dead, that they might be judged according to men in the flesh, *but live according to God in the spirit.*" **(1 Peter 4:6)**

"Knowing that Christ being raised from the dead dieth no more; death hath no more dominion over him." **(Romans 6:9)**

> *Note: Death is the spiritual body leaving the physical body. This scripture clearly states that Christ's physical body and spiritual bodies will never separate again. His physical body will never die again.*

> *Note: "If the idea of an embodied God is repugnant, then why are the central doctrines and singularly most distinguishing characteristics of all Christianity the Incarnation, the Atonement, and the physical Resurrection of the Lord Jesus Christ? If having a body is not only not needed but not desirable by Deity, why did the Redeemer of mankind redeem His body, redeeming it from the grasp of death and the grave, guaranteeing it would never again be separated from His spirit in time or eternity?"[1]*

"Who is the *image* of the *invisible* God, the firstborn of every creature." **(Colossians 1:15)**

> *Note: The word "image" translates into the Greek term, "eikon," which is the same term the Savior used in referring to Caesar's picture on a Roman coin (Matthew 22:20). Just as the "image" on the coin was a physical likeness of Caesar, the Son is a physical likeness of His Father. The same word is used in the Greek Old Testament when God is said to have created man "in his own image" (Genesis 1:27). To ignore the physical aspects of this "image" is to ignore the context within which this term is used throughout the scriptures.*

"God is a Spirit: and they that worship him must worship him in spirit and in truth." **(John 4:24)**

> *Note: What is a spirit? What do the scriptures tell us is the true nature of a spirit? When the apostles saw Jesus walking on the Sea of Galilee, they were afraid and frightened, proclaiming, "It is a spirit" (Matthew 14:26). When the Savior after His Resurrection, appeared to His Apostles they were again afraid "and supposed that they had seen a spirit" (Luke 24:37). The Apostles believed and knew that a spirit was in the form of a man, or they would not have mistaken the Savior for one. John did not proclaim that God is "only" a spirit, he said that "God is a Spirit." God is a spirit in the same sense as man is a spirit.*

> *Note: What John meant here is that we must worship God in a spirit of unity, love, and righteousness.*

FOOD FOR THOUGHT

The scriptures also say:

"He [the Lord] shall *cover thee with his feathers*, and under his wings shalt thou trust: his truth shall be thy shield and buckler." **(Psalms 91:4)**

> *Note: Does this mean that <u>God has feathers</u>?*

"For the Lord thy God is a *consuming fire*, even a *jealous* God." **(Deuteronomy 4:24)**

> *Note: Does this mean that <u>God is fire</u> or that He has the ungodly attribute of jealousy?*

"He that loveth not knoweth not God; for *God is love*." **(1 John 4:8)**

> *Note: Does this mean that God is nothing more than the emotion of Love?*

"He [the Lord] *is the Rock*, his work is perfect: for all his ways are judgment: a God of truth and without iniquity, just and right is he." **(Deuteronomy 32:4)**

> *Note: Does this mean that God is a rock?*

Of course, the answer to all of these above is "of course not." Some scriptures are obviously figurative, and some are to be taken literally. The reader of scripture must be very careful when interpreting the meaning of the scripture, as you can see above. The reader must do thorough scriptural research to determine whether (1) there are other scriptures to support the interpretation, and (2) the scripture can be supported by historical documentation.

"*Jesus cried and said*, He that believeth on me, believeth not on me, but on him that sent me. And *he that seeth me seeth him that sent me*." **(John 12:44–45)**

See chapter 30: **"Man Has Both a Physical & Spiritual Body"**
See chapter 21: **"God — Who Is He?"**

CHAPTER 21

GOD — WHO IS HE?

GOD IS OUR LITERAL FATHER

WE ARE HIS OFFSPRING

MANKIND AND JESUS ARE BROTHERS

"For in him we live, and move, and have our being; as certain also of your own poets have said, For we are also his offspring. Forasmuch then as we are the offspring of God, we ought not to think that the Godhead is like unto gold, or silver, or stone, graven by art and man's device." **(Acts 17:28–29)**

Modern Christian churches have no explanation as to who God is, what he is, or why he is. Most if not all, except for maybe a few, Christian churches teach that God just created mankind. If so why did he do this? Was he bored, lonely, or just wanted something to do? Did he have a purpose, a reason? They can't explain why he created us. Well let's see what the Bible teaches us about this . . .

GOD — WHO IS HE?

GOD IS OUR LITERAL FATHER — WE ARE HIS OFFSPRING — MANKIND AND JESUS ARE BROTHERS

Scriptures used by some Christian faiths to substantiate their belief and teaching that mankind is the creation of God and not his literal children.

"And the Lord God formed man of the dust of the ground, and breathed into his nostrils the breath of life; and man became a living soul." **(Genesis 2:7)**

"But now, O Lord, thou art our father; we are the clay, and thou our potter; and we all are the work of thy hand." **(Isaiah 64:8)**

"All things were made by him; and without him was not any thing made that was made." **(John 1:3)**

"That is, They which are the children of the flesh, these are not the children of God: but the children of the promise are counted for the seed." **(Romans 9:8)**

"For ye are all the children of God by faith in Christ Jesus." **(Galatians 3:26)**

"But when the fulness of the time was come, God sent forth his Son, made of a woman, made under the law, To redeem them that were under the law, that we might receive the adoption of sons." **(Galatians 4:4–5)**

"For as many as are led by the Spirit of God, they are the sons of God." **(Romans 8:14)**

NOW THE REST OF THE STORY . . . (scriptures that further explain or clarify the topic)

"Furthermore we have had fathers of our flesh which corrected us, and we gave them reverence: shall we not much rather be in subjection unto the *Father of spirits*, and live?" **(Hebrews 12:9)**

NOW SEE . . .

"For in him we live, and move, and have our being; as certain also of your own poets have said, *For we are also his offspring.* Forasmuch then as *we are the offspring of God*, we ought not to think that the Godhead is like unto gold, or silver, or stone, graven by art and man's device." **(Acts 17:28–29)**

"They shall not labour in vain, nor bring forth for trouble; for *they are the seed* of the blessed *of the Lord*, and *their offspring* with them." **(Isaiah 65:23)**

> *Note: Acts 17:28–29 and Isaiah 65:23 clearly show that "offspring" means literally children. See Isaiah 61:9 for further definition of "seed." See Revelation 22:16 for further definition of "offspring."*

"*Ye are the children of the Lord your God*: ye shall not cut yourselves, nor make any baldness between your eyes for the dead." **(Deuteronomy 14:1)**

"I have said, *Ye are gods*; and *all of you are children of the most High*." **(Psalms 82:6)**

"Then the Jews took up stones again to stone him. Jesus answered them, Many good works have I shewed you from my Father; for which of those works do ye stone me? The Jews answered him, saying, For a good work we stone thee not; but for blasphemy; and because that thou, being a man, makest thyself God. Jesus answered them, *Is it not written in your law, I said, Ye are gods?* If he called them gods, unto whom the word of God came, and the scripture cannot be broken; Say ye of him, whom the Father hath sanctified, and sent into the world, Thou blasphemest; because *I said, I am the Son of God?*" **(John 10:31–36)**

"Yet the number of the children of Israel shall be as the sand of the sea, which cannot be measured nor numbered; and it shall come to pass, that in the place where it was said unto them, Ye are not my people, there it shall be said unto them, *Ye are the sons of the living God*." **(Hosea 1:10)**

"For the earnest expectation of the creature waiteth for the manifestation of *the sons of God*."**(Romans 8:19)**

"The Spirit itself beareth witness with our spirit, that *we are the children of God*." **(Romans 8:16)**

"*And if children*, then heirs; *heirs of God*, and *joint-heirs with Christ*; if so be that we suffer with him, that we may be also glorified together." **(Romans 8:17)**

> **Note: Joint heirs with Christ of what? Everything Our Heavenly Father has.**

"Be ye therefore perfect, even as *your Father* which is in heaven is perfect." **(Matthew 5:48)**

> **Note: We are instructed to be as perfect as our Heavenly Father is perfect. If we are to become as perfect as He is, will we then become as He is, a god?**

"Behold, what manner of love the Father hath bestowed upon us, that we should be called the sons of God: therefore the world knoweth us not, because it knew him not. Beloved, now are we the sons of God, and it doth not yet appear what we shall be: but we know that, *when he shall appear, we shall be like him; for we shall see him as he is*." **(1 John 3:2–3)**

"After this manner therefore pray ye: *Our Father* which art in heaven, Hallowed be thy name." **(Matthew 6:9)**

"One God and *Father of all*, who is above all, and through all, and in you all." **(Ephesians 4:6)**

"And not for that nation only, but that also he should gather together in one *the children of God* that were scattered abroad." **(John 11:52)**

"For this cause I bow my knees *unto the Father* of our Lord Jesus Christ, *Of whom the whole family in heaven and earth is named*." **(Ephesians 3:14–15)**

"Which was the son of Enos, which was the son of Seth, which was the son of Adam, *which was the son of God.*" (**Luke 3:38**)

> *Note: If Adam is the son of God; then all of Adam's descendants are also the "sons & daughters of God."*
>
> *Read Luke 3:21–38.*

"And no man hath ascended up to heaven, but he that came down from heaven, even the Son of man which is in heaven." (**John 3:13**)

Conclusion

Mankind are the "Literal Children of God."

Mankind are the "Offspring of God."

God is literally our Father.

See chapter 30: **"Man Has Both a Physical & Spiritual Body"**
See chapter 20: **"God Has a Physical Body"**
See chapter 37: **"Premortal Existence of Spirits"**

CHAPTER 22

GODHEAD — TRINITY
THREE SEPARATE BEINGS

"I go unto the Father: for my Father is greater than I." **(John 14:28)**

Not until the council of Constantinople (AD 381) was the concept of one God existing in three coequal persons, of one undivided substance, formally ratified. The concept of the Trinity was further debated at the Councils of Ephesus (AD 431) and finally at Chalcedon (AD 451), where it became canon law. It wasn't until the fifteenth century that the disputations came to an end and the Nicene Creed became completely ratified and dogma. This chapter will help you to explain the Godhead.

GODHEAD — TRINITY
THREE SEPARATE BEINGS

Scriptures used by some Christian faiths to substantiate their belief and teaching that God the Father, Jesus Christ, and the Holy Ghost are one and the same being and substance:

"But after that the kindness and love of God our Savior toward man appeared." **(Titus 3:4)**

> *Note: Some claim that this scripture shows that God the Father and Jesus Christ our Savior are one and the same personage. (See "Jesus Christ is Jehovah" in this book)*

"I and my Father are one." **(John 10:30)**

> *Note: In the original Greek texts the word "one" appears in the neuter gender which indicates oneness in attributes, power or purpose. For it to imply a oneness of being, personality, or identity, the masculine form of the word would be required.*[1]

NOW SEE . . .

"For this cause shall a man leave his father and mother, and cleave to his wife; And they twain shall be one flesh: so then they are no more twain, but one flesh." **(Mark 10:7–8)**

> *Note: Again in the original Greek texts the word "one" appears in the neuter gender, oneness in purpose.*

"For there are three that bear record in heaven, the Father, the Word, and the Holy Ghost: and these three are one." **(1 John 5:7)**

> *Note: If there really was only one in Heaven then the verse would only need to read that there is one that bear's record; but it does not say that. It says there "are three" that bear record in heaven.*

"In the beginning was the Word, and the Word was with God, and the Word was God. The same was in the beginning with God. All things were made by him; and without him was not any thing made that was made." **(John 1:1–3)**

"And the Word was made flesh, and dwelt among us, (and we beheld his glory, the glory as of the only begotten of the Father,) full of grace and truth." **(John 1:14)**

> *Note: The important word and phrase here in John 1:1–3, is "with God." This scripture is saying that the "Word" was "with" God; NOT that the Word is God the Father. Those who misunderstand the Trinity try to use this scripture to prove that God the Father and the Word (Jesus Christ) are one and the same personage.*

> *Note: The New World Translation of the Bible, John 1:1–3 reads, "In the beginning was the Word, and the Word was with God, and the Word was a god. This one was in the beginning with God. All things came into*

existence through him, and apart from him not even one thing came into existence."

Note: Per John 1:1–3, Jesus Christ (the Word) created everything. Would he not then have to be a "<u>god</u>" to do this? How could he have "created all things" without having the knowledge, ability, and power to do so?

Note: John 1:14 confirms that the "Word" is Jesus Christ.

"Take heed therefore unto yourselves, and to all the flock, over the which the Holy Ghost hath made you overseers, to feed the church of God, which he hath purchased with his own blood." (**Acts 20:28**)

Note: The phrase "with his own blood," notice that "his" is not capitalized. In the Bible wherever the word "his" is used to mean God with a capital "G" or personally identifying "God" the Father, the "h" in "his" is always a capitalized "H." In this case "with his own blood" is referring to His son, Jesus. Just as you are "the blood" of your father, Jesus is the blood of his father. The same applies to the words "he" and "him" when referring to the Son. (John 1:1–3)

NOW THE REST OF THE STORY . . . (scriptures that further explain or clarify the topic)

"Verily I say unto you, All sins shall be forgiven unto the sons of men, and blasphemies wherewith soever they shall blaspheme: *But he that shall blaspheme against the Holy Ghost hath never forgiveness*, but is in danger of eternal damnation." (**Mark 3:28–29**)

"Wherefore I say unto you, All manner of sin and blasphemy shall be forgiven unto men: *but the blasphemy against the Holy Ghost shall not be forgiven unto men.* And *whosoever speaketh a word against the Son of man*, it shall be forgiven him: *but whosoever speaketh against the Holy Ghost, it shall not be forgiven him*, neither in this world, neither in the world to come." (**Matthew 12:31–32**; see also **Luke 12:10**)

Note: Mark 3:28–29 and Matthew 12:31–32 conclusively show that God the Father, Jesus Christ, and the Holy Ghost are NOT one and the same personage or undivided substance (as so states the Nicene Creed and most of Christianity). For if they were, then a sin or blaspheme against God the Father or the Son of Man (Jesus Christ), would then be a sin against the Holy Ghost also and unforgiveable. If not so, then Matthew would not have had to make this distinction.

Note: Mark 3:28–29 and Matthew 12:31–32 also show conclusively that the Holy Ghost is NOT just a force or an influence, but an actual personage of the Godhead.

"But of that day and hour knoweth no man, no, not the angels of heaven, *but my Father only.*" (**Matthew 24:36**)

"But of that day and that hour knoweth no man, no, not the angels which are in heaven, *neither the Son*, but the Father." (**Mark 13:32**)

> *Note: If the Father and the Son are of one undivided substance and being, how can one have knowledge of something and the other does not?*

"For *the Father judgeth no man, but hath committed all judgment unto the Son.*" (**John 5:22**)

> *Note: If the Father and the Son are the same being or of the same undivided substance, how can one be something, a judge, and the other is not? How can one judge and the other not?*

"For I came down from heaven, *not to do mine own will*, but the will of him that sent me." (**John 6:38**; see also **John 5:30, John 4:34, Mark 14:36, Luke 22:42**)

> *Note: If the Father and the Son are the same being or of the same undivided substance, how can one do something that is not the will of the other?*

"And he was withdrawn from them about a stone's cast, and kneeled down, and prayed, Saying, *Father, if thou be willing*, remove this cup from me: nevertheless *not my will*, but thine, be done." (**Luke 22:41–42**)

> *Note: If the Father and the Son are the same being or of the same undivided substance, why did he have to pray to his Father to "remove this cup from me"? He could have just done it himself.*

"I go unto the Father: for *my Father is greater than I.*" (**John 14:28**)

> *Note: If the Father and the Son are the same being or of the same undivided substance, how can one be greater than the other? The Athanasian Creed states that <u>neither</u> the Father, the Son, nor the Holy Ghost is greater than the other.*

"Then answered Jesus and said unto them, Verily, verily, I say unto you, *The Son can do nothing of himself, but what he seeth the Father do*: for what things soever he doeth, these also doeth the Son likewise." (**John 5:19**; see also **verse 20**)

> *Note: If God the Father and Christ were one being and substance, how could one not do something unless he saw the other do it first?*

"Jesus answered them, and said, My doctrine is not mine, *but his that sent me.* If any man will do His will, he shall know of the doctrine, *whether it be of God, or whether I speak of myself.*" (**John 7:16–17**)

> *Note: If God the Father and Christ were one being and substance, the doctrine would be Christ's also.*

"For I have not spoken of myself; but *the Father which sent me, he gave me a commandment*, what I should say, and what I should speak. And I know that his commandment is life everlasting: whatsoever I speak therefore, even as the Father said unto me, so I speak." (**John 12:49–50**)

> *Note: If God the Father and Christ were one being and substance, why would one need to give the other a commandment?*

"And he went a little further, and fell on his face, and prayed, saying, O my Father, if it be possible, let this cup pass from me: nevertheless *not as I will, but as thou wilt.*" **(Matthew 26:39)**

> *Note: Is Christ praying unto himself? If the Father and the Son are of one undivided substance and one being, then he MUST be praying unto himself. For a time, Christ's will was not the Father's will, therefore two separate persons.*

"And about the ninth hour Jesus cried with a loud voice, saying, Eli, Eli, lama sabachthani? that is to say, *My God, my God, why hast thou forsaken me?*" **(Matthew 27:46**; see also **Mark 15:34)**

> *Note: Is Christ asking himself why has he forsaken himself? If God the Father and Christ were one being and substance then not only would he be forsaking himself, he would also know the answer to his question and not have to ask it.*

"But that the world may know that *I love the Father*; and as the Father gave me commandment, even so I do. Arise, let us go hence." **(John 14:31)**

> *Note: Is Jesus in love with himself? If the Father and the Son are of one undivided substance and one being, then he MUST love himself.*

"And he saith unto them, Ye shall drink indeed of my cup, and be baptized with the baptism that I am baptized with: but to sit on my right hand, and on my left, *is not mine to give, but it shall be given to them for whom it is prepared of my Father.*" **(Matthew 20:23)**

> *Note: If God the Father and Christ were one being and substance, why can one give what the other cannot?*

"Jesus saith unto her, Touch me not; for I am not yet ascended to my Father: but go to my brethren, and say unto them, I ascend unto *my Father, and your Father; and to my God, and your God.*" **(John 20:17)**

> *Note: Is Christ to ascend unto himself? Is he both his own father and his own god? If God the Father and Jesus Christ are of one undivided substance and one being, then this must be so. But NO. These scriptures clearly show that God the Father and Jesus Christ are two distinct and individual personages and beings. Christ clearly demonstrates a hierarchy of beings. Our Heavenly Father and our Savior cannot be the same being or undivided substance, since the Father is the God of Jesus Christ, His son.*

> *Note: The Savior clearly says that his Father is also our Father, yet we are not one in substance or being with Him. Hebrews 12:9 & Acts 17:29 says that God is "the Father of our spirits and that we are His offspring."*

"And said, Behold, I see the heavens opened, and the Son of man *standing on the right hand of God.*" **(Acts 7:56)**

"Who is gone into heaven, and is *on the right hand of God*; angels and authorities and powers being made subject unto him." **(1 Peter 3:22)**

> *Note: In Acts 7:56 and 1 Peter 3:22, Stephan saw two separate individuals standing next to each other, angels and "authorities and powers" being made subject unto Jesus Christ.*

"For it is written, As I live, saith the Lord, *every knee shall bow to me*, and *every tongue shall confess to God."* **(Romans 14:11)**

> *Note: The Lord said "to me" and "to God." Two separate beings.*

"Neither pray I for these alone, but for them also which shall believe on me through their word; *That they all may be one; as thou, Father, art in me, and I in thee, that they also may be one in us*: that the world may believe that thou hast sent me. And the glory which thou gavest me I have given them; *that they may be one, even as we are one: I in them, and thou in me*, that they may be made perfect in one; and that the world may know that thou hast sent me, and hast loved them, as thou hast loved me." **(John 17:20–23)**

> *Note: Christ is asking the Father that His Apostles and "everyone which shall believe in him," that may be one, "as Christ and the Father are one." Is he asking that the Father, Christ, the Apostles, and all that believe in Him, all meld into one being, into one undivided substance? NO!*
>
> *He is asking that they all will be one in purpose, spirit, righteousness, and love that exists between the Father, the Son, and the Holy Ghost.*
>
> *If we are to interpret the oneness of the Father and the Son as a reference to their physical identity or their oneness of essence, then we must ascribe this same oneness to all of Christ's disciples.*

"At that day ye shall know that *I am in my Father*, and *ye in me*, and *I in you*." **(John 14:20)**

> *Note: Christ is clearly showing that He, his Father, and the Apostles are One in Purpose and NOT one in substance nor personage.*

"As concerning therefore the eating of those things that are offered in sacrifice unto idols, we know that an idol is nothing in the world, and that there is none other God but one. For though there be that are called gods, whether in heaven or in earth, (*as there be gods many, and lords many*,) But to us there is but *one God, the Father*, of whom are all things, and we in him; and *one Lord Jesus Christ*, by whom are all things, and we by him." **(1 Corinthians 8:4–6)**

> *Note: In verse 6, note the words "and we in him." Now see John 17:20–23 above, where Christ says "that they may be one, even as we are one: I in them, and thou in me, that they may be made perfect in one." Paul is clearly showing "One in Purpose, NOT One in Substance."*

"And God said, *Let us make man in our* image, after *our* likeness: . . . So God created man in his own image, in the image of God created he him; male and female created he them." (**Genesis 1:26–27**)

> *Note: "Our" is plural . . . NOT singular. Clearly indicating the plurality of individuals.*

> *Note: The operative word in this verse is the Hebrew verb "tsalam," "to create in one's own image." Tsalam in modern Hebrew is used to mean "photocopy," or to create an exact duplicate of something.*

"And Adam lived an hundred and thirty years, and begat *a son in his own likeness, after his image*; and called his name Seth." (**Genesis 5:3**)

"And the Lord God said, Behold, the man is become as one of *us*." (**Genesis 3:22**)

> *Note: "Us" is plural . . . NOT singular. Clearly indicating the plurality of individuals.*

"For there is one God, and *one mediator* between God and men, the man Christ Jesus." (**1 Timothy 2:5**)

> *Note: The Son is the mediator or advocate who stands between us and our Heavenly Father, indicating at least two separate beings. A mediator is a third party who mediates between two or more others. If Jesus and God were indeed one being and undivided substance, then there would be no third-party mediator.*

"My little children, these things write I unto you, that ye sin not. And if any man sin, we have an *advocate with the Father*, Jesus Christ the righteous." (**1 John 2:1**)

> *Note: An "Advocate" just like a "Mediator" is a third party; one cannot be an advocate or a mediator for one's self.*

"If I had not done among them the works which none other man did, they had not had sin: but now have they both seen and hated *both me and my Father*." (**John 15:24**)

> *Note: The words "both" me "and" my Father, clearly indicates two separate beings or persons, and would not have been spoken this way if this clarification was not needed and intended.*

"If I bear witness of myself, *my witness is not true*." (**John 5:31**)

"The Pharisees therefore said unto him, *Thou bearest record of thyself; thy record is not true*." (**John 8:13**)

"It is also written in your law, that the testimony of two men is true. I am one that bear witness of myself, and *the Father* that sent me beareth witness of me." (**John 8:17–18**)

> *Note: The Savior taught that in order to prove His divinity He needed the testimony of two or three witnesses <u>other than Himself</u>. If the Father was not a separate being from Jesus, then Jesus would have violated His foundational statement, "<u>If I bear witness of myself, my witness is not true</u>," and Jewish law.*

"And this is life eternal, that they might know thee the only true God, *and* Jesus Christ, whom thou hast sent." (**John 17:3**)

"For there are certain men crept in unawares, who were before of old ordained to this condemnation, ungodly men, turning the grace of our God into lasciviousness, and denying the only Lord God, *and* our Lord Jesus Christ." (**Jude 1:4**)

"*But unto the Son he saith*, Thy throne, *O God*, is for ever and ever." (**Hebrews 1:8**)

"To him that overcometh will I grant to sit with me in *my throne*, even as I also overcame, and am set down with my Father in *his throne*." (**Revelation 3:21**)

> *Note: The words "my throne" and "his throne" show two separate persons, beings, and thrones.*

The term "trinity" is NOT once used by Heavenly Father, Jesus Christ, the Lord's prophets, or the Apostles. Nowhere within the pages of the Holy Bible can any terminology such as "trinity," "triad," "triune," or anything like it be found. Nor is there any scripture within the Holy Bible that says the Father, the Son, and the Holy Ghost are one being.

The term "trinity," or the Latin term "trinitas," was first used by Tertullian, a lawyer by trade, Christian by faith, and a theologian, who lived from AD 160 to 220. The term first appeared in his work, "Against Praxeas," around AD 210, over 110 years after the death of the last Apostle.[2]

The New Catholic Encyclopedia indicates that a solid Trinitarian doctrine was not *derived* and *combined* into *orthodoxy* by the whole Catholic church until at least another hundred years. The formulation of *one God in three Persons* was not solidly established, not fully assimilated into Christian life and its profession of faith, prior to the end of the fourth century. Among the Apostolic Fathers, there had been nothing even remotely approaching such a concept or perspective (emphases added).

Harper's Bible Dictionary records that *"the formal **doctrine of the Trinity** as it was defined by the great church councils of the fourth and fifth centuries is **not to be found in the [New Testament]**"* (emphasis added).

The doctrine of the Trinity was not part of the early Christian New Testament message. It cannot be denied that not only the word "Trinity," but even the explicit idea of the Trinity is nowhere found in the apostolic witness of the faith. The doctrine of the Trinity, is not a Biblical doctrine.

It is important to remember that many of the early converts to Christianity were of the Jewish faith. The Jewish converts had a major difficulty with the doctrine taught by the Apostles and believed by the early Christians, of God the Father, Jesus Christ, and the Holy Ghost, all being individual and equal members of the Godhead; this was blasphemy as the Jewish converts believed in only one god. Early Church "Fathers" living prior to the Council of Nicaea such as Clement, Ignatius, Hermas, Justin Martyr, and Origen, believed and taught the Father, Son, and Holy Ghost were three distinct persons.[3]

Because of the contention between different Christian groups over this matter, the Roman Emperor Constantine, who assumed control of the Christian Church as a means to solidify his own political rule, called for a council in the city of Nicaea (AD 325) over which he would rule, to settle this doctrinal rift. From this council was drawn up the Creed of Nicaea.

Not until the council of Constantinople (AD 381) was the concept of one God existing in three coequal persons, of one undivided substance formally ratified. The concept of the Trinity was further debated at the Councils of Ephesus (AD 431) and finally at Chalcedon (AD 451) where it became canon law.[4]

It wasn't until the fifteenth century that the disputations came to an end and the Nicene Creed became completely ratified and dogma.

John 14:1–21 Teaches Us Much about the Godhead

1. Let not your heart be troubled: ye believe in God, believe also in me.

> *Note: if God the Father and Jesus Christ were indeed of one essence or being, then verse 1 above would be unnecessary, as anyone who believed in God the Father would automatically believe in Jesus Christ.*

2. In my Father's house are many mansions: if it were not so, I would have told you. I go to prepare a place for you.

3. And if I go and prepare a place for you, I will come again, and receive you unto myself; that where I am, there ye may be also.

4. And whither I go ye know, and the way ye know.

5. Thomas saith unto him, Lord, we know not whither thou goest; and how can we know the way?

6. Jesus saith unto him, I am the way, the truth, and the life: *no man cometh unto the Father, but by me.*

> *Note: Verse 6 above clearly explains that no one can come unto the Father except through the Savior; not even through the Father directly. If they are one and the same how could this be?*

7. If ye had known me, ye should have known *my Father* also: and from henceforth ye know him, and have seen him.

8. Philip saith unto him, Lord, shew us the Father, and it sufficeth us.

9. Jesus saith unto him, Have I been so long time with you, and yet hast thou not known me, Philip? *he that hath seen me hath seen the Father*; and how sayest thou then, Shew us the Father?

> *Note: Many claim that verse 9 proves that the Father and Christ are one and the same person.*

10. Believest thou not that *I am in the Father, and the Father in me?* the words that I speak unto you I speak not of myself: but *the Father* that dwelleth in me, *he doeth the works.*

> **Note: If the Father and the Son are the same, how could the Father be doing the works and not the Son?**

11. Believe me that I am in the Father, and the Father in me: or else believe me for the very works' sake.

12. Verily, verily, I say unto you, He that believeth on me, the works that I do shall he do also; and greater works than these shall he do; because I go unto *my Father.*

13. And whatsoever ye shall ask in my name, that will I do, that the Father may be glorified in the Son.

14. If ye shall ask any thing in my name, I will do it.

15. If ye love me, keep my commandments.

16. *And I will pray the Father, and he shall give you another Comforter, that he may abide with you for ever;*

17. Even the Spirit of truth; whom the world cannot receive, because it seeth him not, neither knoweth him: but ye know him; for he dwelleth with you, *and shall be in you.*

18. I will not leave you comfortless: I will come to you.

19. Yet a little while, and the world seeth me no more; but ye see me: because I live, ye shall live also.

20. At that day ye shall know that *I am in my Father, and ye in me, and I in you.*

21. He that loveth me not keepeth not my sayings: and the word which ye hear is not mine, *but the Father's which sent me.*

> **Note: If God the Father and Christ were one being and substance, the "words" would be Christ's also.**

JOHN 17. THE GREAT INTERCESSORY PRAYER

Jesus prays for His Apostles and all the Saints. Jesus explains how the Father and the Son are one.

1. These words spake Jesus, and lifted up his eyes to heaven, and said, Father, the hour is come; glorify thy Son, that thy Son also may glorify thee:

2. As thou hast given him *power over all flesh,* that he should give eternal life to as many as thou hast given him.

3. And this is life eternal, *that they might know thee the only true God,* and Jesus Christ, whom thou hast sent.

4. I have glorified thee on the earth: I have finished the work which thou gavest me to do.

5. And now, O Father, glorify thou me with thine own self *with the glory which I had with thee before the world was.*

6. I have manifested thy name unto the men which thou gavest me out of the world: thine they were, and thou gavest them me; and they have kept thy word.

7. Now they have known that all things whatsoever thou hast given me are of thee.

8. For I have given unto them the words which thou gavest me; and they have received them, and have known surely that I came out from thee, and they have believed that thou didst send me.

9. I pray for them: I pray not for the world, but for them which thou hast given me; for they are thine.

10. And all mine are thine, and thine are mine; and I am glorified in them.

11. And now I am no more in the world, but these are in the world, and I come to thee. Holy Father, keep through thine own name those whom thou hast given me, *that they may be one, as we are.*

12. While I was with them in the world, I kept them in thy name: those that thou gavest me I have kept, and none of them is lost, but the son of perdition; that the scripture might be fulfilled.

13. And now come I to thee; and these things I speak in the world, that they might have my joy fulfilled in themselves.

14. I have given them thy word; and the world hath hated them, because they are not of the world, even as I am not of the world.

15. I pray not that thou shouldest take them out of the world, but that thou shouldest keep them from the evil.

16. *They are not of the world, even as I am not of the world.*

17. Sanctify them through thy truth: thy word is truth.

18. *As thou hast sent me* into the world, even *so have I also sent them* into the world.

19. And for their sakes I sanctify myself, that they also might be sanctified through the truth.

20. Neither pray I for these alone, but for them also which shall believe on me through their word;

21. *That they all may be one; as thou, Father, art in me, and I in thee, that they also may be one in us*: that the world may believe that thou hast sent me.

22. And the glory which thou gavest me I have given them; that *they may be one, even as we are one*:

23. *I in them, and thou in me, that they may be made perfect in one*; and that the world may know that thou hast sent me, and hast loved them, as thou hast loved me.

24. Father, I will that they also, whom thou hast given me, be with me where I am; that they may behold my glory, which thou hast given me: for thou lovedst me before the foundation of the world.

25. O righteous Father, the world hath not known thee: but I have known thee, and these have known that thou hast sent me.

26. And I have declared unto them thy name, and will declare it: *that the love wherewith thou hast loved me may be in them, and I in them.*

It wasn't long after the death of the Jesus Christ and the Apostles, that uninspired theologians and philosophers wasted little time in changing the simple and pure teachings of Jesus Christ in order to establish a church of their own liking. Complicated doctrines such as that of the "Trinity" gave these men power over the believers.

OTHER SCRIPTURES YOU MAY WANT TO READ . . .

Matthew 3:13–17
Matthew 19:16–17
Mark 1:10–11
Luke 12:10

Luke 3:21–23
John 8:13
1 Corinthians 11:3
Ephesians 4:4–6

CONCLUSION

God the Father, Jesus Christ, and the Holy Ghost

Are three separate beings and personages,

Three who are one — only in purpose.

The Nicene and Athanasian Creeds are man-made doctrines not supported by scripture.

See chapter 21: **"God —Who Is He?"**
See chapter 28: **"Jesus Christ — Who Is He?"**
See chapter 27: **"Jehovah Is Jesus Christ"**
See chapter 25: **"Holy Ghost"**
See article: "The Only True God and Jesus Christ" by Elder Jeffrey R. Holland (*Ensign*, November 2007, 40–42)

CHAPTER 23

GOD'S LAW OF HEALTH

"Know ye not that ye are the temple of God, and that the Spirit of God dwelleth in you? If any man defile the temple of God, him shall God destroy; for the temple of God is holy, which temple ye are." **(1 Corinthians 3:16–17)**

What is "God's Law of Health"? Does it just cover things like harmful drugs, alcohol, or Tobacco? Are we abusing and defiling our body, our "temple of God," when we abuse food and become obese? What about laziness or lack of exercise which may lead to being overweight and poor health?

GOD'S LAW OF HEALTH

Scriptures used by some Christian faiths to substantiate their belief and teaching about God's Laws regarding health, especially what one should or should not eat or drink:

There is much controversy and argument among various Christian faiths regarding this subject. Some Christian faiths adhere strictly to the law of Moses, while other claim that Jesus Christ abolished these Old Testament laws. The problem; Which law do we follow? Is clouded by the age-old problem of Bible interpretation, and whose interpretation does one choose to follow. And yet there is another problem in Modern-day Christianity on this subject; some pastors and churches choosing to ignore the subject altogether. Why would they do this you ask? Because mankind enjoys his food, drink, tobacco, and let's not forget mind-altering drugs, more than he or she loves God.

NOW THE REST OF THE STORY . . . (scriptures that further explain or clarify the topic)

Our purpose here is not to argue for or against the Law if Moses, but to present scriptures that we should take to heart that will help us to be better sons and daughters of our Heavenly Parents, better husbands and wives, and better parents to our children.

"Know ye not that ye are the temple of God, and that the Spirit of God dwelleth in you? *If any man defile the temple of God, him shall God destroy*; for the temple of God is holy, *which temple ye are.*" (**1 Corinthians 3:16–17**; see also **1 Corinthians 6:19–20**)

"Beloved, I wish above all things that thou mayest *prosper and be in health*, even as thy soul prospereth." (**3 John 1:2**)

"*Do not drink wine nor strong drink*, thou, nor thy sons with thee, when ye go into the tabernacle of the congregation, lest ye die: it shall be a statute for ever throughout your generations." (**Leviticus 10:9**)

"Now therefore beware, I pray thee, and *drink not wine nor strong drink*, and eat not any unclean thing." (**Judges 13:4**)

"*Wine is a mocker, strong drink is raging*: and whosoever is deceived thereby is not wise." (**Proverbs 20:1**)

"Woe unto them that rise up early in the morning, *that they may follow strong drink; that continue until night, till wine inflame them*! And the harp, and the viol, the tabret, and pipe, and wine, are in their feasts: but they regard not the work of the Lord, neither consider the operation of his hands." (**Isaiah 5:11–12**)

"And put a knife to thy throat, *if thou be a man given to appetite.*" (**Proverbs 23:2**)

"*And God said*, Behold, I have given you *every herb bearing seed*, which is upon the face of all the earth, and *every tree*, in the which is the fruit of a tree yielding seed; to you it shall be for meat. And to *every beast* of the earth, and to *every fowl* of the air, and to *everything that creepeth upon the earth*, wherein there is life, I have given *every green herb* for meat: and it was so." **(Genesis 1:29–30)**

"*Every moving thing that liveth shall be meat for you*; even as the green herb have I given you all things." **(Genesis 9:3)**

"Whether therefore ye eat, or drink, or whatsoever ye do, *do all to the glory of God.*" **(1 Corinthians 10:31)**

"*The sleep of a labouring man is sweet*, whether he eat little or much: but the abundance of the rich will not suffer him to sleep." **(Ecclesiastes 5:12)**

"*If ye love me, keep my commandments.*" **(John 14:15)**

CHAPTER 24

HEAVEN – HELL
DEGREES OF GLORY

"Not every one that saith unto me, Lord, Lord, shall enter into the kingdom of heaven; but he that doeth the will of my Father which is in heaven. Many will say to me in that day, Lord, Lord, have we not prophesied in thy name? and in thy name have cast out devils? and in thy name done many wonderful works? And then will I profess unto them, I never knew you: depart from me, ye that work iniquity." **(Matthew 7:21–23)**

What is Heaven? Where is it? How many Heavens are there? What will Heaven be like? What is Hell? Where is it at? Is a sentence to Hell for all eternity? What will Hell be like? Not all Christian churches agree on this. Let's take a look at what the Bible says . . .

Heaven — Hell — Degrees of Glory

Scriptures used by some Christian faiths to substantiate their belief and teaching about Heaven; and that those who are sent to Hell are doomed to remain in Hell for all eternity:

"Then shall he say also unto them on the left hand, Depart from me, ye cursed, into everlasting fire, prepared for the devil and his angels." (**Matthew 25:41**)

"And these shall go away into everlasting punishment: but the righteous into life eternal." (**Matthew 25:46**)

"And *the devil* that deceived them *was cast into the lake of fire* and brimstone, *where the beast and the false prophet are*, and shall be tormented day and night for ever and ever." (**Revelation 20:10**)

> **Note: It is the devil and the false prophet that shall be tormented day and night forever and ever.**

"But I say unto you, That whosoever is angry with his brother without a cause shall be in danger of the judgment: and whosoever shall say to his brother, Raca, shall be in danger of the council: but whosoever shall say, Thou fool, shall be in danger of hell fire." (**Matthew 5:22**)

Now the Rest of the Story . . . (scriptures that further explain or clarify the topic)

Heaven

"And *no man* hath ascended up to heaven, *but he that came down from heaven*, even the Son of man which is in heaven." (**John 3:13**)

"Not every one that saith unto me, Lord, Lord, shall enter into the kingdom of heaven; but he that doeth the will of my Father which is in heaven. Many will say to me in that day, Lord, Lord, have we not prophesied in thy name? and in thy name have cast out devils? and in thy name done many wonderful works? *And then will I profess unto them, I never knew you: depart from me, ye that work iniquity."* (**Matthew 7:21–23**)

"And one of the malefactors which were hanged railed on him, saying, If thou be Christ, save thyself and us. But the other answering rebuked him, saying, Dost not thou fear God, seeing thou art in the same condemnation? And we indeed justly; for we receive the due reward of our deeds: but this man hath done nothing amiss. And he said unto Jesus, Lord, remember me when thou comest into thy kingdom. *And Jesus said unto him,* Verily I say unto thee, *To day shalt thou be with me in paradise."* (**Luke 23:39–43**)

"Jesus saith unto her, Mary. She turned herself, and saith unto him, Rabboni; which is to say, Master. Jesus saith unto her, Touch me not; *for I am not yet ascended to my Father*: but go to my brethren, and say unto them, I ascend unto my Father, and your Father; and to my God, and your God." (**John 20:16–17**)

> *Note: In Luke 23:39-43, we learn that Christ promised one of the men being crucified next to Him that* "Today shalt thou be with me in paradise." *Yet three days later he tells Mary, in John 20:16-17, that He has not yet ascended to His Father which is in Heaven. This tells us that "paradise" is not Heaven; Christ is telling us that He went to "paradise" the day he died, but had not been to heaven three days later.*

DEGREES OF GLORY

"*I knew a man in Christ* above fourteen years ago, (whether in the body, I cannot tell; or whether out of the body, I cannot tell: God knoweth;) such an one caught up to *the third heaven*." (**2 Corinthians 12:2**)

"There are also celestial bodies, and bodies terrestrial: but *the glory of the celestial* is one, and *the glory of the terrestrial* is another. There is one glory of the sun, and another glory of the moon, and another glory of the stars: for one star differeth from another star in glory. *So also is the resurrection of the dead.* It is sown in corruption; it is raised in incorruption." (**1 Corinthians 15:40–42**)

> *Note: 2 Corinthians 12:2 and 1 Corinthians 15:40–42 unmistakably tell us that "salvation" is nothing like the Protestant definition of "universal salvation for all" by the "Grace of God." These verses inform us that there are different "degrees of salvation and glory" or exaltation. What does man have to do to achieve salvation to one of these "degrees of glory"?*

THE SPIRIT PRISON — HELL

"Who shall be punished with everlasting destruction *from the presence of the Lord*, and from the glory of his power." (**2 Thessalonians 1:9**)

"*For Christ* also hath once suffered for sins, the just for the unjust, that he might bring us to God, being put to death in the flesh, but quickened by the Spirit: By which also *he went and preached unto the spirits in prison*; Which sometime were disobedient, when once the longsuffering of God waited in the days of Noah, while the ark was a preparing, wherein few, that is, eight souls were saved by water." (**1 Peter 3:18–20**)

> *Note: Why would Christ during the three days he was dead, and before his resurrection, go to the "spirits in prison" and preach to them? Answer: because they cannot be judged for something they knew nothing about. They needed to be given knowledge of Christ and the Gospel.*

NOW SEE . . .

"For to this end Christ both died, and rose, and revived, that he might be *Lord both of the dead and living*." (**Romans 14:9**)

"*For this cause was the gospel preached also to them that are dead, that they might be judged according to men in the flesh*, but live according to God in the spirit." (**1 Peter 4:6**)

"Therefore my heart is glad, and my glory rejoiceth: my flesh also shall rest in hope. For *thou wilt not leave my soul in hell*; neither wilt thou suffer thine Holy One to see corruption." **(Psalms 16:9–10)**

"For great is thy mercy toward me: and *thou hast delivered my soul from the lowest hell.*" **(Psalms 86:13**; see also **Acts 2:25–31)**

> *Note: In Psalms 16:9–10 and 86:13, David is rejoicing because God will not leave his soul in hell.*

"For David speaketh concerning him, I foresaw the Lord always before my face, for he is on my right hand, that I should not be moved: Therefore did my heart rejoice, and my tongue was glad; moreover also my flesh shall rest in hope: Because *thou wilt not leave my soul in hell*, neither wilt thou suffer thine Holy One to see corruption." **(Acts 2:25–27)**

"Men and brethren, let me freely speak unto you of the patriarch David, that he is both dead and buried, and his sepulchre is with us unto this day. Therefore being a prophet, and knowing that God had sworn with an oath to him, that of the fruit of his loins, according to the flesh, he would raise up Christ to sit on his throne; He seeing this before spake of the resurrection of Christ, that *his soul was not left in hell*, neither his flesh did see corruption." **(Acts 2:29–31)**

"Jesus said unto her, I am the resurrection, and the life: *he that believeth in me, though he were dead, yet shall he live*: And whosoever liveth and believeth in me shall never die. Believest thou this?" **(John 11:25–26)**

ALL SINS SHALL BE FORGIVEN UNTO THE SONS OF MEN

"Verily I say unto you, *All sins shall be forgiven unto the sons of men*, and blasphemies wherewith soever they shall blaspheme: *But he that shall blaspheme against the Holy Ghost hath never forgiveness*, but is in danger of eternal damnation." **(Mark 3:28–29)**

"Wherefore I say unto you, *All manner of sin and blasphemy shall be forgiven unto men: but the blasphemy against the Holy Ghost shall not be forgiven unto men. And whosoever speaketh a word against the Son of man*, it shall be forgiven him: *but whosoever speaketh against the Holy Ghost, it shall not be forgiven him*, neither in this world, neither in the world to come." **(Matthew 12:31–32**; see also **Luke 12:10)**

See chapter 19: **"Forgiveness"**
See chapter 45: **"Salvation for All Mankind"**
See chapter 40: **"Repentance"**
See chapter 7: **"Baptism for the Dead"**

CHAPTER 25

HOLY GHOST

"If ye love me, keep my commandments. And I will pray the Father, and he shall give you another Comforter, that he may abide with you for ever; Even the Spirit of truth; whom the world cannot receive, because it seeth him not, neither knoweth him: but ye know him; for he dwelleth with you, and shall be in you. I will not leave you comfortless: I will come to you." **(John 14:15–18)**

Some Christian churches teach that the Holy Ghost is not a personage of the godhead, but only the influence, power, and love of God the Father.

HOLY GHOST

Scriptures used by some Christian faiths to substantiate their belief and teaching about the Holy Ghost:

"Now when they heard this, they were pricked in their heart, and said unto Peter and to the rest of the apostles, Men and brethren, what shall we do? Repent, and be baptized every one of you in the name of Jesus Christ, for the remission of sins, and you shall receive the gift of the Holy Ghost." (**Acts 2:37–38**)

> *Note: Some churches use this scripture to teach that the Holy Ghost is bestowed automatically when baptized and that there is no need for a separate "confirmation" or "laying on of hands" procedure.*

For those churches that do practice a separate "confirmation ceremony" (such as the Catholic Church) it is usually performed when a person reaches the age of "discretion or accountability," usually between seven to fifteen years of age.

In the **Catholic Church** the sacrament of Confirmation builds on the sacraments of Baptism, Penance, and Holy Communion, completing the process of initiation into the Catholic community. Confirmation, a sacrament of initiation, establishes young adults as full-fledged members of the faith.

This sacrament is called *Confirmation* because the faith given in Baptism is now confirmed and made strong. During Baptism, the child's parents and godparents make promises to renounce Satan and believe in God and the Church on the child's behalf. At Confirmation, you renew those same promises, this time speaking for yourself.

The **Catholic ritual of Confirmation**: When you're confirmed, you get to choose a Confirmation name to add to your first and middle names, your new name must be a Christian name such as one of the canonized saints or a hero from the Bible. The Confirmation ceremony may take place at Mass or outside of Mass and is performed usually by a bishop. Here's what happens at the actual ritual of Confirmation: (1) You stand or kneel before the bishop; (2) Your sponsor lays one hand on your shoulder and speaks your confirmation name; (3) The bishop anoints you by using oil of Chrism (a consecrated oil) to make the Sign of the Cross on your forehead while saying your Confirmation name and "Be sealed with the gift of the Holy Spirit"; (4) You respond, "Amen"; (5) The bishop then says, "Peace be with you"; (6) You respond, "And with your spirit" or "And also with you."

Now you are an adult in the eyes of the Catholic Church. Being confirmed in the church means accepting responsibility for your faith and destiny, and means that you must do what's right on your own.[1]

"And Jesus, when he was baptized, went up straightway out of the water: and, lo, the heavens were opened unto him, and he saw *the Spirit of God* descending like a dove, and lighting upon him: And lo a voice from heaven, saying, *This is my beloved Son*, in whom I am well pleased." (**Matthew 3:16–17**)

"Now when the apostles which were at Jerusalem heard that Samaria had received the word of God, they sent unto them Peter and John: Who, when they were come down, prayed for them, that they might receive the Holy Ghost: (For as yet he was fallen upon none of them: only they were baptized in the name of the Lord Jesus.) *Then laid they their hands on them, and they received the Holy Ghost.*" (**Acts 8:14–17**)

"He said unto them, *Have ye received the Holy Ghost since ye believed?* And they said unto him, We have not so much as heard whether there be any Holy Ghost. And he said unto them, Unto what then were ye baptized? And they said, Unto John's baptism. Then said Paul, John verily baptized with the baptism of repentance, saying unto the people, that they should believe on him which should come after him, that is, on Christ Jesus. *When they heard this, they were baptized in the name of the Lord Jesus.* And *when Paul had laid his hands upon them, the Holy Ghost came on them*; and they spake with tongues, and prophesied." (**Acts 19:2–6**)

> Note: In Acts 19:2–6, these believers had not yet been baptized in the name of Jesus Christ by someone with the authority and priesthood to do so. Paul therefore rebaptized them "in the name of Jesus Christ" and then "laid his hands upon them" and bestowed the Gift of the Holy Ghost onto them.

"Therefore leaving the principles of the doctrine of Christ, let us go on unto perfection; not laying again the foundation of repentance from dead works, and of faith toward God, Of *the doctrine of baptisms, and of laying on of hands*, and of resurrection of the dead, and of eternal judgment. And this will we do, if God permit. For it is impossible for those who were once enlightened, and have tasted of the heavenly gift, and were made partakers of the Holy Ghost, And have tasted the good word of God, and the powers of the world to come, If they shall fall away, to renew them again unto repentance; seeing they crucify to themselves the Son of God afresh, and put him to an open shame." (**Hebrews 6:1–6**)

> Note: Hebrews 6:1-6, is discussing the Gift of the Holy Ghost being given "by the laying on of hands"; and also discusses the unforgivable sin against the Holy Ghost as taught in Matthew 12:31-32 and Luke 12:10.

"Wherefore I say unto you, All manner of sin and blasphemy shall be forgiven unto men: but *the blasphemy against the Holy Ghost shall not be forgiven unto men.* And *whosoever speaketh a word against the Son of man*, it shall be forgiven him: *but whosoever speaketh against the Holy Ghost, it shall not be forgiven him*, neither in this world, neither in the world to come." (**Matthew 12:31–32**; see also **Luke 12:10**)

"If ye love me, keep my commandments. And I will pray the Father, and he shall give you *another Comforter*, that he may abide with you for ever; *Even the Spirit of truth*; whom the world cannot receive, because it seeth him not, neither knoweth him: but ye know him; for he dwelleth with you, and shall be in you. I will not leave you comfortless: I will come to you." (**John 14:15–18**)

"But the Comforter, *which is the Holy Ghost*, whom the Father will send in my name, he shall teach you all things, and bring all things to your remembrance, whatsoever I have said unto you." (**John 14:26**)

CHAPTER 26

HOW CAN I
KNOW THE TRUTH?
TESTIMONY

"Whereof the Holy Ghost also is a witness to us: for after that he had said before, This is the covenant that I will make with them after those days, saith the Lord, I will put my laws into their hearts, and in their minds will I write them." **(Hebrews 10:15–16)**

Gaining a testimony of the gospel, of Jesus Christ, God the Father, and the Church, doesn't happen just for the asking. Gaining and growing a testimony takes sincere effort, it takes living the gospel principles, prayer and more prayer, and, most important, a sincere heart that wants to know the truth.

How Can I Know the Truth?
Testimony

Scriptures used by some questioning whether or not you can know the truth of things:

"The heart is deceitful above all things, and desperately wicked: who can know it?" **(Jeremiah 17:9)**

Now the Rest of the Story . . . (scriptures that further explain or clarify the topic)

"Whereof *the Holy Ghost also is a witness to us*: for after that he had said before, *This is the covenant that I will make with them* after those days, saith the Lord, *I will put my laws into their hearts, and in their minds* will I write them." **(Hebrews 10:15–16)**

"Now *the God of hope fill you with all joy and peace in believing*, that ye may abound in hope, *through the power of the Holy Ghost*." **(Romans 15:13)**

"And I will pray the Father, and he shall give you another *Comforter*, that he may abide with you for ever." **(John 14:16)**

"But the Comforter, which is *the Holy Ghost*, whom the Father will send in my name, *he shall teach you all things*, and bring all things to your remembrance, whatsoever I have said unto you." **(John 14:26)**

"But when the Comforter is come, whom I will send unto you from the Father, even the Spirit of truth, which proceedeth from the Father, *he shall testify of me*." **(John 15:26)**

"Howbeit when he, *the Spirit of truth*, is come, he *will guide you into all truth*: for he shall not speak of himself; but whatsoever he shall hear, that shall he speak: and he will shew you things to come." **(John 16:13)**

"*Ask*, and it shall be given you; *seek*, and ye shall find; *knock*, and it shall be opened unto you: For every one that asketh receiveth; and he that seeketh findeth; and to him that knocketh it shall be opened." **(Matthew 7:7–8)**

"Jesus said unto him, If thou canst believe, *all things are possible to him that believeth*." **(Mark 9:23)**

"Now *faith is* the substance of things hoped for, the evidence of things not seen." **(Hebrews 11:1)**

"(*For we walk by faith, not by sight*.)" **(2 Corinthians 5:7)**

"For if the word spoken by angels was steadfast, and every transgression and disobedience received a just recompence of reward; How shall we escape, if we neglect so great salvation; which at the first began to be spoken by the Lord, and was confirmed unto us by them that heard him; *God also bearing them witness, both with signs and wonders, and with divers miracles, and gifts of the Holy Ghost, according to his own will?"* **(Hebrews 2:2–4)**

"If any of you lack wisdom, let him ask of God, that giveth to all men liberally, and upbraideth not; and it shall be given him. *But let him ask in faith, nothing wavering.* For he that wavereth is like a wave of the sea driven with the wind and tossed." **(James 1:5–6)**

"Prove all things; hold fast that which is good." **(1 Thessalonians 5:21)**

"Behold, I stand at the door, and knock: if any man hear my voice, and open the door, I will come in to him, and will sup with him, and he with me." **(Revelation 3:20)**

Food for Thought

The Apostles all died horrible deaths! Regarding the Apostles, it is not so important as to how they died. What is important, is the fact that they were all willing to die for their faith. If Jesus had not been resurrected, the Apostles and many of the disciples would have known it. People will not die for something they know to be a lie. *The fact that all of the apostles and many of the disciples, were willing to die horrible deaths, refusing to renounce their faith in Christ, is tremendous evidence that they had truly witnessed the resurrection of Jesus Christ.*

After all of this . . . How do I know it is true?
It's simple. Through the Holy Ghost,

God told me it's true.

See chapter 4: "**Apostles**" (Death of the Apostles)
See chapter 25: "**Holy Ghost**"
See chapter 43: "**Revelation**"

CHAPTER 27

JEHOVAH IS JESUS CHRIST

"And I appeared unto Abraham, unto Isaac, and unto Jacob, by the name of God Almighty, but by my name JEHOVAH was I not known to them." **(Exodus 6:3)**

Most post Protestant Reformation Christian churches teach that God the Father is Jehovah. The Jehovah's Witnesses have even changed the wording in their New World Translation of the Bible to reflect such. This chapter will help you to show that Jesus Christ is Jehovah.

JEHOVAH IS JESUS CHRIST
(NOT GOD THE FATHER)

Scriptures used by some Christian faiths to substantiate their belief and teaching Jehovah is God the Father:

"And I appeared unto Abraham, unto Isaac, and unto Jacob, by the name of God Almighty, but by my name JEHOVAH was I not known to them." **(Exodus 6:3)**

"That men may know that thou, whose name alone is JEHOVAH, art the most high over all the earth." **(Psalm 83:18)**

"Behold, God is my salvation; I will trust, and not be afraid: for the Lord JEHOVAH is my strength and my song; he also is become my salvation." **(Isaiah 12:2)**

"Trust ye in the Lord for ever: for in the Lord JEHOVAH is everlasting strength." **(Isaiah 26:4)**

"And Abraham called the name of that place Jehovah-jireh: as it is said to this day, In the mount of the Lord it shall be seen." **(Genesis 22:14)**

"And Moses built an altar, and called the name of it Jehovah-nissi." **(Exodus 17:15)**

"Then Gideon built an altar there unto the Lord, and called it Jehovah-shalom: unto this day it is yet in Ophrah of the Abi-ezrites." **(Judges 6:24)**

NOW THE REST OF THE STORY . . . (scriptures that further explain or clarify the topic)

"And I appeared unto Abraham, unto Isaac, and unto Jacob, by the name of God Almighty, but by my name *JEHOVAH* was I not known to them." **(Exodus 6:3)**

"And *God said unto Moses*, I Am That I Am: and he said, Thus shalt thou say unto the children of Israel, *I Am* hath sent me unto you." **(Exodus 3:14)**

"Jesus answered, If I honour myself, my honour is nothing: it is my Father that honoureth me; of whom ye say, that he is your God: . . . Your father Abraham rejoiced to see my day: and he saw it, and was glad. Then said the Jews unto him, Thou art not yet fifty years old, and hast thou seen Abraham? *Jesus said unto them,* Verily, verily, I say unto you, *Before Abraham was, I am.*" **(John 8:54–58**; verse 55 not shown for brevity)

> *Note: God in Exodus 3:14, said that he was "I AM." Jesus Christ said in John 8:54–58 that he is "I AM." This confirms that the God of the Old Testament is Jesus Christ and that Jesus Christ is Jehovah.*

CONCLUSION
Jesus Christ, who is "I Am," is "Jehovah."

"That they may see, and know, and consider, and understand together, that the hand of the Lord hath done this, and *the Holy One of Israel hath created it.*" **(Isaiah 41:20)**

"Fear not, thou worm Jacob, and ye men of Israel; I will help thee, saith the Lord, and *thy redeemer, the Holy One of Israel.*" **(Isaiah 41:14)**

"But now thus *saith the Lord that created thee*, O Jacob, and he that formed thee, O Israel, Fear not: for I have redeemed thee, I have called thee by thy name; thou art mine. . . . For *I am the Lord thy God, the Holy One of Israel, thy Savior*: I gave Egypt for thy ransom, Ethiopia and Seba for thee." **(Isaiah 43:1–3**; verse 2 not shown for brevity)

> **Note:** *The Holy One of Israel, thy Redeemer, thy Savior, thy God, is Jesus Christ. See also, Isaiah 30:15, 48:17, 60:14, Ezekiel 39:7, Jeremiah 50:29, Psalms 71:22, 89:18. Now see Isaiah 43:11 below:*

"I, even I, am the Lord; and *beside me there is no savior.*" **(Isaiah 43:11)**

"Looking for that blessed hope, and the glorious appearing of *the great God* and *our Savior Jesus Christ.*" **(Titus 2:13**; see also **1 Timothy 1:1, 2 Peter 1:1, 2 Peter 1:11, 2 Peter 3:18, Philippians 3:20, Luke 2:11)**

"Be it known unto you all, and to all the people of Israel, that *by the name of Jesus Christ of Nazareth*, whom ye crucified, whom God raised from the dead, . . . Neither is there salvation in any other: *for there is none other name under heaven given among men, whereby we must be saved.*" **(Acts 4:10, 12**; verse 11 has been omitted for brevity)

CONCLUSION
Jesus Christ, "the Holy One of Israel," "the Creator," "the Redeemer," "the Savior," is "Jehovah."

"Therefore *I will judge you*, O house of Israel, every one according to his ways, *saith the Lord God*. Repent, and turn yourselves from all your transgressions; so iniquity shall not be your ruin." **(Ezekiel 18:30)**

"For *the Father judgeth no man, but hath committed all judgment unto the Son.*" **(John 5:22)**

"*In the beginning was the Word*, and the Word was with God, and the Word was God. The same was in the beginning with God. *All things were made by him*; and without him was not any thing made that was made." **(John 1:1–3)**

"*And the Word was made flesh, and dwelt among us*, (and we beheld his glory, the glory as of the only begotten of the Father,) full of grace and truth." **(John 1:14)**

CONCLUSION

Jesus Christ who "made all things," who "judgeth all," <u>is</u> "Jehovah."

"And he said unto them, The sabbath was made for man, and not man for the sabbath: Therefore *the Son of man is Lord also of the sabbath*." **(Mark 2:27–28)**

"And he said unto them, That the *Son of man* is Lord also of the sabbath." **(Luke 6:5)**

"And hath given him authority to execute judgment also, *because he is the Son of man*." **(John 5:27**; see also **John 5:22–27)**

"Also I say unto you, Whosoever shall confess me before men, him shall the Son of man also confess before the angels of God." **(Luke 12:8)**

"When Jesus came into the coasts of Cæsarea Philippi, he asked his disciples, saying, Whom do men say that *I the Son of man am?*" **(Matthew 16:13)**

"Saying, The *Son of man* must be delivered into the hands of sinful men, *and be crucified*, and the third day rise again." **(Luke 24:7)**

"Wherefore I say unto you, All manner of sin and blasphemy shall be forgiven unto men: but the blasphemy against the Holy Ghost shall not be forgiven unto men. And *whosoever speaketh a word against the Son of man, it shall be forgiven him*: but whosoever speaketh against the Holy Ghost, it shall not be forgiven him, neither in this world, neither in the world to come." **(Matthew 12:31–32)**

CONCLUSION

Jesus Christ, the "Son of Man," <u>is</u> Jehovah.

"*Thus saith God the Lord*, he that created the heavens, and stretched them out; he that spread forth the earth, and that which cometh out of it; he that giveth breath unto the people upon it, and spirit to them that walk therein: . . . *I am the Lord: that is my name*: and my glory will I not give to another, neither my praise to graven images." **(Isaiah 42:5–8**; verses 6–7 not shown for brevity)

> *Note: See chapter 15: "Creation — Who Created the Heavens and the Earth?"*

"And being found in fashion as a man, he humbled himself, and became obedient unto death, even the death of the cross. Wherefore God also hath highly exalted him, and given him a name which is above every name: That at the name of Jesus every knee should bow, of things in heaven, and things in earth, and things under the earth; And that every tongue should confess that *Jesus Christ is Lord*, to the glory of God the Father." (**Philippians 2:8–11**)

"My doctrine shall drop as the rain, my speech shall distil as the dew, as the small rain upon the tender herb, and as the showers upon the grass: Because I will publish the name of the Lord: ascribe ye greatness unto our God. *He is the Rock*, his work is perfect: for all his ways are judgment: a God of truth and without iniquity, just and right is he." (**Deuteronomy 32:2–4**)

"Moreover, brethren, I would not that ye should be ignorant, how that all our fathers were under the cloud, and all passed through the sea; And were all baptized unto Moses in the cloud and in the sea; And did all eat the same spiritual meat; And did all drink the same spiritual drink: for they drank of that spiritual Rock that followed them: *and that Rock was Christ.*" (**1 Corinthians 10:1–4**)

"And I will feed them that oppress thee with their own flesh; and they shall be drunken with their own blood, as with sweet wine: and all flesh shall know that *I the Lord am thy Saviour and thy Redeemer, the mighty One of Jacob.*" (**Isaiah 49:26**)

CONCLUSION

"The LORD" of the Old Testament, the "I Am," "The Holy One of Israel," "Our Savior," "Our Redeemer," the "Creator" who "made all things," who "Judgeth All," is Jesus Christ, who is "Jehovah"!

See chapter 28: "**Jesus Christ — Who Is He?**"
See chapter 15: "**Creation — Who Created the Heavens and the Earth?**"

CHAPTER 28

JESUS CHRIST — WHO IS HE?

"While he yet spake, behold, a bright cloud overshadowed them: and behold a voice out of the cloud, which said, This is my beloved Son, in whom I am well pleased; hear ye him." **(Matthew 17:1–5)**

Jesus Christ — Who Is He?

Scriptures used by some Christian faiths to substantiate their belief and teaching as to who Jesus Christ is:

See the chapter "**Godhead — Trinity — Three Separate Beings.**"

Now the Rest of the Story . . . (scriptures that further explain or clarify the topic)

"And Jesus, when he was baptized, went up straightway out of the water: and, lo, the heavens were opened unto him, and he saw the Spirit of God descending like a dove, and lighting upon him: *And lo a voice from heaven, saying, This is my beloved Son, in whom I am well pleased.*" (**Matthew 3:16–17**)

"When Jesus came into the coasts of Cæsarea Philippi, he asked his disciples, saying, Whom do men say that I the Son of man am? . . . He saith unto them, But whom say ye that I am? And Simon Peter answered and said, *Thou art the Christ, the Son of the living God.* And Jesus answered and said unto him, Blessed art thou, Simon Bar-jona: for flesh and blood hath not revealed it unto thee, but my Father which is in heaven." (**Matthew 16:13, 15–17**; read verses 13–19)

"While he yet spake, behold, a bright cloud overshadowed them: and behold a voice out of the cloud, which said, *This is my beloved Son*, in whom I am well pleased; hear ye him." (**Matthew 17:1–5**; verses 1–4 omitted for brevity)

"*These words spake Jesus*, and lifted up his eyes to heaven, and said, *Father*, the hour is come; *glorify thy Son*, that thy Son also may glorify thee: As thou hast given him power over all flesh, that he should give eternal life to as many as thou hast given him. And this is life eternal, that they might know thee the only true God, and *Jesus Christ*, whom thou hast sent. I have glorified thee on the earth: I have finished the work which thou gavest me to do. And now, O *Father, glorify thou me with thine own self with the glory which I had with thee before the world was.*" (**John 17:1–5**)

"Watch therefore: for ye know not what hour your Lord doth come. . . . Therefore be ye also ready: for in such an hour as ye think not *the Son of man* cometh." (**Matthew 24:42–44**)

"Wherefore I say unto you, All manner of sin and blasphemy shall be forgiven unto men: but the blasphemy against the Holy Ghost shall not be forgiven unto men. And whosoever speaketh a word against *the Son of man*, it shall be forgiven him: but whosoever speaketh against the Holy Ghost, it shall not be forgiven him, neither in this world, neither in the world to come." (**Matthew 12:31–32**; see also **Luke 12:10**)

"If I had not done among them the works which none other man did, they had not had sin: but now have they both seen and hated *both me and my Father.*" (**John 15:24**)

> *Note: The words "both" and the phrase "me and my Father," clearly indicates two separate beings or persons and would not have been spoken this way if this clarity was not needed and intended.*

"Ye have heard how I said unto you, I go away, and come again unto you. If ye loved me, ye would rejoice, because I said, I go unto the Father: for *my Father* is greater than I." (**John 14:28**)

"Jesus saith unto her, Touch me not; for I am not yet ascended to my Father: but go to my brethren, and say unto them, I ascend unto *my Father*, and your Father; and to *my God*, and your God." (**John 20:17**)

"God, who at sundry times and in divers manners spake in time past unto the fathers by the prophets, Hath in these last days spoken unto us by *his Son*, whom he hath appointed heir of all things, by whom also he made the worlds." (**Hebrews 1:2**)

"*For the Father judgeth no man, but hath committed all judgment unto the Son*: That all men should honour the Son, even as they honour the Father. He that honoureth not the Son honoureth not the Father which hath sent him. Verily, verily, I say unto you, *He that heareth my word*, and believeth on him that sent me, hath everlasting life, and shall not come into condemnation; but is passed from death unto life. Verily, verily, I say unto you, The hour is coming, and now is, when *the dead shall hear the voice of the Son of God*: and they that hear shall live. For as the Father hath life in himself; so hath he given to the Son to have life in himself; And hath given him authority to execute judgment also, *because he is the Son of man.*" (**John 5:22–27**)

> *Note: Some Christian faiths teach that Jesus is the "Son of Man" because his mother Mary is of the human race, also known as "man"; making him a son of man. So then the Father gave Jesus "authority to execute judgment," because he is the son of man, a "human," over all mankind because he Jesus, is of the human race. Are we not all as humans "the sons of man"? Do we then qualify for this authority of judgment? Could this not mean that Jesus is the "Son of Man" because God the Father is known as "Man of Holiness," making Jesus the son of "Man" or God the Father? The title "the Son of man" is just another way of saying "the Son of God the Father."*

"Even as the *Son of man* came not to be ministered unto, but to minister, and to give his life a ransom for many." (**Matthew 20:28**)

"And the high priest stood up in the midst, and asked Jesus, saying, . . . *Art thou the Christ, the Son of the Blessed?* And Jesus said, *I am*: and ye shall see the Son of man sitting on the right hand of power, and coming in the clouds of heaven." (**Mark 14:60, 62**; verse 61 omitted for brevity)

"Seeing then that we have a great high priest, that is passed into the heavens, *Jesus the Son of God*, let us hold fast our profession." (**Hebrews 4:14**)

"Then the Jews took up stones again to stone him. *Jesus answered them*, Many good works have I shewed you from my Father; for which of those works do ye stone me? The Jews answered him, saying, For a good work we stone thee not; but for blasphemy; and because that thou, being a man, makest thyself God. Jesus answered them, *Is it not written in your law, I said, Ye are gods?* If he called them gods, unto whom the word of God came, and the scripture cannot be broken; Say ye of him, whom the Father hath sanctified, and sent into the world, Thou blasphemest; because *I said, I am the Son of God?*" **(John 10:31–36)**

"And in the synagogue there was a man, which had a spirit of an unclean devil, and cried out with a loud voice, Saying, Let us alone; what have we to do with thee, thou Jesus of Nazareth? art thou come to destroy us? I know thee who thou art; *the Holy One of God*." **(Luke 4:33–34)**

"And Jesus being full of the Holy Ghost returned from Jordan, and was led by the Spirit into the wilderness, Being forty days tempted of the devil. And in those days he did eat nothing: and when they were ended, he afterward hungered. And the devil said unto him, *If thou be the Son of God*, command this stone that it be made bread. And Jesus answered him, saying, It is written, That man shall not live by bread alone, but by every word of God. And the devil, taking him up into an high mountain, shewed unto him all the kingdoms of the world in a moment of time. And the devil said unto him, All this power will I give thee, and the glory of them: for that is delivered unto me; and to whomsoever I will I give it. If thou therefore wilt worship me, all shall be thine. And Jesus answered and said unto him, Get thee behind me, Satan: for it is written, Thou shalt worship the Lord thy God, and him only shalt thou serve. And he brought him to Jerusalem, and set him on a pinnacle of the temple, and said unto him, If thou be the Son of God, cast thyself down from hence: For it is written, *He shall give his angels charge over thee, to keep thee*: And in their hands they shall bear thee up, lest at any time thou dash thy foot against a stone. *And Jesus answering said* unto him, It is said, *Thou shalt not tempt the Lord thy God*." **(Luke 4:1–12)**

CONCLUSION

Jesus Christ is "the Son of God."

"The next day John seeth Jesus coming unto him, and saith, Behold the Lamb of God, *which taketh away the sin of the world*." **(John 1:29)**

"And she shall bring forth a son, and thou shalt call his name JESUS: for *he shall save his people from their sins*." **(Matthew 1:21)**

"*Who gave himself a ransom for all*, to be testified in due time." **(1 Timothy 2:6)**

"For I delivered unto you first of all that which I also received, how that *Christ died for our sins* according to the scriptures." **(1 Corinthians 15:3)**

"And they sung a new song, saying, Thou art worthy to take the book, and to open the seals thereof: for thou wast slain, and *hast redeemed us to God by thy blood* out of every kindred, and tongue, and people, and nation." **(Revelation 5:9)**

"Jesus saith unto him, I am the way, the truth, and the life: *no man cometh unto the Father, but by me.*" **(John 14:6)**

"Jesus said unto her, *I am the resurrection, and the life*: he that believeth in me, though he were dead, yet shall he live." **(John 11:25)**

"And not only so, but we also joy in God through our Lord Jesus Christ, by whom we have now *received the atonement.*" **(Romans 5:11)**

"And we have seen and do testify that *the Father sent the Son to be the Saviour of the world.*" **(1 John 4:14)**

"Be it known unto you all, and to all the people of Israel, that *by the name of Jesus Christ* of Nazareth, whom ye crucified, whom God raised from the dead, even by him doth this man stand here before you whole. This is the stone which was set at nought of you builders, which is become the head of the corner. Neither is there salvation in any other: *for there is none other name under heaven given among men, whereby we must be saved.*" **(Acts 4:10–12)**

Conclusion

Jesus Christ is our Redeemer and our Savior.

"In the beginning was *the Word*, and the Word was *with God*, and the *Word was God.* The same was in the beginning with God. All things were made by him; and without him was not any thing made that was made." **(John 1:1–3)**

"And the Word was made flesh, and dwelt among us, (and we beheld his glory, the glory as of the only begotten of the Father,) full of grace and truth." **(John 1:14)**

> *Note: The important word and phrase here in John 1:1–3 is "with God." This scripture is saying that the "Word" was "with" God; NOT that the Word is God the Father. Those who misunderstand the Trinity try to use this scripture to prove that God the Father and the Word (Jesus Christ) are one and the same personage.*

> *Note: In the New World Translation of the Bible, John 1:1–3 reads, "In the beginning was the Word, and the Word was with God, and the Word was a god. This one was in the beginning with God. All things came into existence through him, and apart from him not even one thing came into existence."*

> *Note: Per John 1:1–3, Jesus Christ (the Word) created everything. Would he not then have to be a "god" to do this? How could he have "created all things" without having the knowledge, ability, and power to do so?*

> *Note: John 1:14 confirms that the "Word" is Jesus Christ.*

"Looking for that blessed hope, and the glorious appearing of *the great God* and *our Savior Jesus Christ.*" (**Titus 2:13**)

> *Note: The defining word here is "and," indicating two separate events (hope and appearing) and beings (God and Jesus).*

"*But unto the Son he saith,* Thy throne, *O God,* is for ever and ever." (**Hebrews 1:8**)

Conclusion

Jesus Christ is a god.

See chapter 15: "**Creation — Who Created the Heavens and the Earth?**"
See chapter 22: "**Godhead — Trinity — Three Separate Beings**"
See chapter 27: "**Jehovah Is Jesus Christ**"

CHAPTER 29

JUDGMENT

"And I saw the dead, small and great, stand before God; and the books were opened: and another book was opened, which is the book of life: and the dead were judged out of those things which were written in the books, according to their works. And the sea gave up the dead which were in it; and death and hell delivered up the dead which were in them: and they were judged every man according to their works." **(Revelation 20:12–15)**

Is just believing in God and Jesus Christ, going to church on Sundays, keeping the Ten Commandments, and basically being a good person enough? Will we be judged for what we don't do, for what we should have done and didn't do? Who will judge us? Let's see what the Bible says . . .

JUDGMENT

Scriptures used by some Christian faiths to substantiate their belief and teaching that "Belief and Faith" in Jesus Christ and "The Grace of God" is all that is required for Salvation:

"That whosoever believeth in him should not perish, but have eternal life." **(John 3:15)**

"He that believeth and is baptized shall be saved; but he that believeth not shall be damned." **(Mark 16:16)**

"For whosoever shall call upon the name of the Lord shall be saved." **(Romans 10:13)**

"And from Jesus Christ, who is the faithful witness, and the first begotten of the dead, and the prince of the kings of the earth. Unto him that loved us, and washed us from our sins in his own blood." **(Revelation 1:5)**

"In whom we have redemption through his blood, the forgiveness of sins, according to the riches of his grace." **(Ephesians 1:7**; see also **Colossians 1:14)**

NOW THE REST OF THE STORY . . . (scriptures that further explain or clarify the topic)

"For we must all appear before the judgment seat of Christ; *that every one may receive the things done in his body*, according to that he hath done, *whether it be good or bad*." **(2 Corinthians 5:10)**

"*Our God* shall come, and shall not keep silence: a fire shall devour before him, and it shall be very tempestuous round about him. He shall call to the heavens from above, and to the earth, *that he may judge his people*. Gather my saints together unto me; those that have made a covenant with me by sacrifice. And the heavens shall declare his righteousness: *for God is judge himself*. Selah." **(Psalms 50:3–6)**

"For *the Father judgeth no man, but hath committed all judgment unto the Son*." **(John 5:22)**

"Then answered Peter and said unto him, Behold, we have forsaken all, and followed thee; what shall we have therefore? And Jesus said unto them, Verily I say unto you, *That ye which have followed me*, in the regeneration when the Son of man shall sit in the throne of his glory, ye also shall sit upon twelve thrones, *judging the twelve tribes of Israel*." **(Matthew 19:27–28**; see also **Luke 22:30)**

"Jesus said unto her, I am the resurrection, and the life: *he that believeth in me, though he were dead, yet shall he live*: And whosoever liveth and believeth in me shall never die. Believest thou this?" **(John 11:25–26)**

"Behold, *I will send you Elijah the prophet before the coming of the great and dreadful day of the Lord*: And he shall turn the heart of the fathers to the children, and the heart of the children to their fathers, *lest I come and smite the earth with a curse.*" **(Malachi 4:4–6)**

"For the Son of man shall come in the glory of his Father with his angels; and *then he shall reward every man according to his works.*" **(Matthew 16:27)**

"And I saw the dead, small and great, stand before God; and the books were opened: and another book was opened, which is the book of life: and the dead were judged out of those things which were written in the books, *according to their works.* And the sea gave up the dead which were in it; and death and hell delivered up the dead which were in them: and they were judged every man *according to their works.*" **(Revelation 20:12–15)**

"Wherefore by their fruits ye shall know them. *Not everyone that saith unto me, Lord, Lord, shall enter into the kingdom of heaven*; but he that doeth the will of my Father which is in heaven. Many will say to me in that day, Lord, Lord, have we not prophesied in thy name? and in thy name have cast out devils? and in thy name done many wonderful works? And then will I profess unto them, I never knew you: depart from me, ye that work iniquity." **(Matthew 7:20–23)**

"For I bear them record that they have a zeal of God, *but not according to knowledge.* For they being *ignorant of God's righteousness,* and going about *to establish their own righteousness,* have not submitted themselves unto the righteousness of God. For Christ is the end of the law for righteousness to every one that believeth." **(Romans 10:2–4)**

"*For if God spared not the angels that sinned, but cast them down to hell,* and delivered them into chains of darkness, to be reserved unto judgment; *And spared not the old world, but saved Noah* the eighth person, a preacher of righteousness, bringing in the flood upon the world of the ungodly; *And turning the cities of Sodom and Gomorrha into ashes condemned them* with an overthrow, making them an ensample unto those that after should live ungodly." **(2 Peter 2:4–6)**

"*And the angels which kept not their first estate,* but left their own habitation, he hath reserved in everlasting chains under darkness unto the judgment of the great day." **(Jude 1:6)**

"*For it had been better for them not to have known the way of righteousness,* than, after they have known it, to turn from the holy commandment delivered unto them." **(2 Peter 2:21)**

"For *he shall have judgment without mercy,* that hath shewed no mercy; and mercy rejoiceth against judgment." **(James 2:13)**

"But I say unto you, That every idle word that men shall speak, *they shall give account thereof in the day of judgment.*" **(Matthew 12:36)**

"Ye have heard that it was said by them of old time, Thou shalt not kill; and *whosoever shall kill [murder] shall be in danger of the judgment.*" **(Matthew 5:21)**

"Of the doctrine of baptisms, and of laying on of hands, and of resurrection of the dead, *and of eternal judgment.*" **(Hebrews 6:2)**

"*For God shall bring every work into judgment,* with every secret thing, *whether it be good, or whether it be evil.*" **(Ecclesiastes 12:14)**

"But I say unto you, That *whosoever is angry with his brother without a cause shall be in danger of the judgment*: and whosoever shall say to his brother, Raca, shall be in danger of the council: but whosoever shall say, Thou fool, shall be in danger of hell fire." **(Matthew 5:22)**

"Judge not, that ye be not judged. *For with what judgment ye judge, ye shall be judged*: and with what measure ye mete, it shall be measured to you again." **(Matthew 7:1–2**; see also **Luke 6:37)**

"A false witness shall not be unpunished, and *he that speaketh lies shall perish.*" **(Proverbs 19:9)**

"But after thy hardness and impenitent heart treasurest up unto thyself wrath against the day of wrath and revelation of the righteous judgment of God; *Who will render to every man according to his deeds.*" **(Romans 2:5–6)**

See chapter 1: "**Accountability**"
See chapter 19: "**Forgiveness**"
See chapter 24: "**Heaven — Hell — Degrees of Glory**"
See chapter 40: "**Repentance**"

CHAPTER 30

MAN HAS BOTH A PHYSICAL & SPIRITUAL BODY

"For as the body without the spirit is dead, so faith without works is dead also."
(**James 2:26**)

As a whole, Modern-Day Christianity does not believe that mankind has a spirit body, a mirror image of his or her physical self, composed entirely of spirit, the offspring of a Heavenly Father.

Man Has Both a Physical & Spiritual Body

Scriptures used by some Christian faiths to substantiate their belief and teaching that Mankind does not have a spiritual body:

The Bible scriptures used by these faiths to substantiate their belief are far-reaching at best, and requires a vast amount of stretched commentary to explain. Therefore, they will not be listed or discussed in this chapter. What the vast majority of modern-day Christians do not believe in, is the pre-existence as taught by the LDS Church and the Bible. Therefore, they do not believe in a pre-existent spiritual body being a part of the physical body of man.

Now the Rest of the Story . . . (scriptures that further explain or clarify the topic)

"The Spirit itself beareth witness with our spirit, that *we are the children of God.*" **(Romans 8:16)**

"Furthermore we have had fathers of our flesh which corrected us, and we gave them reverence: shall we not much rather be in subjection unto the *Father of spirits,* and live?" **(Hebrews 12:9)**

"For in him we live, and move, and have our being; as certain also of your own poets have said, For *we are also his offspring.* Forasmuch then as we are *the offspring of God,* we ought not to think that the Godhead is like unto gold, or silver, or stone, graven by art and man's device." **(Acts 17:28–29)**

"For ye are bought with a price: therefore glorify God *in your body,* and *in your spirit,* which are God's." **(1 Corinthians 6:20)**

> *Note: This scripture reads "in your body and in your spirit"; not in "God's body or in God's spirit," or in anyone else's body or spirit. It teaches us that we have our own body and our own spirit.*

"For what man knoweth the things of a man, save *the spirit of man which is in him?* even so the things of God knoweth no man, but the Spirit of God." **(1 Corinthians 2:11)**

"To the general assembly and church of the firstborn, which are written in heaven, and to God the Judge of all, and to the *spirits of just men* made perfect." **(Hebrews 12:23)**

"Who knoweth the *spirit of man* that goeth upward, and the spirit of the beast that goeth downward to the earth?" **(Ecclesiastes 3:21)**

"The *spirit of a man* will sustain his infirmity; but a wounded spirit who can bear?" **(Proverbs 18:14)**

> Note: How can a spirit be wounded unless it has substance, form, shape, and intellect?

"The *spirit of man* is the candle of the LORD, searching all the inward parts of the belly." **(Proverbs 20:27)**

"But *there is a spirit in man*: and the inspiration of the Almighty giveth them understanding." **(Job 32:8)**

> Note: The inspiration of the Almighty gives man's spirit understanding.

"And they fell upon their faces, and said, O God, *the God of the spirits of all flesh*, shall one man sin, and wilt thou be wroth with all the congregation?" **(Numbers 16:22)**

"Let the Lord, *the God of the spirits of all flesh*, set a man over the congregation." **(Numbers 27:16)**

"O Lord, by these things men live, and in all these things is *the life of my spirit*: so wilt thou recover me, and make me to live." **(Isaiah 38:16)**

DEATH IS BROUGHT ABOUT WHEN MAN'S SPIRIT BODY LEAVES HIS PHYSICAL BODY

"For as *the body without the spirit is dead*, so faith without works is dead also." **(James 2:26)**

"And they stoned Stephen, calling upon God, and saying, Lord Jesus, *receive my spirit*." **(Acts 7:59)**

"And when Jesus had cried with a loud voice, he said, Father, *into thy hands I commend my spirit*: and having said thus, *he gave up the ghost*." **(Luke 23:46)**

> Note: When Christ's spirit body left his physical body, the physical body died. The "resurrection" is when the spirit body and the physical body are reunited.

"For this cause was the gospel preached also to them that are dead, that they might be judged according to men in the flesh, but *live according to God in the spirit*." **(1 Peter 4:6)**

"By which also he went and preached unto the *spirits in prison*." **(1 Peter 3:19)**

"And all wept, and bewailed her: but he said, Weep not; she is not dead, but sleepeth. And they laughed him to scorn, knowing that she was dead. And he put them all out, and took her by the hand, and called, saying, Maid, arise. *And her spirit came again, and she arose straightway*: and he commanded to give her meat." **(Luke 8:52–55**; for the full story, read **Luke 8:41–56)**

"And he stretched himself upon the child three times, and cried unto the Lord, and said, O Lord my God, I pray thee, *let this child's soul come into him again.* And the Lord heard the voice of Elijah; *and the soul of the child came into him again, and he revived.*" **(1 Kings 17:21–22)**

"Then shall the dust return to the earth as it was: *and the spirit shall return unto God who gave it.*" **(Ecclesiastes 12:7)**

"And fear not them which kill the body, *but are not able to kill the soul*: but rather fear him which is able to *destroy both soul and body* in hell." **(Matthew 10:28)**

"For what shall it profit a man, if he shall gain the whole world, *and lose his own soul?*" **(Mark 8:36)**

"Who shall change our vile body, *that it may be fashioned like unto his glorious body*, according to the working whereby he is able even to subdue all things unto himself." **(Philippians 3:21)**

"It is sown a natural body; it is raised a spiritual body. *There is a natural body, and there is a spiritual body.*" **(1 Corinthians 15:44)**

See chapter 21: **"God — Who Is He?"**

CHAPTER 31

MAN-MADE CHURCHES

THE PHILOSOPHIES OF MEN
MINGLED WITH SCRIPTURE

"For I bear them record that they have a zeal of God, but not according to knowledge. For they being ignorant of God's righteousness, and going about to establish their own righteousness, have not submitted themselves unto the righteousness of God. For Christ is the end of the law for righteousness to every one that believeth." **(Romans 10:2–4)**

Now there are some very important questions that we all should ask: Where did these men, pastors, priests, reverends get the authority to start their church? Where did they receive the authority to teach their doctrine? Did Heavenly Father or His son Jesus Christ appear to them and personally instruct them to form a church and what to teach?

MAN-MADE CHURCHES

THE PHILOSOPHIES OF MEN
MINGLED WITH SCRIPTURE

Scriptures used by some Christian faiths to substantiate their belief and teaching that anyone can start a church and preach what he or she believes to be the truth:

There are no Bible scriptures that give this authority. Instead, protestant faiths rely on the concepts of "The Priesthood of All Believers"; see the chapters "Priesthood of God — Authority" and "Bible Supreme Authority — Sola Scriptura" for more information and scriptures.

NOW THE REST OF THE STORY . . . (scriptures that further explain or clarify the topic)

Old Testament priests were chosen by God, not self-appointed; the same for New Testament Apostles who were chosen by the Savior. The Savior ordained the Apostles to the priesthood and gave them the authority to choose and ordain Priests, Bishops, Elders, etc. The Apostles then gave this authority to those who they ordained to various priesthood offices. Those who were then and are now chosen, are ordained for a purpose: to serve God with their lives.

"*Woe be unto the pastors* that destroy and scatter the sheep of my pasture! saith the Lord." (**Jeremiah 23:1**)

"*I have not sent these prophets*, yet they ran: *I have not spoken to them*, yet they prophesied. But *if they had stood in my counsel*, and had *caused my people to hear my words*, then they should have turned them from their evil way, and from the evil of their doings." (**Jeremiah 23:21**)

"For every high priest taken from among men is ordained for men in things pertaining to God, that he may offer both gifts and sacrifices for sins: Who can have compassion on the ignorant, and on them that are out of the way; for that he himself also is compassed with infirmity. And by reason hereof he ought, as for the people, so also for himself, to offer for sins. *And no man taketh this honour unto himself, but he that is called of God, as was Aaron.* So also Christ glorified not himself to be made an high priest; but he that said unto him, Thou art my Son, to day have I begotten thee. As he saith also in another place, *Thou art a priest for ever after the order of Melchisedec.*" (**Hebrews 5:1–6**)

"*For God is not the author of confusion*, but of peace, as in all the churches of the saints." **(1 Corinthians 14:33)**

> Note: **With over 30,000 different Christian faiths, all interpreting the Bible differently and teaching what they believe about God and His son, is this not "confusion"?**

"Now I beseech you, brethren, by the name of our Lord Jesus Christ, *that ye all speak the same thing*, and *that there be no divisions among you*; but *that ye be perfectly joined together in the same mind and in the same judgment.*" **(1 Corinthians 1:10)**

"Now this I say, that every one of you saith, I am of Paul; and I of Apollos; and I of Cephas; and I of Christ. *Is Christ divided?* Was Paul crucified for you? Or were ye baptized in the name of Paul?" **(1 Corinthians 1:12–18)**

> Note: **Paul is reprimanding some of the early members of the church because they called themselves after certain disciples of Christ rather than after the name of Christ. They were forming their own churches. Teaching their own doctrines. (1 Corinthians 14:33; 1 Corinthians 1:10; 1 Corinthians 1:12–18)**

"There is *one body*, and *one Spirit*, even as ye are called in one hope of your calling; One Lord, one faith, one baptism." **(Ephesians 4:4–5)**

"Not every one that saith unto me, Lord, Lord, shall enter into the kingdom of heaven; but he that doeth the will of my Father which is in heaven. *Many will say to me in that day*, Lord, Lord, have we not prophesied in thy name? and in thy name have cast out devils? and in thy name done many wonderful works? *And then will I profess unto them, I never knew you: depart from me, ye that work iniquity.*" **(Matthew 7:21–23)**

"I marvel that ye are *so soon removed from him that called you into the grace of Christ unto another gospel*: Which is not another; but there be some that trouble you, *and would pervert the gospel of Christ.* But though we, or an angel from heaven, preach any other gospel unto you than that which we have preached unto you, let him be accursed." **(Galatians 1:6–9)**

"For I bear them record that they have a zeal of God, *but not according to knowledge.* For they *being ignorant of God's righteousness*, and *going about to establish their own righteousness*, have not submitted themselves unto the righteousness of God. For Christ is the end of the law for righteousness to every one that believeth." **(Romans 10:2–4)**

"Ye hypocrites, well did Esaias prophesy of you, saying, This people draweth nigh unto me with their mouth, and honoureth me with their lips; but their heart is far from me. But in vain they do worship me, *teaching for doctrines the commandments of men.*" **(Matthew 15:7–9**; see also **Mark 7:7–9)**

"From which some having swerved have turned aside unto vain jangling; *Desiring to be teachers of the law; understanding neither what they say, nor whereof they affirm.*" **(1 Timothy 1:6–7)**

"They profess that they know God; *but in works they deny him,* being abominable, and disobedient, and unto every good work reprobate." (**Titus 1:16**)

"But there were false prophets also among the people, even as *there shall be false teachers among you, who privily shall bring in damnable heresies,* even denying the Lord that bought them, and bring upon themselves swift destruction. And many shall follow their pernicious ways; by reason of whom the way of truth shall be evil spoken of. *And through covetousness shall they with feigned words make merchandise of you.*" (**2 Peter 2:1–3**)

"*We have also a more sure word of prophecy*; whereunto ye do well that ye take heed, as unto a light that shineth in a dark place, until the day dawn, and the day star arise in your hearts: Knowing this first, *that no prophecy of the scripture is of any private interpretation.* For the prophecy came not in old time by the will of man: but holy men of God spake as they were moved by the Holy Ghost." (**2 Peter 1:19–21**)

"*And he gave some, apostles; and some, prophets; and some, evangelists; and some, pastors and teachers*; For the perfecting of the saints, for the work of the ministry, for the edifying of the body of Christ: *Till we all come in the unity of the faith,* and of the knowledge of the Son of God, unto a perfect man, unto the measure of the stature of the fullness of Christ: *That we henceforth be no more children, tossed to and fro, and carried about with every wind of doctrine,* by the sleight of men, and cunning craftiness, whereby they lie in wait to deceive." (**Ephesians 4:11–14**)

"Verily, verily, I say unto you, *He that entereth not by the door into the sheepfold, but climbeth up some other way, the same is a thief and a robber.*" (**John 10:1**)

> *Note: As much as someone may want to make Christianity easier or stricter, or teach the Savior's doctrines to his own interpretation; he or she only becomes guilty of John 10:1.*

"Beware lest any man spoil you through philosophy and vain deceit, after the tradition of men, after the rudiments of the world, *and not after Christ.*" (**Colossians 2:8**)

"The earth also is defiled under the inhabitants thereof; because *they have transgressed the laws, changed the ordinance, broken the everlasting covenant.*" (**Isaiah 24:5**)

"For I know this, that *after my departing shall grievous wolves enter in among you,* not sparing the flock. Also of your own selves shall men arise, speaking perverse things, *to draw away disciples after them.*" (**Acts 20:28–30**)

"Now I beseech you, brethren, mark them which cause divisions and offences contrary to the doctrine which ye have learned; and avoid them. *For they that are such serve not our Lord Jesus Christ, but their own belly*; and by good words and fair speeches deceive the hearts of the simple." (**Romans 16:17–18**)

The scriptures teach authority of doctrine, teaching, priesthood, etc., from the top down. For example; God gives authority to his prophets, and His son Jesus Christ.

Then he gives them the doctrines he wants them to teach his children on the earth. His children then pass those teaching on to those who have not heard it.

Protestantism does just the reverse. It teaches Christianity from the bottom up. Protestant churches teach what the pastor wants to teach. The pastor interprets the scriptures and doctrine and decides for himself just what he wants to teach. He is not directed by higher authorities in the denomination.

In most Protestant churches the congregation advertises for and chooses a pastor based on what it wants taught. If the pastor is not willing to teach what the congregation desires he or she is not hired. When a pastor is located that will teach as the congregation requires, they then enter into negotiations to determine just how much the congregation is willing to pay for the pastor's salary, housing, etc. If they come to an agreement, the pastor is hired.

If at any time during the pastor's employment by the congregation the pastor locates another church that will pay him more, he or she resigns, abandons the congregation, and then moves on to the new higher paying church.

On the flip side of the same coin, if the pastor does not please the congregation with his style, teachings, or doctrine; the congregation fires the pastor and looks for another to take his or her place.

In other words, each congregation dictates what God's doctrine and teaching are or will be. They define God and his word, as they want it to be, from the bottom up.

If at any time any member of the congregation decides that he or she does not like what the pastor preaches, how he or she preaches, defines what God is, or His doctrine; that member just moves on to another church or congregation that does.

This is not the way Jesus Christ formed His church. He received His doctrine from God the Father, passed it on to his Apostles whom He ordained to the priesthood and to whom He gave the keys to the Kingdom of Heaven, along with instructions to preach His doctrines to the children of the world.

The Apostles were given the authority and power to organize churches, ordain worthy men to the priesthood as priests, bishops, deacons, etc. If and when any of these churches or members began to teach doctrines that were other than exactly what Christ and the Apostles taught, they were chastised and instructed to discontinue teaching false doctrine or their priesthood authority would be taken away from them. Man does not have the authority to change the doctrine or teaching of Heavenly Father or Jesus Christ, period.

The Savior spoke and prophesized about those pastors who shall take authority upon themselves and shall teach false doctrines, when He said: "Many will say to me in that day, Lord, Lord, have we not prophesied in thy name? and in thy name have cast out devils? And in thy name done many wonderful works? And then I will profess unto them, I never knew you: depart from me, ye that work iniquity" (**Matthew 7:21–23**; verse 21 not shown for brevity).

OTHER SCRIPTURES YOU MAY WANT TO READ . . .

Exodus 28:1–4

Exodus 40:12–16

Matthew 21:33–43

2 Thessalonians 2:3–4

2 Timothy 3:1–8

2 Timothy 4:3–4

2 Corinthians 11:4, 12–15

See chapter 38: **"Priesthood of God — Authority"**

See chapter 11: **"Bible — Supreme Authority — Sola Scriptura"**

See chapter 3: **"Apostasy of the Christian Church"**

CHAPTER 32

MARRIAGE

"Nevertheless neither is the man without the woman, neither the woman without the man, in the Lord. For as the woman is of the man, even so is the man also by the woman; but all things of God." **(1 Corinthians 11:11–12)**

What does God say about marriage? Is it a suggestion that a man and woman marry? Is marriage a requirement? Can a man and a woman just live together? Is marriage a commandment?

Marriage

Scriptures used by some Christian faiths to substantiate their belief and teaching that there is no marriage or family unit in Heaven, and that there is no requirement to get married in this world:

"But they which shall be accounted worthy to obtain that world, and the resurrection from the dead, neither marry, nor are given in marriage." **(Luke 20:35)**

Now the Rest of the Story . . . (scriptures that further explain or clarify the topic)

Part 1 — Marriage and Families in Heaven

"For in the resurrection they neither marry, nor are given in marriage, but are as the angels of God in heaven." **(Matthew 22:30)**

> *Note: We must begin reading with verse 23, which says . . .*

"The same day came to him the Sadducees, *which say that there is no resurrection,* and asked him."

> *Note: This very important verse is often ignored. The Sadducees were a Jewish sect that DID NOT believe in the Resurrection.*

Now read verses 24 through 28 in your Bible.

Now Read Verse 29 . . .

"Jesus answered and said unto them, *Ye do err, not knowing the scriptures, nor the power of God."* **(Matthew 22:29)**

> *Note: Not believing in the Resurrection, the Sadducees priests did not perform marriages for "time and all eternity." They performed marriages for "time" only or for "until death do you part."*

Now Read Matthew 22:30, 31 & 32 Together . . .

"For in the resurrection they neither marry, nor are given in marriage, but are as the angels of God in heaven. But as touching the resurrection of the dead, *have ye not read that which was spoken unto you by God,* I am the God of Abraham, and the God of Isaac, and the God of Jacob? God is not the God of the dead, but of the living." **(Matthew 22:30–32)**

As Mathew 16:19 & 18:18 tell us below . . . *All marriages must be performed on the Earth, by the priesthood of God, and if so . . . will be bound in Heaven for time and all eternity.*

"And *I will give unto thee the keys of the kingdom of heaven*: and *whatsoever thou shalt bind on earth shall be bound in heaven*: and whatsoever thou shalt loose on earth shall be loosed in heaven." (**Matthew 16:19**; see also **Matthew 18:18**)

> *Note: In this scripture the Savior is speaking to the Apostles, whom he ordained to the "priesthood of God," and gave to them the Authority to ordain others to the priesthood.*

> *Note: Nowhere in the Bible does any scripture use the phrase "until death do you part" regarding marriage.*

PART 2 — REQUIREMENT TO GET MARRIED IN THIS WORLD

"So God created man in his own image, in the image of God created he him; male and female created he them. And *God blessed them*, and God said unto them, *Be fruitful, and multiply*, and *replenish the earth*, and subdue it: and have dominion over the fish of the sea, and over the fowl of the air, and over every living thing that moveth upon the earth." (**Genesis 1:27–28**)

> *Note: It is against God's commandments for a man and a woman to fornicate and/or commit adultery to have children and replenish the earth. Yet he commanded them to "Be fruitful and multiply," to have children. God married Adam and Eve in the Garden of Eden. He would not do it any other way. He would not violate his own commandments. See Hebrews 13:4 below.*

"And said, *For this cause shall a man leave father and mother*, and shall *cleave to his wife*: and they twain shall be one flesh? Wherefore they are no more twain, but one flesh. *What therefore God hath joined together, let not man put asunder*." (**Matthew 19:5–6**)

> *Note: A man is to leave his mother and father, and cleave (marry) to his wife. Verse 6 states that God joined them together in marriage.*

"But *from the beginning of the creation God made them male and female.* For this cause shall a man leave his father and mother, and cleave to his wife; *And they twain shall be one flesh*: so then they are no more twain, but one flesh. *What therefore God hath joined together, let not man put asunder.*" (**Mark 10:6–9**)

> *Note: A man is to leave his mother and father, and cleave (marry) to his wife. Verse 9 states that God joined them together in marriage.*

"*And the Lord God said, It is not good that the man should be alone*; I will make him an help meet for him." (**Genesis 2:18**)

> *Note: Why would God say that "it is NOT good that the man should be alone" and then make a woman for him if He did not want them to be married?*

"And the Lord God caused a deep sleep to fall upon Adam, and he slept: and he took one of his ribs, and closed up the flesh instead thereof; And the rib, which the Lord God had taken from man, made he a woman, and brought her unto the man. And Adam said, This is now bone of my bones, and flesh of my flesh: she shall be called Woman, because she was taken out of Man. *Therefore shall a man leave his father and his mother, and shall cleave unto his wife: and they shall be one flesh.* And they were both naked, the man and his wife, and were not ashamed." **(Genesis 2:21–25)**

"Nevertheless *neither is the man without the woman, neither the woman without the man, in the Lord.* For as the woman is of the man, even so is the man also by the woman; but all things of God." **(1 Corinthians 11:11–12)**

> *Note: This scripture is NOT a suggestion. It is a direct commandment from God for marriage.*

"*Marriage is honorable in all,* and the bed undefiled: but whoremongers and adulterers God will judge." **(Hebrews 13:4)**

"And I will give unto thee the keys of the kingdom of heaven: and *whatsoever thou shalt bind on earth shall be bound in heaven*: and whatsoever thou shalt loose on earth shall be loosed in heaven." **(Matthew 16:19**; see also **Matthew 18:18)**

> *Note: This scripture given to Peter and the Twelve Apostles states that Christ gave them the keys to the kingdom of heaven and told them that whatsoever they bind on earth shall be bound in heaven. Marriage is a binding contract performed by the priesthood which Peter and all the Twelve Apostles held. At that time in history there was no such thing as a "civil" marriage in the Jewish community; marriages were only performed in churches by priesthood holders (the authority to act in God's name). Thus a marriage performed by the priesthood (the authority to act in God's name) is both binding on Earth and in Heaven.*

"A bishop then must be blameless, *the husband of one wife*, vigilant, sober, of good behaviour, given to hospitality, apt to teach." **(1 Timothy 3:2)**

> *Note: This does not say "only one wife" nor "at least one wife." Remember that polygamy was practiced among the Jews during this period. What it does say, without a doubt, is that a bishop must be married. How can a bishop teach and council about marriage and family matters if he is not married and has no experience in marriage?*

"Now the Spirit speaketh expressly, that in the latter times some shall depart from the faith, giving heed to seducing spirits, and doctrines of devils; Speaking lies in hypocrisy; having their conscience seared with a hot iron; *Forbidding to marry*, and commanding to abstain from meats, which God hath created to be received with thanksgiving of them which believe and know the truth." **(1 Timothy 4:1–3)**

"And Adam was not deceived, but *the woman being deceived was in the transgression.* Notwithstanding *she shall be saved in childbearing*, if they continue in faith and charity and holiness with sobriety." **(1 Timothy 2:14–15)**

> *Note: It is obvious here that to be saved the woman must bear children. God commanded both male and female not to commit adultery nor fornication, so again, to fulfill this requirement of bearing children, a man and a woman must be married.*

"I will therefore that the *younger women marry, bear children*, guide the house, give none occasion to the adversary to speak reproachfully. For some are already turned aside after Satan." **(1 Timothy 5:14–15)**

"And Jesus answering said unto them, *The children of this world marry, and are given in marriage.*" **(Luke 20:34)**

> Note: *This is a commandment, not an observation nor a suggestion. See 1 Corinthians 11:11–12 and 1 Timothy 4:1–3 and 5:14–15 above.*

"And he arose out of the synagogue, and entered into Simon's house. *And Simon's wife's mother* was taken with a great fever; and they besought him for her." **(Luke 4:38)**

> Note: *Peter's name was Simon. Jesus calls him Simon many times. All biblical scholars acknowledge that the apostle Peter (Simon) was married.*

"Likewise, ye husbands, dwell with them [wives] according to knowledge, giving honour unto the wife, as unto the weaker vessel, and as *being heirs together of the grace of life*; that your prayers be not hindered." **(1 Peter 3:7)**

"But I say unto you, *That whosoever shall put away his wife, saving for the cause of fornication, causeth her to commit adultery*: and whosoever shall marry her that is divorced committeth adultery." **(Matthew 5:32**; see also **Mark 10:10–13)**

> Note: *"Whosoever shall marry her that is divorced committeth adultery" applies only to someone marrying another who was divorced for committing fornication or adultery.*

PART 3 — THE FIRST MARRIAGE WAS IN THE GARDEN OF EDEN AND PERFORMED BY GOD THE FATHER

"And the Lord God caused a deep sleep to fall upon Adam, and he slept: and he took one of his ribs, and closed up the flesh instead thereof; And the rib, which the LORD God had taken from man, made he a woman, and brought her unto the man. And Adam said, This is now bone of my bones, and flesh of my flesh: she shall be called Woman, because she was taken out of Man. *Therefore shall a man leave his father and his mother, and shall cleave unto his wife: and they shall be one flesh.*" **(Genesis 2:21–24)**

> Note: *This is where God the Father marries Adam and Eve.*

"And they were both naked, *the man and his wife*, and were not ashamed." **(Genesis 2:25)**

"And when the woman saw that the tree was good for food, and that it was pleasant to the eyes, and a tree to be desired to make one wise, she took of the fruit thereof, and did eat, and gave also unto *her husband* with her; and he did eat." **(Genesis 3:6)**

"Unto the woman he *[the Lord]* said, I will greatly multiply thy sorrow and thy conception; in sorrow thou shalt bring forth children; and thy desire shall be to *thy husband*, and he shall rule over thee." **(Genesis 3:16)**

"And Adam called *his wife's* name Eve; because she was the mother of all living." **(Genesis 6:20)**

"And Adam knew *Eve his wife*; and she conceived, and bare Cain, and said, I have gotten a man from the Lord." **(Genesis 4:1**; see also **Genesis 4:2, 25)**

> *Note:* In every one of the above verses, the words **"wife"** and **"husband"** are used; not boyfriend, nor girlfriend, nor partner, nor any term suggesting that they were not married. Now, since there was no one else with Adam and Eve on the Earth at this time but God, only God could have, and did marry them.

CHAPTER 33

ORIGINAL SIN
ADAM'S TRANSGRESSION

"And Adam was not deceived, but the woman being deceived was in the transgression." **(1 Timothy 2:14)**

The notion of original sin, as it is usually understood today in traditional Christianity, is a distinctly late invention that evolved from the controversies of the fourth and fifth centuries. This chapter will help you to explain that No man, woman nor child, shall be punished for the sins of another.

Original Sin
Adam's Transgression

Nowhere in the Bible is the term "Original Sin" found. Nowhere in scripture does it say that mankind will be punished for "Adam's Transgression." Nowhere in scripture does it say that anyone will be punished for another's sins. The concept of Original Sin is no more than another example of "the philosophies of men, mingled with scripture."[1]

Scriptures used by some Christian faiths to substantiate their belief and teaching on Original Sin:

"Wherefore, as by one man sin entered into the world, and death by sin; and so death passed upon all men, for that all have sinned." (**Romans 5:12**)

"Therefore as by the offence of one judgment came upon all men to condemnation; even so by the righteousness of one the free gift came upon all men unto justification of life. For as by one man's disobedience many were made sinners, so by the obedience of one shall many be made righteous." (**Romans 5:18–19**)

NOW THE REST OF THE STORY . . . (scriptures that further explain or clarify the topic)

PART 1 — ADAM'S TRANSGRESSION AND ORIGINAL SIN

"And *Adam was not deceived*, but the woman being deceived was in the transgression." (**1 Timothy 2:14**)

"And [Then] the Lord God said, "Behold, the man is [has] become as [like] *one of us to know [in knowing] good and evil*. And now, lest he put forth [reach out] his hand and take also of the tree of life and eat, and live forever." (**Genesis 3:22 KJV; ESV** verbiage in brackets.)

"But *your iniquities* have separated [made a separation] between you and your God, and *your sins* have hid [hidden] his face from you, [so] that he will [does] not hear." (**Isaiah 59:2 KJV; ESV** verbiage in brackets.)

> *Note: In Isaiah 59:2 ponder the words "your iniquities" and "your sins"; man is punished for his sins only, not for the sins of another. In Genesis 3:22, two things came into the world because of "Eve's Transgression" (1 Timothy 2:14): (1) Adam and Eve "became like God" now having knowledge of "good and evil," which Adam and Eve did not possess prior to partaking of the fruit, and (2) "physical death." Adam and Eve were immortal prior to partaking of the fruit. Adam made the ONLY logical decision possible as Eve would now be cast out of the Garden of Eden. God had married Adam and Eve and commanded them to have children*

(Genesis 1:27–28), which, prior to Eve's eating the forbidden fruit of the Tree of Knowledge of Good and Evil, they had not done. Adam therefore knew he, too, had to eat of the forbidden fruit.

"And they fell upon their faces, and said, O God, the God of the spirits of all flesh, *shall one man sin, and wilt thou be wroth with all the congregation?*" (**Numbers 16:22**)

> *Note: Read all of Numbers 16 and you will see that God was not wroth with the innocent of the congregation. He instructed the innocent to leave, and He only punished those who were wicked or who rebelled against Him. Now ask yourself: if God did not punish the innocent in Numbers 16, why would He punish all the innocent children, grandchildren, great-grandchildren, great-great-grandchildren, etc., for the transgressions of Adam and Eve?*

Part 2 — Little Children and Original Sin

"But Jesus said, *Suffer little children*, and forbid them not, to come unto me: *for of such is the kingdom of heaven.*" (**Matthew 19:14 KJV**)

> *Note: the word "Suffer" here means to "let, allow, or permit"; it has nothing to do with pain or agony.*

Now See the ESV . . .

"But Jesus said, "Let the *little children* come to me and do not hinder them, *for to such belongs the kingdom of heaven.*" (**Matthew 19:14 ESV**)

> *Note: Reread the ESV rendition of this scripture: "for to such <u>belongs the kingdom of heaven.</u>" Little children are innocent and do not need to be baptized as infants. Obviously they are not born in sin.*

"But the children of the murderers he slew not: according unto that which is written in the book of the law of Moses, wherein the Lord commanded, saying, The fathers shall not be put to death for the children, nor the children be put to death for the fathers; but *every man shall be put to death for his own sin.*" (**2 Kings 14:6**; see also **2 Chronicles 25:4**)

"*The soul that sinneth, it shall die. The son shall not bear the iniquity of the father, neither shall the father bear the iniquity of the son*: the righteousness of the righteous shall be upon him, and the wickedness of the wicked shall be upon him." (**Ezekiel 18:20**)

Conclusion

No man, woman, or child shall be punished for the sins of another.

THE COUNCIL OF CARTHAGE AD 418 AND THE DOCTRINE OF "ORIGINAL SIN"

The notion of original sin, as it is usually understood today in traditional Christianity, is a distinctly late invention that evolved from the controversies of the fourth and fifth centuries. Tertullian (second century AD), who was very concerned with the idea of sin, says nothing of the doctrine of original sin. Indeed, very few of the Church Fathers up to the fourth century show any interest in it at all. It was not clearly enunciated until Augustine (fourth/fifth century) needed it in his battle with the Christian Pelagians, who denied the doctrine, and it came to be associated with the Council of Carthage in AD 418.[2]

CHAPTER 34

PLAN OF SALVATION

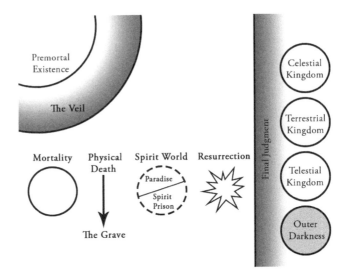

The Plan of Salvation

Our Eternal Life

Many of us spend our lives looking for something to hold on to, something that will last. We look for ways to avoid aging or to become famous or rich. But we eventually realize that mortal life is temporary. Friends and family members grow old and die, the famous are soon forgotten, and wealth is lost as quickly as it is won.

Our hope and happiness lie in knowing who we are, where we came from, and where we can go. We are eternal beings, spirit children of an eternal God. Our lives can be compared to a three-act play: premortal life (before we came to earth), mortal life (our time here on earth), and postmortal life (where we go after we die). God has had a plan for our lives since the beginning of the first act—a plan that, if followed, provides comfort and guidance now, as well as salvation and eternal happiness in our postmortal life.

Understanding the following can help us live a happier life now and in eternity.

God Is Our Father

God is the Father of our spirits. We are created in His image. We have a divine nature and destiny.

See chapter 21: **"God — Who Is He?"**
See chapter 20: **"God Has a Physical Body"**
See chapter 22: **"Godhead — Trinity — Three Separate Beings"**

We Lived with God

Before we were born, we lived with God, the Father of our spirits. All persons on earth are literally brothers and sisters in the family of God.

See chapter 37: **"Premortal Existence of Spirits."**
See chapter 30: **"Man Has Both a Physical & Spiritual Body."**

Earth Life Is Part of God's Plan

Our life on earth has purpose. Coming to earth is part of God's plan to enable our eternal progression, for us to gain a physical body, to learn self-discipline, to be tried and tested, to build and demonstrate faith, to learn to make righteous choices, and to learn to choose between good and evil.

See chapter 32: **"Marriage"**
See chapter 48: **"Sexuality"**
See chapter 26: **"How Can I Know the Truth? Testimony"**
See chapter 25: **"Holy Ghost"**

Jesus Christ Is the Way

Our Heavenly Father sent His Son, Jesus Christ, to be our Savior and show us the way to live according to God's plan.

See chapter 28: **"Jesus Christ — Who Is He?"**
See chapter 5: **"Atonement of Jesus Christ"**
See chapter 15: **"Creation — Who Created the Heavens and the Earth?"**

We Can Find Happiness

Following God's plan for us is the surest way to find happiness and endure life's challenges.

See chapter 6: **"Baptism"**
See chapter 18: **"Faith, Grace & Works — Sincere Belief Is Not Enough"**
See chapter 40: **"Repentance"**
See chapter 19: **"Forgiveness"**
See chapter 14: **"The Commandments — Not Just Ten!"**

We Can Live with God Again

Our lives will not end when we die. Our lives after death are determined by the way we live our lives now.

See chapter 16: **"Death"**
See chapter 42: **"Resurrection of the Physical Body"**
See chapter 24: **"Heaven — Hell — Degrees of Glory"**
See chapter 45: **"Salvation for All Mankind"**
See chapter 46: **"Salvation for the Dead"**

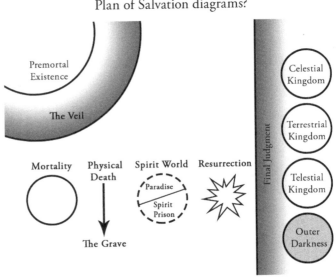

What is missing in this and all
Plan of Salvation diagrams?

Answer: Jesus Christ!
Without Him, there is no salvation.

Plan of Salvation Websites

http://middleagedmormonman.com/home/2016/02/plan-salvation-whats-missing
https://www.lds.org/topics/plan-of-salvation?lang=eng&old=true

Images for LDS Plan of Salvation

A simple Google image search for "LDS Plan of Salvation" will provide countless examples.

CHAPTER 35

PLURAL MARRIAGE

"And Sarai Abram's wife took Hagar her maid the Egyptian, after Abram had dwelt ten years in the land of Canaan, and gave her to her husband Abram to be his wife." **(Genesis 16:3)**

Nowhere in the Old Testament or New Testament does God, His prophets, Jesus or any Apostle say that plural marriage is a sin. Nor is there a commandment in the Bible prohibiting plural marriage. However, there is a history of plural marriage among God's chosen people.

Plural Marriage

Scriptures used by some Christian faiths to substantiate their belief and teaching that plural marriage is a sin:

"A bishop then must be blameless, the husband of one wife, vigilant, sober, of good behaviour, given to hospitality, apt to teach." (**1 Timothy 3:2**)

> *Note: This does not say "only one wife" nor "at least one wife." Remember that polygamy was practiced among the Jews during this period. What it does say, without a doubt, is that a bishop must be married. How can a bishop teach and council about marriage and family matters if he is not married and has no experience in marriage?*

"If any be blameless, the husband of one wife, having faithful children not accused of riot or unruly." (**Titus 1:6**)

> *Note: This does not say "only one wife" nor "at least one wife." Titus 1:5–9 must be read to understand the full purpose of this verse; Paul is talking about the requirements given to Titus for the ordaining of elders in the church. Notice also in this verse the requirement of "faithful children not accused of riot or unruly" to be ordained an elder in the church.*
>
> *Note: Timothy 3:2 and Titus 1:6 above state "the husband of one wife" in a list of qualifications for spiritual leadership for bishops and church leaders. They say nothing about other church members or non-members.*

"Nevertheless, to avoid fornication, let every man have his own wife, and let every woman have her own husband." (**1 Corinthians 7:2**)

> *Note: Not including verses 1 through 4 distorts what Paul was talking about and the meaning of this scripture. Paul is saying "to avoid fornication" every man should have his own wife and every woman should have her own husband.*

Now the Rest of the Story . . .

Nowhere in the Old Testament or New Testament does God, His prophets, Jesus, or any Apostles say that plural marriage is a sin. Nor is there a commandment in the Bible prohibiting plural marriage.

"And Nathan said to David, Thou art the man. *Thus saith the Lord God of Israel*, I anointed thee king over Israel, and I delivered thee out of the hand of Saul; And *I gave thee* thy master's house, and *thy master's wives* into thy bosom, and gave thee the house of Israel and of Judah; and if that had been too little, I would moreover have given unto thee such and such things. Wherefore hast thou despised the commandment of the Lord, to do evil in his sight? *thou hast killed Uriah the Hittite* with the sword, *and hast taken his wife to be thy wife*, and hast slain him with the sword of the children of

Ammon. Now therefore the sword shall never depart from thine house; *because thou hast despised me, and hast taken the wife of Uriah the Hittite to be thy wife. Thus saith the Lord, Behold,* I will raise up evil against thee out of thine own house, and *I will take thy wives before thine eyes, and give them unto thy neighbour,* and he shall lie with thy wives in the sight of this sun. For thou didst it secretly: but I will do this thing before all Israel, and before the sun. And David said unto Nathan, I have sinned against the Lord. And Nathan said unto David, *The Lord also hath put away thy sin; thou shalt not die."* (**2 Samuel 12:7–13**)

> *Note: King David had many wives, according to the Bible, although only eight of them are named. David's first wife was* **Michal,** *the daughter of* King Saul. *The other five named wives of David were* **Ahinoam, Maacah, Haggith, Abital,** *and* **Eglah** *(2 Samuel 3:2–5; 1 Chronicles 3:1–3). According to 2 Samuel 5:13, David married more wives in Jerusalem, but how many is unknown. David did not sin by having multiple wives. David's sin was one of "murder" by having Uriah killed so that he could take Uriah's wife* **Bathsheba** *to be his wife.*

"But king *Solomon* loved many strange women, together with the daughter of Pharaoh, women of the Moabites, Ammonites, Edomites, Zidonians, and Hittites. . . . And he *had seven hundred wives, princesses, and three hundred concubines*: and his wives turned away his heart." (**1 Kings 11:1, 3**)

"And Lamech took unto him *two wives*: the name of the one was Adah, and the name of the other Zillah." (**Genesis 4:19**)

"And *Sarai* Abram's wife *took Hagar* her maid the Egyptian, after Abram had dwelt ten years in the land of Canaan, *and gave her to her husband Abram to be his wife.*" (**Genesis 16:3**)

> *Note: Abraham had two wives: Sarai and Hagar.*

"And Jacob served seven years for *Rachel*; and they seemed unto him but a few days, for the love he had to her. And Jacob said unto Laban, Give me my wife, for my days are fulfilled, that I may go in unto her. . . . And it came to pass in the evening, that he (Laban) took *Leah* his daughter, and brought her to him (Jacob); and he went in unto her . . . And it came to pass, that in the morning, behold, it was Leah: and he said to Laban, What is this thou hast done unto me? did not I serve with thee for Rachel? wherefore then hast thou beguiled me? . . . Fulfil her week, and we will give thee this also for the service which thou shalt serve with me yet seven other years. And Jacob did so, and fulfilled her week: and he gave him Rachel his daughter to wife also." (**Genesis 29:20–21, 23, 25, 27–30**; for the full story, read verses 20–30)

> *Note: Jacob also had two wives: Leah and Rachel.*

"And she (Rachel) gave him *Bilhah* her handmaid to wife: and Jacob went in unto her. . . . When Leah saw that she had left bearing, she took *Zilpah* her maid, and gave her Jacob to wife." (**Genesis 30:4, 9**; for the full story, read verses 1–13)

> *Note: Rachel gives Bilhah and Leah gives Zilpah to Jacob as wives.*

"*If a man have two wives*, one beloved, and another hated, and they have born him children, both the beloved and the hated; and if the firstborn son be hers that was hated: Then it shall be, when he maketh his sons to inherit that which he hath, that he may not make the son of the beloved firstborn before the son of the hated, which is indeed the firstborn: But he shall acknowledge the son of the hated for the firstborn, by giving him a double portion of all that he hath: for he is the beginning of his strength; the right of the firstborn is his." (**Deuteronomy 21:15–17**)

Note: *The above are just a few scriptures pro and con regarding plural marriage. Modern Day Revelation is the best defense for the church's short practice of plural marriage and for the discontinuance of it.*

CHAPTER 36

PREACH WITHOUT CHARGE

"What is my reward then? Verily that, when I preach the gospel, I may make the gospel of Christ without charge, that I abuse not my power in the gospel."
(1 Corinthians 9:18)

Where in the Bible do we find the Savior instructing his Apostles or any disciple to charge money to any they may preach to? Or to demand anything for their services? Nowhere.

PREACH WITHOUT CHARGE

Scriptures used by some Christian faiths to substantiate their belief and teaching that a pastor can charge for his preaching the Word of God:

"Let the elders that rule well be counted worthy of double honour, especially they who labour in the word and doctrine. For the scripture saith, Thou shalt not muzzle the ox that treadeth out the corn. And, The labourer is worthy of his reward." (**1 Timothy 5:17–18**)

> *Note: "Honour" does not mean "money" or payment; neither does "reward." The "reward" for preaching and bringing others to Christ is NOT money.*
> *Note: What is the reward? See 1 Corinthians 9:18 for the answer.*

"Thou shalt not muzzle the ox when he treadeth out the corn." (**Deuteronomy 25:4**)

> *Note: See 1 Corinthians 9:18 for the answer.*

"And in the same house remain, eating and drinking such things as they give: for the labourer is worthy of his hire. Go not from house to house." (**Luke 10:7**)

> *Note: Luke says Jesus admonished those He sent to preach NOT to go from "house to house" seeking of more gain. Jesus said "eating and drinking such things as they give" and nothing about requiring money.*

"Provide neither gold, nor silver, nor brass in your purses, Nor scrip for your journey, neither two coats, neither shoes, nor yet staves: for the workman is worthy of his meat." (**Matthew 10:10**)

> *Note: "For the workman is worthy of his meat"; the word "meat" as used in the Bible, means food or meal. It does not mean money or payment (Bible Dictionary, "meat").*

NOW THE REST OF THE STORY . . . (scriptures that further explain or clarify the topic)

"What is my reward then? Verily that, when I preach the gospel, *I may make the gospel of Christ without charge*, that I abuse not my power in the gospel." (**1 Corinthians 9:18**)

> *Note: Read 1 Corinthians verses 1–18 for a better understanding.*

"And he said unto them, When I sent you without purse, and scrip, and shoes, lacked ye any thing? And they said, Nothing. Then said he unto them, But now, he that hath a purse, let him take it, and likewise his scrip: and he that hath no sword, let him sell his garment, and buy one." (**Luke 22:35–36**)

"I have coveted no man's silver, or gold, or apparel. Yea, ye yourselves know, that *these hands have ministered unto my necessities*, and to them that were with me." (**Acts 20:33–34**)

"Neither did we eat any man's bread for nought; *but wrought with labour and travail night and day*, that we might not be chargeable to any of you: Not because we have not power, but *to make ourselves an ensample unto you to follow us*. For even when we were with you, this we commanded you, that if any would not work, neither should he eat." **(2 Thessalonians 3:8–10)**

"For I think that *God hath set forth us the apostles* last, as it were appointed to death: for we are made a spectacle unto the world, and to angels, and to men. . . . Even unto this present hour we both *hunger*, and *thirst*, and are *naked*, and are buffeted, and have no certain dwelling place; And *labour, working with our own hands*: being reviled, we bless; being persecuted, we suffer it: "Behold, the third time I am ready to come to you; and *I will not be burdensome to you*: for *I seek not yours*, but you: for the children ought not to lay up for the parents, but the parents for the children. And *I will very gladly spend and be spent for you*; though the more abundantly I love you, the less I be loved. But be it so, I did not burden you: nevertheless, being crafty, I caught you with guile. Did I make a gain of you by any of them whom I sent unto you?" **(2 Corinthians 12:14–17**; see also **1 Corinthians 4:9–12)**

"A bishop then must be blameless, the husband of one wife, vigilant, sober, of good behaviour, given to hospitality, apt to teach; Not given to wine, no striker, *not greedy of filthy lucre*; but patient, not a brawler, not covetous." **(1 Timothy 3:2–3)**

> *Note: Merriam-Webster Unabridged Dictionary definition of "filthy lucre": "Ministers are enjoined not to be worldly minded, and not to be given to filthy lucre (money)."*

"The elders which are among you I exhort, who am also an elder, and a witness of the sufferings of Christ, and also a partaker of the glory that shall be revealed: Feed the flock of God which is among you, taking the oversight thereof, not by constraint, but willingly; *not for filthy lucre*, but of a ready mind; Neither as being lords over God's heritage, but *being ensamples to the flock*." **(1 Peter 5:1–3)**

Unfortunately, many preachers have made themselves wealthy, lived lavish lifestyles, owned expensive homes, expensive cars, lavish jewelry, and built monuments unto themselves and their glory—all from the donations of their flock.

"Not every one that saith unto me, Lord, Lord, shall enter into the kingdom of heaven; but he that doeth the will of my Father which is in heaven. *Many will say to me in that day*, Lord, Lord, have we not prophesied in thy name? and in thy name have cast out devils? and in thy name done many wonderful works? *And then will I profess unto them, I never knew you: depart from me, ye that work iniquity*." **(Matthew 7:21–23)**

See chapter 31: **"Man-Made Churches"**

CHAPTER 37

PREMORTAL EXISTENCE OF SPIRITS

"Furthermore we have had fathers of our flesh which corrected us, and we gave them reverence: shall we not much rather be in subjection unto the Father of spirits, and live?" **(Hebrews 12:9)**

The doctrine of premortal existence was not only taught in the early church it continued until the mid-sixth century, when the teachings of Origen concerning the premortal life were condemned by the Catholic church edict known as the *Anathemas Against Origen*, at the Second Council of Constantinople in AD 553.

PREMORTAL EXISTENCE OF SPIRITS

<hr>

Scriptures used by some Christian faiths to substantiate their belief and teaching that mankind did not exist in any form prior to their earthly existence:

"The burden of the word of the Lord for Israel, saith the Lord, which stretcheth forth the heavens, and layeth the foundation of the earth, and formeth the spirit of man within him." (**Zechariah 12:1**)

> *Note: Modern-day Christianity claims that the "spirit of man" does not exist until GOD forms it and places it into him or her.*

<hr>

NOW THE REST OF THE STORY . . . (scriptures that further explain or clarify the topic)

"And we know that all things work together for good to them that love God, to them who are the called according to his purpose. *For whom he did foreknow*, he also did predestinate to be conformed to the image of his Son, that he might be the firstborn among many brethren. Moreover whom *he did predestinate*, them he also called: and whom he called, them he also justified: and whom he justified, them he also glorified." (**Romans 8:28–30**)

God tells Jeremiah: "Then the word of the Lord came unto me, saying, *Before I formed thee in the belly I knew thee*; and before thou camest forth out of the womb I sanctified thee, *and I ordained thee a prophet unto the nations*." (**Jeremiah 1:4–5**)

> *Note: God did not say, "I knew 'of' thee." He said, "I <u>knew</u> thee," which is a past-tense personal relationship.*

"Ye have not chosen me, but I have chosen you, and ordained you, that ye should go and bring forth fruit, and that your fruit should remain: that whatsoever ye shall ask of the Father in my name, he may give it you. These things I command you, that ye love one another. If the world hate you, ye know that it hated me before it hated you. If ye were of the world, the world would love his own: but because ye are not of the world, but *I have chosen you out of the world*, therefore the world hateth you." (**John 15:16–19**)

"Now there was a day when *the sons of God came to present themselves before the Lord*, and Satan came also among them." (**Job 1:6**)

God asks Job: "*Where wast thou when I laid the foundations of the earth?* declare, if thou hast understanding. Who hath laid the measures thereof, if thou knowest? or who hath stretched the line upon it? When the morning stars sang together, *and all the sons of God shouted for joy?*" (**Job 38:4–5, 7**)

"Furthermore we have had fathers of our flesh which corrected us, and we gave them reverence: shall we not much rather be in subjection unto the *Father of spirits*, and live?" (**Hebrews 12:9**)

"For in him we live, and move, and have our being; as certain also of your own poets have said, *For we are also his offspring*. Forasmuch then as *we are the offspring of God*, we ought not to think that the Godhead is like unto gold, or silver, or stone, graven by art and man's device." (**Acts 17:28–29**)

> *Note: Imagine . . . "we are the offspring of God."*

"I have said, *Ye are gods*; and *all of you are children of the most High*." (**Psalms 82:6**)

> *Note: Read this scripture again and ponder it. "Ye are gods" . . . "You are children of the most High."*

"And no man hath ascended up to heaven, *but he that came down from heaven*, even the Son of man which is in heaven." (**John 3:13**)

"*The Lord possessed me in the beginning* of his way, before his works of old. I was set up from everlasting, from the beginning, *or ever the earth was*. When there were no depths, I was brought forth; when there were no fountains abounding with water. Before the mountains were settled, before the hills was I brought forth: *While as yet he had not made the earth*, nor the fields, nor the highest part of the dust of the world. *When he prepared the heavens, I was there*: when he set a compass upon the face of the depth: When he established the clouds above: when he strengthened the fountains of the deep: When he gave to the sea his decree, that the waters should not pass his commandment: when he appointed the foundations of the earth: *Then I was by him, as one brought up with him*: and I was daily his delight, rejoicing always before him; Rejoicing in the habitable part of his earth; and my delights were with the sons of men." (**Proverbs 8:22–31**)

> *Note: Many will teach, mistakenly, that this is Jesus Christ speaking. But we know that this cannot be as verse 26 says, "<u>While as yet he had not made the earth</u>"; since Jesus Christ made the Earth, we know from this verse and verses 27, 28, and 29, that this is not Christ speaking. We know that Solomon wrote some of the Proverbs but we do not know who all the authors were.*

"And as Jesus passed by, he saw a man which was blind from his birth. And his disciples asked him, saying, Master, *who did sin, this man*, or his parents, *that he was born blind?* Jesus answered, Neither hath this man sinned, nor his parents: but that the works of God should be made manifest in him." (**John 9:1–3**)

> *Note: The disciples had been taught and understood the Savior's teaching of our preexistence prior to coming to this Earth, otherwise how would they have known to even ask the question "who did sin, this man, or his parents?" How could this man or any man have sinned before he was born on this Earth unless he had lived somewhere else before?*

"Paul, a servant of God, and an apostle of Jesus Christ, according to the faith of God's elect, and the acknowledging of the truth which is after godliness; In *hope of eternal life*, which God, that cannot lie, *promised before the world began*." (**Titus 1:1–2**)

> *Question: How could one be foreordained, predestinated, known before the Earth was formed, before he or she was conceived in the belly,*

ordained and chosen "out of the world," be the literal "Offspring of God," the Children of God, have something promised to them by God, if he or she had not existed with God somewhere else before coming to this Earth?

"Blessed be the God and Father of our Lord Jesus Christ, who hath blessed us with all spiritual blessings *in heavenly places* in Christ: According as *he hath chosen us in him before the foundation of the world*, that we should be holy and without blame before him in love: *Having predestinated us* unto the adoption of children by Jesus Christ to himself, according to the good pleasure of his will." **(Ephesians 1:3–5)**

"For this cause I bow my knees unto the Father of our Lord Jesus Christ, *Of whom the whole family in heaven and earth is named.*" **(Ephesians 3:14–15)**

"Then shall the dust return to the earth as it was: *and the spirit shall return unto God who gave it.*" **(Ecclesiastes 12:7)**

"*God; Who hath* saved us, and *called us with an holy calling*, not according to our works, but according to his own purpose and grace, *which was given us* in Christ Jesus *before the world began.*" **(2 Timothy 1:8–9**; only the last word of verse 8 is shown for clarity and brevity**)**

"And the angels *which kept not their first estate*, but left their own habitation, he hath reserved in everlasting chains under darkness unto the judgment of the great day." **(Jude 1:6)**

"I write unto you, little children, because your sins are forgiven you for his name's sake. I write unto you, *fathers, because ye have known him that is from the beginning.* I write unto you, young men, because ye have overcome the wicked one. I write unto you, *little children, because ye have known the Father.*" **(1 John 2:12–13)**

The Anathemas against Origen

The doctrine of premortal existence was not only taught in the early church it continued until the mid-sixth century, when the teachings of Origen concerning the premortal life were condemned by the Catholic church edict known as the *Anathemas Against Origen*, at the Second Council of Constantinople in AD 553. A council composed of approximately 165 bishops, although Pope Vigilius, who was in Constantinople at the time, refused to attend it. As a result of this condemnation, the writings of Origen, about 6,000 works, supporting his teachings were either destroyed outright or ordered translated with the appropriate adjustments to eliminate conflict with then current Catholic doctrine. In Origen the Christian Church had its first theologian. He was the greatest textual critic of the early Church. He is considered one of the greatest biblical scholars of the early Church, having written commentaries on most of the books of the Bible, though few exist today. Origen was largely responsible for the collection of usage information regarding the texts which became the New Testament. Origen is regarded today by the Catholic Church as a Church Father, but not a saint.[1]

See chapter 21: "**God — Who Is He?**"
See chapter 30: "**Man Has Both a Physical & Spiritual Body**"
See chapter 20: "**God Has a Physical Body**"

CHAPTER 38

PRIESTHOOD OF GOD AUTHORITY

"And I will give unto thee the keys of the kingdom of heaven: and whatsoever thou shalt bind on earth shall be bound in heaven: and whatsoever thou shalt loose on earth shall be loosed in heaven." **(Matthew 16:13–19)**

The Catholic Church believes in a divine priesthood authority to act in the name of God; while Protestant churches do not. Protestant churches believe that the Bible gives all the authority to start their own church, to preach and interpret the Word of God.

PRIESTHOOD OF GOD — AUTHORITY

Scriptures used by some Christian faiths to substantiate their belief and teaching that there is no ecclesiastical priesthood, justifying their belief and teaching for "The Priesthood of All believers":

"But ye are a chosen generation, a royal priesthood, an holy nation, a peculiar people; that ye should shew forth the praises of him who hath called you out of darkness into his marvelous light." **(1 Peter 2:9)**

"And hast made us unto our God kings and priests: and we shall reign on the earth." **(Revelation 5:10)**

> *Note: Question . . . Are you a "king" because of this verse?*

"And ye shall be unto me a kingdom of priests, and an holy nation. These are the words which thou shalt speak unto the children of Israel." **(Exodus 19:6)**

> *Note: Did you notice the last sentence of this verse? This verse is directed to the nation of Israel only.*

THE PRIESTHOOD OF ALL BELIEVERS

The "universal priesthood" or the "priesthood of all believers" is a Protestant Christian doctrine stating that ordinary Christians share a common priesthood. The exact meaning of this belief and its implications varies widely among denominations.

The origins of the doctrine within Protestantism are somewhat obscure. The idea was found in a radical form in Lollard thought. Martin Luther incorporated it in his writings for the purpose of reforming the Christian Church, it became not only a central tenet of Protestantism, but a foundational concept of Protestantism. The Bible passage considered to be the basis of this belief is the First Epistle of Peter, 2:9.[1]

Some groups during the Reformation believed that priesthood authority was still needed, but was lost from the earth. Roger Williams believed, "There is no regularly constituted church of Christ on earth, nor any person qualified to administer any church ordinances; nor can there be until new apostles are sent by the Great Head of the Church for whose coming I am seeking." Another group, the Seekers, believed that the Roman Catholic Church had lost its authority through corruption and waited for Christ to restore his true church and authority.[2]

Most Protestants today recognize only Christ as their mediator between themselves and God (1 Timothy 2:5). The Epistle to the Hebrews calls Jesus the supreme "high priest," who offered himself as a perfect sacrifice (Hebrews 7:23–28). Protestants believe that through Christ they have been given direct access to God, just like a priest; thus the doctrine is called the "priesthood of all believers." God is equally accessible to all the faithful, and every Christian has equal potential to minister for God.[3]

NOW THE REST OF THE STORY . . . (scriptures that further explain or clarify the topic)

Old Testament priests were chosen by God, not self-appointed; the same for New Testament Apostles who were chosen by the Savior. The Savior ordained the Apostles to the priesthood and gave them the authority to choose and ordain Priests, Bishops, Elders, etc. The Apostles then gave this authority to those who they ordained to the various priesthood offices. Those who were then and are now chosen, are ordained for a purpose: to serve God with their lives.

"And when he was come into the temple, the chief priests and the elders of the people came unto him as he was teaching, and said, *By what authority doest thou these things? and who gave thee this authority?*" (**Matthew 21:23**; see also **Mark 11:28**)

> Note: *The chief priests recognized that one must hold the priesthood and have authority to act in the name of God.*

"For every *high priest* taken from among men *is ordained for men in things pertaining to God*, that he may offer both gifts and sacrifices for sins: Who can have compassion on the ignorant, and on them that are out of the way; for that he himself also is compassed with infirmity. And by reason hereof he ought, as for the people, so also for himself, to offer for sins. *And no man taketh this honour unto himself, but he that is called of God, as was Aaron.* So also Christ glorified not himself to be made an high priest; but he that said unto him, Thou art my Son, to day have I begotten thee. As he saith also in another place, *Thou art a priest for ever after the order of Melchisedec.*" (**Hebrews 5:1–6**)

AND HOW WAS AARON ORDAINED?

"And thou shalt bring Aaron and his sons unto the door of the tabernacle of the congregation, and wash them with water. And *thou shalt put upon Aaron the holy garments, and anoint him, and sanctify him; that he may minister unto me in the priest's office.* And thou shalt bring his sons, and clothe them with coats: And thou shalt anoint them, as thou didst anoint their father, that they may minister unto me in the priest's office: for *their anointing shall surely be an everlasting priesthood throughout their generations.* Thus did Moses: according to all that the Lord commanded him, so did he." (**Exodus 40:12–16**)

"Whither the forerunner is for us entered, even *Jesus, made an high priest* for ever after *the order of Melchisedec.*" (**Hebrews 6:20**)

"If therefore perfection were by the *Levitical priesthood*, (for under it the people received the law,) what further need was there that *another priest should rise after the order of Melchisedec*, and not be called after the order of Aaron? For the priesthood being changed, there is made of necessity a change also of the law." **(Hebrews 7:11–12)**

"And when it was day, he called unto him his disciples: and *of them he chose twelve*, whom also *he named apostles*; Simon, (whom he also named Peter,) and Andrew his brother, James and John, Philip and Bartholomew, Matthew and Thomas, James the son of Alphæus, and Simon called Zelotes, And Judas the brother of James, and Judas Iscariot, which also was the traitor." **(Luke 6:13–16**; see also **Matthew 10:1–4)**

"*Ye have not chosen me*, but *I have chosen you, and ordained you*, that ye should go and bring forth fruit, and that your fruit should remain: that whatsoever ye shall ask of the Father in my name, he may give it you." **(John 15:16)**

> *Note: Jesus said, "Ye have not chosen me, but I have chosen you, and ordained you." Of all Jesus's disciples He alone chose who the Twelve Apostles would be and He ordained them, not the other way around. The Apostles were given authority to chose who would be ordained as priests, bishops, etc.; they did not go to the Apostles and request to be chosen.*

"Then he called his twelve disciples together, *and gave them power and authority* over all devils, and to cure diseases. And he sent them to preach the kingdom of God, and to heal the sick." **(Luke 9:1–2)**

"And *I will give unto thee the keys of the kingdom of heaven*: and whatsoever thou shalt bind on earth shall be bound in heaven: and whatsoever thou shalt loose on earth shall be loosed in heaven." **(Matthew 16:19)**

> *Note: This is where Peter received the keys to the Kingdom of Heaven, and powers of the priesthood.*

"Verily I say unto you, *Whatsoever ye shall bind on earth shall be bound in heaven: and whatsoever ye shall loose on earth shall be loosed in heaven.*" **(Matthew 18:18)**

> *Note: This is where the Apostles received the keys to the Kingdom of Heaven, and powers of the priesthood.*

"Then said Jesus to them again, Peace be unto you: *as my Father hath sent me, even so send I you.* And when he had said this, he breathed on them, and saith unto them, Receive ye the Holy Ghost: Whose so ever sins ye remit, they are remitted unto them; and whose so ever sins ye retain, they are retained." **(John 20:21–23)**

> *Note: Jesus who ordained the Apostles to the priesthood also gave them the "authority and power" to forgive sins! Does the Protestant "priesthood of all believers" have this authority and power? No!*

"And *he ordained twelve*, that they should be with him, and *that he might send them forth to preach*, And to have power to heal sicknesses, and to cast out devils." **(Mark 3:14–15)**

> *Note: Note the wording "he ordained" and "he might send." No one but Christ had the power or the authority to ordain or send themselves or anyone else, until Christ gave this authority to his Apostles.*

"Wherefore of these men which have companied with us all the time that the Lord Jesus went in and out among us, Beginning from the baptism of John, unto that same day that he was taken up from us, *must one be ordained* to be a witness with us of his resurrection. And they appointed two, Joseph called Barsabas, who was surnamed Justus, and Matthias. And they prayed, and said, *Thou, Lord, which knowest the hearts of all men, shew whether of these two thou hast chosen*, That he may take part of this ministry and apostleship, from which Judas by transgression fell, that he might go to his own place. And they gave forth their lots; and *the lot fell upon Matthias*; and he was numbered with the eleven apostles." **(Acts 1:21–26)**

> Note: *The eleven remaining Apostles realize that with the death of Judas Iscariot, another Apostle must be chosen to take his place among them. Matthias is chosen, called, and ordained an Apostle to replace Judas Iscariot.*

"Now there were in the church that was at Antioch certain prophets and teachers; as Barnabas, and Simeon that was called Niger, and Lucius of Cyrene, and Manaen, which had been brought up with Herod the tetrarch, and Saul. As they ministered to the Lord, and fasted, *the Holy Ghost said, Separate me Barnabas and Saul* for the work whereunto *I have called them*. And when they had fasted and prayed, and *laid their hands on them*, they sent them away." **(Acts 13:1–3)**

> Note: *Saul (Paul) and Barnabas are called and ordained Apostles.*

"Then *the twelve called* the multitude of the disciples unto them, and said, It is not reason that we should leave the word of God, and serve tables. Wherefore, brethren, look ye out among you seven men of honest report, full of the Holy Ghost and wisdom, whom we may appoint over this business. But we will give ourselves continually to prayer, and to the ministry of the word. And the saying pleased the whole multitude: *and they chose* Stephen, a man full of faith and of the Holy Ghost, and Philip, and Prochorus, and Nicanor, and Timon, and Parmenas, and Nicolas a proselyte of Antioch: *Whom they set before the apostles*: and when they had prayed, *they laid their hands on them*. And the word of God increased; and the number of the disciples multiplied in Jerusalem greatly; and a great company of *the priests* were obedient to the faith." **(Acts 6:2–7)**

> Note: *These men were all ordained to the priesthood by someone who held the priesthood, the Apostles.*

"Paul, *an apostle*, (not of men, neither by man, but *by Jesus Christ, and God the Father*, who raised him from the dead;)" **(Galatians 1:1)**

"For this cause left I thee in Crete, that thou shouldest set in order the things that are wanting, and *ordain elders in every city*, as I had appointed thee." **(Titus 1:5)**

> Note: *Titus ordains these elders by the authority of the priesthood as instructed by the Apostle Paul.*

"Now therefore ye are no more strangers and foreigners, but fellow citizens with the saints, and of the household of God; and are *built upon the foundation of apostles* and *prophets*, Jesus Christ himself being the chief corner stone; in whom all the building fitly framed together groweth unto an holy temple in the Lord: in whom ye also are builded together for an habitation of God through the Spirit." **(Ephesians 2:19–22)**

"And *he gave* some, *apostles*; and some, *prophets*; and some, *evangelists*; and some, *pastors* and *teachers*; For the perfecting of the saints, for the work of the ministry, for the edifying of the body of Christ: *Till we all come in the unity of the faith*, and of the knowledge of the Son of God, unto a perfect man, unto the measure of the stature of the fullness of Christ: *That we henceforth be no more children, tossed to and fro, and carried about with every wind of doctrine, by the sleight of men, and cunning craftiness, whereby they lie in wait to deceive.*" **(Ephesians 4:11–14)**

> Note: "*Till we all come in the unity of the faith,*" nowhere in the New Testament is it stated or indicated, or even hinted at, that the requirement for apostles and prophets was temporary. Quite to the contrary. And why? So the people would not be "*carried about with every wind of doctrine.*" Ephesians 4:11-14, is very clear; apostles, prophets, and the priesthood will be the leaders of Christ's church UNTIL we all come in the unity of the faith. With all the different Christian denominations teaching different doctrines and beliefs there is no unity of the faith yet.

"There is *one body*, and *one Spirit*, even as ye are called in one hope of your calling; One Lord, *one faith*, one baptism." **(Ephesians 4:4–5)**

"After these things *the Lord appointed other seventy* also, and sent them two and two before his face into every city and place, whither he himself would come." **(Luke 10:1)**

"And when they had *ordained them elders in every church*, and had prayed with fasting, they commended them to the Lord, on whom they believed." **(Acts 14:23)**

> Note: The apostles, Barnabas and Paul holding the priesthood and having authority ordained these elders. Ordination to the priesthood must be done by someone already holding the priesthood. Other priesthood officers of Christ's church: "Bishops" (1 Timothy 3, Titus 1:7); "Elders" (Titus 1:5); "Deacons" (Philippians 1:1).

"*Except the Lord build the house, they labour in vain that build it*: except the Lord keep the city, the watchman waketh but in vain." **(Psalms 127:1)**

"*Many pastors have destroyed my vineyard*, they have trodden my portion under foot, they have made my pleasant portion a desolate wilderness." **(Jeremiah 12:10)**

"*Woe be unto the pastors* that destroy and scatter the sheep of my pasture! saith the Lord." **(Jeremiah 23:1)**

"Now this I say, that every one of you saith, I am of Paul; and I of Apollos; and I of Cephas; and I of Christ. *Is Christ divided?* Was Paul crucified for you? Or were ye baptized in the name of Paul?" **(1 Corinthians 1:12–13**; see also verses 14–18**)**

"For *God is not the author of confusion*, but of peace, as in all the churches of the saints." **(1 Corinthians 14:33)**

"Not every one that saith unto me, Lord, Lord, shall enter into the kingdom of heaven; but he that doeth the will of my Father which is in heaven. Many will say to me in that day, Lord, Lord, have we not prophesied in thy name? and in thy name have cast out devils? and in thy name done many wonderful works? *And then will I profess unto them, I never knew you: depart from me, ye that work iniquity."* **(Matthew 7:21–23)**

> *Note: Sincerity is a wonderful attribute, but it is not a substitute for priesthood authority, power, and keys. A citizen, no matter how sincere, cannot give valid parking tickets. Why? Because he does not have the authority to do so. The same applies to the priesthood of God. A Christian minister, no matter how sincere, who was not called and ordained to the priesthood of God, by someone ordained to that priesthood, does not have priesthood authority or power. You cannot take this authority upon yourself just because you want it. Simon Magnus is a perfect example of this. (See Acts 8:17–20 below.)*

"Then laid they their hands on them, and they received the Holy Ghost. And when Simon saw that through laying on of the apostles' hands the Holy Ghost was given, *he offered them money, Saying, Give me also this power,* that on whomsoever I lay hands, he may receive the Holy Ghost. But Peter said unto him, Thy money perish with thee, because thou hast thought that the gift of God may be purchased with money." **(Acts 8:17–20)**

No matter how much it may be desired, no one can purchase the authority and power of the priesthood; nor by paying for and attending a college or divinity school can the priesthood be obtained. The only way to obtain the priesthood of God, is to be called of God and ordained to the priesthood by someone holding the priesthood and having the authority of God to ordain another.

"*For the Son of man* is as a man taking a far journey, who left his house, and *gave authority to his servants,* and to every man his work, and *commanded the porter to watch."* **(Mark 13:34)**

> *Note: This scripture teaches a very important doctrine and lesson. "The Son of Man" (Jesus Christ), gave <u>HIS authority</u> to <u>HIS servants</u> (priesthood holders, church leaders), and <u>HE commanded</u> them. He did not give authority to just anyone who may want it. Only someone duly ordained to the priesthood can bestow the priesthood onto someone else.*

"Surely the Lord God will do nothing, but he revealeth his secret *unto his servants the prophets."* **(Amos 3:7)**

"Jesus Christ the same yesterday, and today, and forever." **(Hebrews 13:8)**

Exodus 28:1–4

Exodus 28:41

Exodus 30:30

Exodus 40:12–16

Numbers 27:18–23

Jeremiah 1:4–9

Jeremiah 3:14–15

Matthew 28:19

Mark 6:7

1 Corinthians 12:12–31

2 Corinthians 11:12–15

Philippians 1:1

Titus 1:5–7

Hebrews 3:1

1 Timothy 3

1 Timothy 4:14

Interesting Note: The Apostle John is said to have died at Ephesus sometime around AD 100. According to the Catholic Church there were four popes during John's lifetime; St. Linus (AD 67–76), St. Anacletus (AD 76–88), St. Clement I (AD 88–97), and St. Evaristus (AD 97–105). Each of these men was a previous bishop before becoming the Pope. Interestingly enough in the hierarchal order of priesthood authority during the time of the original apostles, an apostle has more priesthood authority, oversees, and would ordain bishops, not the other way around. During the time of these four popes, only the Apostle John received revelation for the church. Not one Catholic Pope has yet to claim revelation from God. The Catholic Church teaches that all revelation ceased with the death of the apostles. Yet this last living apostle was under the authority of the bishops who became the pope.

See chapter 11: **"Bible — Supreme Authority — Sola Scriptura"**

Chapter 39

PROPHETS

"And he gave some, apostles; and some, prophets; and some, evangelists; and some, pastors and teachers; For the perfecting of the saints, for the work of the ministry, for the edifying of the body of Christ: Till we all come in the unity of the faith, and of the knowledge of the Son of God, unto a perfect man, unto the measure of the stature of the fullness of Christ: That we henceforth be no more children, tossed to and fro, and carried about with every wind of doctrine, by the sleight of men, and cunning craftiness, whereby they lie in wait to deceive." **(Ephesians 4:11–14)**

Christianity today teaches that God no longer speaks to mankind, that He no longer provides revelation to His church through prophets, and that He ceased to communicate with mankind after the death of John the Revelator.

Where do the scriptures declare that the heavens are closed and that there will be no more revelation from God and no more prophets? Nowhere.

Prophets

Scriptures used by some Christian faiths to substantiate their belief and teaching that Jesus Christ was the last prophet; that there have been and will be no other prophets after Him. Some Christian faiths teach that John the Baptist was the last prophet. These churches also teach that the Bible is the full, complete, and final word of God, therefore there is no need for prophets:

"God, who at sundry times and in divers manners spake in time past unto the fathers by the prophets, Hath in these last days spoken unto us by his Son, whom he hath appointed heir of all things, by whom also he made the worlds." **(Hebrews 1:1–2)**

> *Note: Paul is telling the people of his time that God spoke to His people through the prophets before the arrival of Jesus and that in "these last days" (the days of Jesus's ministry, which the Apostles considered to be the last days), that God spoke to mankind through his Son, Jesus. Paul was not talking about the time frame that modern day Christianity considers to be the "Last Days."*

Jesus said: "For all the prophets and the law prophesied until John." **(Matthew 11:13)**

Jesus said: "The law and the prophets were until John: since that time the kingdom of God is preached, and every man presseth into it." **(Luke 16:16)**

> *Note: Jesus is saying here in Matthew 11:13 and Luke 16:16, that until Him, the law of Moses was in force and God communicated to mankind through the prophets; now that I Jesus am here, I speak for God.*

Now the Rest of the Story . . . (scriptures that further explain or clarify the topic)

"Surely the Lord God will do nothing, *but he revealeth his secret unto his servants the prophets.*" **(Amos 3:7)**

"And he [the Lord] said, Hear now my words: *If there be a prophet among you,* I the Lord will make myself known unto him in a vision, and will speak unto him in a dream." **(Numbers 12:6)**

"Behold, the days come, saith the Lord God, that *I will send a famine in the land,* not a famine of bread, nor a thirst for water, but *of hearing the words of the Lord:* And they shall wander from sea to sea, and from the north even to the east, they shall run to and fro to seek the word of the Lord, *and shall not find it.*" **(Amos 8:11–12)**

> *Note: This is what happens when there are no prophets upon the Earth.*

"Behold, *I will send you Elijah the prophet before the coming of the great and dreadful day of the Lord:* And he shall turn the heart of the fathers to the children, and the heart of the children to their fathers, *lest I come and smite the earth with a curse.*" **(Malachi 4:5–6)**

"Now therefore ye are no more strangers and foreigners, but fellow citizens with the saints, and of the household of God; and are *built upon the foundation of apostles and prophets,* Jesus Christ himself being the chief corner stone; in whom all the building fitly framed together groweth unto an holy temple in the Lord: in whom ye also are builded together for an habitation of God through the Spirit." **(Ephesians 2:19–22)**

"And he said unto me, These sayings are faithful and true: and the Lord God of the *holy prophets* sent his angel to shew unto his servants the things which must shortly be done." **(Revelation 22:6)**

> *Note: See Amos 3:7 above, again.*

"And I saw another angel fly in the midst of heaven, *having the everlasting gospel to preach unto them that dwell on the earth,* and to every nation, and kindred, and tongue, and people." **(Revelation 14:6)**

> *Note: Why would another angel have to bring the gospel to all those who dwell on the Earth if the true, complete, inerrant and uncorrupted gospel was already here?*

"When a prophet *speaketh in the name of the Lord,* if the thing follow not, nor come to pass, that is the thing which the Lord hath not spoken, but the prophet hath spoken it presumptuously: thou shalt not be afraid of him." **(Deuteronomy 18:22)**

> *Note: This scripture tells us how to recognize a true prophet.*

"*He that receiveth a prophet in the name of a prophet shall receive a prophet's reward;* and he that receiveth a righteous man in the name of a righteous man shall receive a righteous man's reward." **(Matthew 10:41)**

PROPHETS BEFORE JESUS CHRIST

Noah (Genesis 6:8–9)
Joseph (Genesis 37:5–10)
Aaron (Exodus 7:1)
Joshua (Joshua 1:1–9)
Moses (Exodus 3:1–4)
Moses (Deuteronomy 34:10)
Samuel (1 Samuel 3:20–21)
Gad (1 Samuel 22:5)
Nathan (2 Samuel 7:2)
Solomon (1 Kings 9:2–9)
Ahijah (1 Kings 14:2)
Jehu (1 Kings 16:7)
Elijah (1 Kings 18:22)
Elisha (1 Kings 4:20–36)

Isaiah (2 Kings 19:2)
Shemaiah (2 Chronicles 12:5)
Iddo (2 Chronicles 13:22)
Oded (2 Chronicles 15:8)
Jonas (Matthew 12:39)
Esaias (Matthew 3:3–4)
Jeremy (Matthew 2:17)
John the Baptist (Matthew 11:9–10)
Zechariah (Ezra 5:1–6)
Haggai (Haggai 1:1–3)
Azur (Jeremiah 28:1)
Ezekiel (Ezekiel 1–48)
Daniel (Daniel 1:17)

Joel (Joel 1:1)
Obadiah (Obadiah 1)
Jonah (Jonah 1–2)
Micah (Micah 1:1)
Nahum (Nahum 1–3)
Habakkuk (Habakkuk 1–3)
Zephaniah (Zephaniah 1–3)
Jeremiah (2 Chronicles 36:12)
Malachi (Malachi 1–4)

The following Prophets are listed in the New Testament as having become prophets after the death of Jesus Christ.

"Now *there were in the church that was at Antioch certain prophets* and teachers; as *Barnabas*, and *Simeon* that was called Niger, and *Lucius of Cyrene*, and *Manaen*, which had been brought up with Herod the tetrarch, and Saul." (**Acts 13:1**)

"And *Judas* and *Silas*, being *prophets* also themselves, exhorted the brethren with many words, and confirmed them." (**Acts 15:32**)

"And in these days came *prophets* from Jerusalem unto Antioch. And there stood up *one of them named Agabus*, and signified by the Spirit that there should be great dearth throughout all the world: which came to pass in the days of Claudius Cæsar." (**Acts 11:27–28**; see also **Acts 21:10**)

CONCLUSION

Jesus Christ and the Apostles were NOT the last prophets.

Christianity today teaches that God no longer talks to mankind, that he no longer provides revelation to His church, and that God ceased to communicate with mankind after the death of John the Revelator.

Where do the scriptures declare that the heavens are closed and that there will be no more revelation from God and no more prophets? Nowhere.

If God loved His children enough anciently to give them prophets who could receive direct revelation that would bless their lives, then He would also do so today. If He did not, then He would be an unjust God, favoring one generation of His children over another. Does God love today's generation of His children less than He did in previous generations of His children? Of course not.

"Jesus Christ the same yesterday, and to day, and for ever." (**Hebrews 13:8**)

"Therefore also said the wisdom of God, *I will send them prophets* and apostles, *and some of them they shall slay and persecute.*" (**Luke 11:49**)

> Note: *The scriptures and history show that mankind has persecuted and killed the prophets and apostles of God throughout the Old Testament, the New Testament, and since.*

"And *he gave* some, *apostles*; and some, *prophets*; and some, *evangelists*; and some, pastors and teachers; For the perfecting of the saints, for the work of the ministry, for the edifying of the body of Christ: *Till we all come in the unity of the faith*, and of the knowledge of the Son of God, unto a perfect man, unto the measure of the stature of the fullness of Christ: *That we henceforth be no more children, tossed to and fro, and carried about with every wind of doctrine, by the sleight of men, and cunning craftiness, whereby they lie in wait to deceive.*" (**Ephesians 4:11–14**)

> *Note: "Till we all come in the unity of the faith," nowhere in the New Testament is it stated or indicated, or even hinted at, that the requirement for prophets was temporary. Quite to the contrary. And why? So the people would not be "carried about with every wind of doctrine."*

> *Ephesians 4:11–14 is very clear: Prophets, Apostles, and the priesthood will be the leaders of Christ's church UNTIL we all come in the unity of the faith. With all the different Christian denominations teaching different doctrines and beliefs, there is no unity of the faith yet.*

"Fear them not therefore: for *there is nothing covered, that shall not be revealed; and hid, that shall not be known.*" (**Matthew 10:26**)

> *Note: How can things not covered and hid be revealed without revelation? And who will this revelation be given to and received by if we have not prophets? This verse tells us that ALL things not revealed will eventually be revealed to Christ's Church, His prophets, His priesthood leaders, and to mankind.*

See chapter 43: "**Revelation**"

CHAPTER 40

REPENTANCE

"But shewed first unto them of Damascus, and at Jerusalem, and throughout all the coasts of Judæa, and then to the Gentiles, that they should repent and turn to God, and do works meet for repentance." **(Acts 26:20)**

Is a simple confession and believing in Christ all that is necessary for repentance?

REPENTANCE

Scriptures used by some Christian faiths to substantiate their belief and teaching about Repentance:

"That if thou shalt confess with thy mouth the Lord Jesus, and shalt believe in thine heart that God hath raised him from the dead, thou shalt be saved. For with the heart man believeth unto righteousness; and with the mouth confession is made unto salvation." **(Romans 10:9–10)**

NOW THE REST OF THE STORY . . . (scriptures that further explain or clarify the topic)

"I tell you, Nay: but, *except ye repent, ye shall all likewise perish.*" **(Luke 13:3)**

"*Repent*, and be baptized every one of you in the name of Jesus Christ, *for the remission of sins*, and you shall receive the gift of the Holy Ghost." **(Acts 2:38**; see also verses 37 & 39)

"*Repent* ye therefore, and be converted, *that your sins may be blotted out*, when the times of refreshing shall come from the presence of the Lord." **(Acts 3:19)**

"From that time Jesus began to preach, and to say, *Repent*: for the kingdom of heaven is at hand." **(Matthew 4:17)**

"But go ye and learn what that meaneth, I will have mercy, and not sacrifice: for I am not come to call the righteous, but *sinners to repentance.*" **(Matthew 9:13)**

"And saying, The time is fulfilled, and the kingdom of God is at hand: *repent* ye, and *believe the gospel.*" **(Mark 1:15)**

"But shewed first unto them of Damascus, and at Jerusalem, and throughout all the coasts of Judæa, and then to the Gentiles, *that they should repent and turn to God, and do works meet for repentance.*" **(Acts 26:20)**

"*For godly sorrow worketh repentance to salvation* not to be repented of: but the sorrow of the world worketh death." **(2 Corinthians 4:10)**

"And I gave her space to repent of her fornication; and she repented not. Behold, I will cast her into a bed, and them that commit adultery with her into great tribulation, *except they repent of their deeds.*" **(Revelation 2:21)**

"If we say that we have no sin, we deceive ourselves, and the truth is not in us. *If we confess our sins, he is faithful and just to forgive us our sins, and to cleanse us from all unrighteousness.* If we say that we have not sinned, we make him a liar, and his word is not in us." **(1 John 1:8–10)**

"*He that covereth his sins shall not prosper*: but whoso confesseth and forsaketh them shall have mercy." **(Proverbs 28:13)**

See chapter 18: "**Faith, Grace & Works — Sincere Belief Is Not Enough**"

CHAPTER 41

RESTORATION OF THE GOSPEL & CHRIST'S CHURCH

"Repent ye therefore, and be converted, that your sins may be blotted out, when the times of refreshing shall come from the presence of the Lord; And he shall send Jesus Christ, which before was preached unto you: Whom the heaven must receive until the times of restitution of all things, which God hath spoken by the mouth of all his holy prophets since the world began." (**Acts 3:19–21**)

The Catholic and Protestant churches do not believe that priesthood authority or Christ's original church have ever been lost or taken away from the Earth. The Catholic Church declares that priesthood authority has been in place since the Apostle Peter and succeeded through the Popes. The Protestant churches do not believe in priesthood authority and believe that the Catholic church corrupted the teachings and doctrines of Christ's original church, which then needed to be reformed or taught again. Neither the Catholic nor Protestant churches believe in revelation from God that would allow for modern day prophets and a restoration of Christ's church.

RESTORATION OF THE GOSPEL & CHRIST'S CHURCH

Scriptures used by some Christian faiths to substantiate their belief and teaching that there is no more revelation, or that God will not send His angels with revelation to his children on this earth:

"But though we, or an angel from heaven, preach any other gospel unto you than that which we have preached unto you, let him be accursed." **(Galatians 1:8)**

"As we said before, so say I now again, If any man preach any other gospel unto you than that ye have received, let him be accursed." **(Galatians 1:9)**

NOW THE REST OF THE STORY . . . (scriptures that further explain or clarify the topic)

"And his disciples asked him, saying, Why then say the scribes that *Elias must first come?* And Jesus answered and said unto them, Elias truly shall first come, *and restore all things.* But I say unto you, That Elias is come already, and they knew him not, but have done unto him whatsoever they listed. Likewise shall also the Son of man suffer of them. Then the disciples understood that he spake unto them of John the Baptist." **(Matthew 17:10–13**; see also **Mark 9:2–13** and **Luke 9:28–36)**

> *Note: During the time of Christ's ministry, just what did John the Baptist restore? Nothing. John preached "baptism and repentance for the remission of sins," which was nothing new to the Israelites as they had been practicing baptism for hundreds of years already. Matthew 17:10–13 tells us that Elias (John) must "come first (return) and restore all things." Mark and Luke do not mention John the Baptist as being "Elias," only Matthew does.*

"The Revelation of Jesus Christ, which God gave unto him, to shew unto his servants things which must shortly come to pass; and *he sent and signified it by his angel* unto his servant John." **(Revelation 1:1)**

"And I saw another angel fly in the midst of heaven, *having the everlasting gospel to preach unto them that dwell on the earth,* and to every nation, and kindred, and tongue, and people." **(Revelation 14:6)**

> *Note: Why would God send an angel to preach the gospel to every nation and people if it was already upon the earth in an uncorrupted form?*

"But though we, or an angel from heaven, preach any other gospel unto you than that which we have preached unto you, let him be accursed." **(Galatians 1:8)**

> *Note: Many churches will use Galatians 1:8 in their defense against the angle Moroni coming to Joseph Smith, or that there is no more revelation,*

or that God will not send His angles with revelation to his children on this earth. How can they explain Revelation 1:1 & 14:6 above?

Note: See the chapter "Angels" in this book.

"Behold, *I will send you Elijah the prophet before the coming of the great and dreadful day of the Lord*: And he shall turn the heart of the fathers to the children, and the heart of the children to their fathers, lest I come and smite the earth with a curse." **(Malachi 4:5–6)**

> *Note: **Can any other church document the return of Elijah the prophet? And if so, what did he do to turn the heart of the fathers to the children, and the heart of the children to their fathers?***

"Repent ye therefore, and be converted, that your sins may be blotted out, when the times of refreshing shall come from the presence of the Lord; And he shall send Jesus Christ, which before was preached unto you: *Whom the heaven must receive until* the times of *restitution of all things*, which God hath spoken by the mouth of all his holy prophets since the world began." **(Acts 3:19–21)**

> *Note: **"the times of refreshing," and the "times of restitution." What do these words and phrases mean? These terms denote a return of something that was once present but that has been taken away or lost, a restoration.***

"That in the *dispensation of the fullness of times* he might gather together in one all things in Christ, both which are in heaven, and which are on earth; even in him." **(Ephesians 1:10)**

"The word of the Lord came again unto me, saying, Moreover, thou son of man, take thee one stick, and *write upon it, For Judah*, and for the children of Israel his companions: then take another stick, and *write upon it, For Joseph*, the stick of Ephraim, and for all the house of Israel his companions: *And join them one to another into one stick*; and they shall become one in thine hand. And when the children of thy people shall speak unto thee, saying, Wilt thou not shew us what thou meanest by these? Say unto them, Thus saith the Lord God; Behold, I will take the stick of Joseph, which is in the hand of Ephraim, and the tribes of Israel his fellows, and will put them with him, even with the stick of Judah, and make them one stick, and they shall be one in mine hand. *And the sticks whereon thou writest shall be in thine hand before their eyes.*" **(Ezekiel 37:15–20)**

> *Note: **What is the Book of Judah? Where is it? The answer: the Bible.***

WHAT IS THE BOOK OF JOSEPH? WHERE IS IT? THE ANSWER . . . THE BOOK OF MORMON.

"One Lord, *one faith*, one baptism." **(Ephesians 4:5)**

> *Note: **Neither Christ nor His Apostles established different churches teaching different doctrines. When the churches did stray, when they did change the doctrines they were taught, they were chastised and warned that if they did not return to the fold and teach the truth, they would lose their authority and priesthood to act in the name of God and Jesus Christ.***

Only seven churches *still remained that were worthy of mention in the book of Revelation, and the seeds of apostasy were evident even in them.* (Revelation 1:11–20; 2:1–5; 3:14–19)

> "Surely the Lord God will do nothing, *but he revealeth his secret unto his servants the prophets.*" (**Amos 3:7**)

See chapter 3: "**Apostasy of the Christian Church**"

CHAPTER 42

RESURRECTION OF THE PHYSICAL BODY

"And though after my skin worms destroy this body, yet in my flesh shall I see God." (**Job 19:26**)

One of the core beliefs of Christians is that after death, at the time of judgement, the physical body will again be reunited with the spirit and resurrected, never again to be separated. Thereafter to enjoy eternal bliss or eternal pain and suffering. Some Christian faiths however believe that only the "spirit of man" will survive the final judgement.

RESURRECTION OF THE PHYSICAL BODY

Scriptures used by some Christian faiths to substantiate their belief and teaching that there is no resurrection of the physical body. Those that hold this belief teach that only the "spirit of man" will survive the final judgment.

"Now this I say, brethren, that flesh and blood cannot inherit the kingdom of God; neither doth corruption inherit incorruption." **(1 Corinthians 15:50)**

"So also is the resurrection of the dead. It is sown in corruption; it is raised in incorruption: It is sown in dishonour; it is raised in glory: it is sown in weakness; it is raised in power: It is sown a natural body; it is raised a spiritual body. There is a natural body, and there is a spiritual body." **(1 Corinthians 15:42–44)**

"All flesh shall perish together, and man shall turn again unto dust." **(Job 34:15)**

> *Note: These churches that teach there is no resurrection of man's physical body, like all Christian churches, teach and believe in the Resurrection of Christ's physical body.*

NOW THE REST OF THE STORY . . . (scriptures that further explain or clarify the topic)

"And though after my skin worms destroy this body, *yet in my flesh shall I see God.*" **(Job 19:26)**

"Marvel not at this: for the hour is coming, in the which *all that are in the graves shall hear his voice, And shall come forth; they that have done good, unto the resurrection of life*; and they that have done evil, unto the resurrection of damnation." **(John 5:28–29)**

"And have hope toward God, which they themselves also allow, that *there shall be a resurrection of the dead, both of the just and unjust.*" **(Acts 24:15)**

"But now is Christ risen from the dead, and become the firstfruits of them that slept. For since by man came death, *by man came also the resurrection of the dead.* For as in Adam all die, even so in Christ shall all be made alive." **(1 Corinthians 15:20–22)**

"Else what shall they do which are baptized for the dead, if the dead rise not at all? why are they then baptized for the dead?" **(1 Corinthians 15:29)**

"And as they thus spake, Jesus himself stood in the midst of them, and saith unto them, Peace be unto you. But they were terrified and affrighted, and supposed that they had seen a spirit. And he said unto them, Why are ye troubled? and why do thoughts arise in your hearts? Behold my hands and my feet, that it is I myself: handle me, and see; for *a spirit hath not flesh and bones, as ye see me have.*" **(Luke 24:36–39)**

> *Note: The first time the Apostles saw Jesus after His Resurrection, they thought that He was a spirit. He then showed them that He was indeed a*

resurrected body of flesh and bones and instructed them to "handle me, and see."

"And he led them out as far as to Bethany, and he lifted up his hands, and blessed them. And it came to pass, while he blessed them, *he was parted from them, and carried up into heaven.* And they worshipped him, and returned to Jerusalem with great joy: And were continually in the temple, praising and blessing God. Amen." **(Luke 24:50–53)**

> *Note: When Christ was resurrected, He took His "glorified physical body" of flesh and bone with Him.*

"For if we have been planted together in the likeness of his death, *we shall be also in the likeness of his resurrection."* **(Romans 6:5)**

> *Note: When we are resurrected, we will take our "glorified physical body" of flesh and bone with us. Just as the Savior did with His Resurrection.*

"And while they looked steadfastly toward heaven as he went up, behold, two men stood by them in white apparel; Which also said, Ye men of Galilee, why stand ye gazing up into heaven? *this same Jesus, which is taken up from you into heaven, shall so come in like manner as ye have seen him go into heaven."* **(Acts 1:10–11)**

> *Note: Jesus was resurrected with His glorified physical body and will return with His glorified physical body.*

"Who shall *change our vile body,* that it may be fashioned *like unto his glorious body,* according to the working whereby he is able even to subdue all things unto himself." **(Philippians 3:21)**

"There are also celestial bodies, and bodies terrestrial: but the *glory of the celestial* is one, and the *glory of the terrestrial* is another. There is one glory of the sun, and another glory of the moon, and another glory of the stars: for one star differeth from another star in glory. *So also is the resurrection of the dead.* It is sown in corruption; it is raised in incorruption." **(1 Corinthians 15:40–42)**

"For the wages of sin is death; but *the gift of God is eternal life through Jesus Christ our Lord."* **(Romans 6:23)**

See chapter 24: **"Heaven — Hell — Degrees of Glory"**
See chapter 40: **"Repentance"**
See chapter 7: **"Baptism for the Dead"**
See chapter 46: **"Salvation for the Dead"**
See chapter 45: **"Salvation for All Mankind"**
See chapter 5: **"Atonement of Jesus Christ"**

CHAPTER 43

REVELATION

"Surely the Lord God will do nothing, but he revealeth his secret unto his servants the prophets." **(Amos 3:7)**

Modern-day Christianity teaches that God no longer provides guidance through revelation to His church, that He ceased to communicate with mankind after the death of John the Revelator. Today's Christianity also teaches that due to this lack of revelation that the teachings recorded in the Bible are ALL of God's teachings and that there can be no more teachings nor doctrine to be revealed.

REVELATION

Christ originally instructed the Apostles that they were to preach ONLY to the house of Israel and NOT to the Gentiles, (Matthew 10:5–6). Then after his death and resurrection he gave Peter, through revelation, a spiritual change order to take the gospel to the Gentiles (Acts 10). Peter's experience taught two important principles of Christ's church: first, the teachings and doctrine of the church could be changed, but ONLY by revelation from Christ, and second, that such revelation will come to and ONLY to the prophet who is God's spokesman on the earth. Simply put, God's church will be governed by divine revelation and order. Without revelation, Christ's church would be no more than a man-run organization governed by the powers of reason and the philosophies of men mingled with scripture.

Scriptures used by some Christian faiths to substantiate their belief and teaching that there is no more revelation from God, and that God will not send His angles with revelation to his children on this earth:

"But though we, or an angel from heaven, preach any other gospel unto you than that which we have preached unto you, let him be accursed." **(Galatians 1:8)**

"As we said before, so say I now again, If any man preach any other gospel unto you than that ye have received, let him be accursed." **(Galatians 1:9)**

> *Note: See Galatians 1:11–12 below.*

"Grace and peace be multiplied unto you through the knowledge of God, and of Jesus our Lord, According as his divine power hath given unto us all things that pertain unto life and godliness, through the knowledge of him that hath called us to glory and virtue." **(2 Peter 1:2–3)**

> *Note: See John 16:12–13 below. In verse 12, Jesus tells His Apostles that He has much more to tell them, to teach them, but that they are not ready to receive them yet and that the Holy Ghost will bring these things to them later.*

"Being born again, not of corruptible seed, but of incorruptible, by the word of God, which liveth and abideth for ever. For all flesh is as grass, and all the glory of man as the flower of grass. The grass withereth, and the flower thereof falleth away: But the word of the Lord endureth for ever. And this is the word which by the gospel is preached unto you." **(1 Peter 1:23–25)**

Protestantism: Protestants generally teach that the modern age is not a period of continuing revelation. Although there are some non-Catholic and Protestant faiths that accept the doctrine of personal or individual revelation.

Roman Catholicism: Vatican II states that "no new public revelation is to be expected before the glorious manifestation of our Lord, Jesus Christ." The notion of progressive or continuing revelation is not held by the Roman Catholic Church or by Eastern Orthodoxy, who instead favor the idea of tradition and development of doctrine, while progressivist and continuationist approaches are specifically condemned in the declaration Dominus Iesus.[1]

Now the Rest of the Story . . . (scriptures that further explain or clarify the topic)

"Fear them not therefore: for *there is nothing covered, that shall not be revealed; and hid, that shall not be known.*" (**Matthew 10:26**)

> *Note: How can things not covered and hid be revealed without revelation? This verse tells us that there are things not covered and hidden, and that ALL things not revealed will eventually be revealed to mankind.*

"The Revelation of Jesus Christ, which God gave unto him, to shew unto his servants things which must shortly come to pass; and he sent and signified it *by his angel* unto his servant John." (**Revelation 1:1**)

"And I saw another angel fly in the midst of heaven, *having the everlasting gospel* to preach unto them that dwell on the earth, and to every nation, and kindred, and tongue, and people." (**Revelation 14:6**)

"But though we, or an angel from heaven, preach any other gospel unto you than that which we have preached unto you, let him be accursed." (**Galatians 1:8**)

> *Note: Many churches will use Galatians 1:8 in their defense against the angle Moroni coming to Joseph Smith, or that there is no more revelation, or that God will not send His angles with revelation to his children on this earth. How can they explain Revelation 1:1 and 14:6 above?*

"For do I now persuade men, or God? or *do I seek to please men?* for if I yet pleased men, I should not be the servant of Christ." (**Galatians 1:10**)

> *Note: Many churches are doing exactly this, the "pleasing of men." The making of Christianity "easy," the making of Christianity "palatable" serves to bring more members into their churches while corrupting the teachings and doctrines of Christ.*

"But I certify you, brethren, that the gospel which was preached of me is not after man. For I neither received it of man, neither was I taught it, but by *the revelation of Jesus Christ.*" (**Galatians 1:11–12**)

> *Note: Paul declares here that he received the gospel he preached by revelation from Jesus Christ, which happened after the Savior's death. Paul was not a disciple or follower of Jesus, he was a persecutor of Christians before his vision of the Savior and his conversion.*

"Behold, *I will send you Elijah the prophet before the coming of the great and dreadful day of the Lord*: And he shall turn the heart of the fathers to the children, and the heart of the children to their fathers, lest I come and smite the earth with a curse." **(Malachi 4:5–6)**

"*I have yet many things to say unto you, but ye cannot bear them now.* Howbeit when he, the Spirit of truth, is come, he will guide you into all truth: for he shall not speak of himself; but whatsoever he shall hear, that shall he speak: and he will shew you things to come." **(John 16:12–13)**

> Note: See John 16:1–11, Jesus is telling the Apostles of His death and Resurrection, that He must now go to His Father, and that the Holy Ghost will come. In verse 12 above, He tells His Apostles that He has much more to tell them, to teach them, but that they are not ready to receive them yet and that the Holy Ghost will bring these things to them later. This verse explains 2 Peter 1:2–3 above.

"*If any of you lack wisdom, let him ask of God,* that giveth to all men liberally, and upbraideth not; *and it shall be given him.* But let him ask in faith, nothing wavering. For he that wavereth is like a wave of the sea driven with the wind and tossed. For let not that man think that he shall receive any thing of the Lord." **(James 1:5–7)**

"And his disciples asked him, saying, Why then say the scribes *that Elias must first come*? And Jesus answered and said unto them, Elias truly shall first come, *and restore all things.* But I say unto you, That Elias is come already, and they knew him not, but have done unto him whatsoever they listed. Likewise shall also the Son of man suffer of them. Then the disciples understood that he spake unto them of John the Baptist." **(Matthew 17:10–13)**

> Note: During the time of Christ's ministry, just what did John the Baptist restore? Nothing. John preached "baptism and repentance for the remission of sins," which was nothing new to the Israelites as they had been practicing baptism for hundreds of years already. Matthew 17:10–13 tells us that Elias (John) must "come first (return) and restore all things."

"That in the *dispensation of the fullness of times* he might *gather together* in one *all things in Christ,* both *which are in heaven,* and *which are on earth*; even in him." **(Ephesians 1:10)**

> Note: We are now in the "Dispensation of the Fullness of Times," and this gathering has not happened yet.

"Surely the Lord God will do nothing, *but he revealeth his secret unto his servants the prophets.*" **(Amos 3:7)**

"*Where there is no vision,* the people perish." **(Proverbs 29:18)**

"And it shall come to pass *in the last days,* saith God, I will pour out of my Spirit upon all flesh: and *your sons and your daughters shall prophesy,* and your young men shall see visions, and your old men shall dream dreams: And on my servants and on my handmaidens I will pour out in those days of my Spirit; *and they shall prophesy.*" **(Acts 2:17–18)**

Where do the scriptures declare that the heavens are closed and that there will be no more revelation from God? Without revelation, all would be guesswork, confusion, and darkness.

Why do we not have any current revelation from God? The good news is . . . We do!

The Lord continues to talk to His children today just as He did anciently. If he loved His children enough anciently, enough to give them prophets who could receive direct revelation that would bless their lives, then He would do so also today. If He did not, then He would be an unjust God, favoring one generation of His children over another. Does God love today's generation of his children less than He did previous generations of His children? Of course not.

"Jesus Christ the same yesterday, and to day, and for ever." **(Hebrews 13:8)**

See chapter 8: "**Bible — Add To or Take Away From**"
See chapter 9: "**Bible Errors — Contradictions — Inerrancy**"
See chapter 10: "**Bible Incomplete — Missing Scripture**"
See chapter 39: "**Prophets**"

CHAPTER 44

SABBATH

"And he said unto them, The sabbath was made for man, and not man for the sabbath: Therefore the Son of man is Lord also of the sabbath." **(Mark 2:27–28)**

The majority of Christians celebrate the sabbath on Sunday, while some do so on Saturday, yet others begin the sabbath on Friday when the sun goes down and finish the sabbath at sundown Saturday, in the Jewish tradition (e.g. Seventh-day Adventists, Seventh Day Baptists).

SABBATH

Scriptures used by some Christian faiths to substantiate their belief and teaching about the Sabbath. Some Christian churches celebrate the Sabbath on Saturday while most do so on Sunday:

"Remember the sabbath day, to keep it holy." **(Exodus 20:8)**

"Six days shalt thou labour, and do all thy work: But the seventh day is the sabbath of the Lord thy God: in it thou shalt not do any work, thou, nor thy son, nor thy daughter, thy manservant, nor thy maidservant, nor thy cattle, nor thy stranger that is within thy gates." **(Exodus 20:9–10)**

"Six days may work be done; but in the seventh is the sabbath of rest, holy to the Lord: whosoever doeth any work in the sabbath day, he shall surely be put to death. Wherefore the children of Israel shall keep the sabbath, to observe the sabbath throughout their generations, for a perpetual covenant." **(Exodus 31:15–16**; see also **Exodus 35:2)**

NOW THE REST OF THE STORY . . . (scriptures that further explain or clarify the topic)

"And upon the first day of the week, when the disciples came together to break bread, Paul preached unto them, ready to depart on the morrow; and continued his speech until midnight." **(Acts 20:7)**

"Now concerning the collection for the saints, *as I have given order to the churches of Galatia,* even so do ye. *Upon the first day of the week* let every one of you lay by him in store, as God hath prospered him, that there be no gatherings when I come." **(1 Corinthians 16:1–2)**

"One man esteemeth one day above another: another esteemeth every day alike. Let every man be fully persuaded in his own mind. *He that regardeth the day, regardeth it unto the Lord;* and he that regardeth not the day, to the Lord he doth not regard it. He that eateth, eateth to the Lord, for he giveth God thanks; and he that eateth not, to the Lord he eateth not, and giveth God thanks." **(Romans 14:5–6)**

"Let no man therefore judge you in meat, or in drink, or *in respect of an holyday,* or of the new moon, *or of the sabbath days*: Which are a shadow of things to come; but the body is of Christ." **(Colossians 2:16–17)**

"And he said unto them, *The sabbath was made for man,* and not man for the sabbath: Therefore *the Son of man is Lord also of the sabbath.*" **(Mark 2:27–28)**

"For I have received of the Lord that which also I delivered unto you, That the Lord Jesus the same night in which he was betrayed took bread: And when he had given thanks, he brake it, and said, Take, *eat: this is my body,* which is broken for you: *this do in remembrance of me.*" **(1 Corinthians 11:23–24)**

"For as often as ye eat this bread, and drink this cup, ye do shew the Lord's death till he come." **(1 Corinthians 11:26)**

"But let a man examine himself, and so let him eat of that bread, and drink of that cup. For *he that eateth and drinketh unworthily, eateth and drinketh damnation to himself*, not discerning the Lord's body." **(1 Corinthians 11:28–29)**

CHAPTER 45

SALVATION FOR
ALL MANKIND

"There are also celestial bodies, and bodies terrestrial: but the glory of the celestial is one, and the glory of the terrestrial is another. There is one glory of the sun, and another glory of the moon, and another glory of the stars: for one star differeth from another star in glory. So also is the resurrection of the dead. It is sown in corruption; it is raised in incorruption." **(1 Corinthians 15:40–42)**

Some Christian churches teach that all mankind will be "saved" if only they believe in Jesus Christ. Others believe that one must be baptized also. And some believe that unless the believer belongs to their particular church, there will be no salvation for them. Some churches teach that unless a person believes in Christ and is baptized, their soul will spend eternity is Hell, even those unfortunates who may have never heard of Christ.

SALVATION FOR ALL MANKIND

Scriptures used by some Christian faiths to substantiate their belief and teachings about Salvation; the Grace of God and faith are all that is needed for salvation:

"For by grace are ye saved through faith; and that not of yourselves: it is the gift of God: Not of works, lest any man should boast." (**Ephesians 2:8–9**)

"He that believeth and is baptized shall be saved; but he that believeth not shall be damned." (**Mark 16:16**)

Now See . . .

"He who has believed and has been baptized shall be saved." (**Mark 16:16 NASV**)

> *Note: The New American Standard Version of the Bible says "He who has believed," past tense. In other words if you "once believed" and now no longer do, it's okay, you will be saved anyway.*

"Verily, verily, I say unto you, He that heareth my word, and believeth on him that sent me, hath everlasting life, and shall not come into condemnation; but is passed from death unto life." (**John 5:24**)

"That if thou shalt confess with thy mouth the Lord Jesus, and shalt believe in thine heart that God hath raised him from the dead, thou shalt be saved." (**Romans 10:9**)

"For whosoever shall call upon the name of the Lord shall be saved." (**Romans 10:13**)

> *Note: Romans 10:9 and 13 are often used by those churches teaching that baptism is not a requirement. See also Ephesians 1:7, Colossians 1:14, and 1 John 1:7.*

"Who are kept by the power of God through faith unto salvation ready to be revealed in the last time." (**1 Peter 1:5**)

"And all flesh shall see the salvation of God." (**Luke 3:6**)

"And he said to the woman, Thy faith hath saved thee; go in peace." (**Luke 7:50**)

"And they said, Believe on the Lord Jesus Christ, and thou shalt be saved, and thy house." (**Acts 16:31**)

"Whoso eateth my flesh, and drinketh my blood, hath eternal life; and I will raise him up at the last day" (**John 6:53–54**)

Now the Rest of the Story . . . (scriptures that further explain or clarify the topic)

"And she shall bring forth a son, and thou shalt call his name *Jesus: for he shall save his people from their sins.*" (**Matthew 1:21**)

"And being made perfect, he became the author of eternal salvation *unto all them that obey him.*" (**Hebrews 5:9**)

"Then said one unto him, Lord, *are there few that be saved?* And he said unto them, Strive to enter in at the strait gate: *for many, I say unto you, will seek to enter in, and shall not be able.*" (**Luke 13:23–24**)

"Esaias also crieth concerning Israel, Though the number of the children of Israel be as the sand of the sea, *a remnant shall be saved.*" (**Romans 9:27**)

"Marvel not at this: for the hour is coming, in the which all that are in the graves shall hear his voice, And shall come forth; *they that have done good, unto the resurrection of life; and they that have done evil, unto the resurrection of damnation.*" (**John 5:28–29**)

"*Jesus said unto her, I am the resurrection, and the life*: he that believeth in me, though he were dead, yet shall he live: And whosoever liveth and believeth in me shall never die. Believest thou this?" (**John 11:25–26**)

"And *no man hath ascended up to heaven, but he that came down from heaven*, even the Son of man which is in heaven." (**John 3:13**)

"Therefore my heart is glad, and my glory rejoiceth: my flesh also shall rest in hope. *For thou wilt not leave my soul in hell*; neither wilt thou suffer thine Holy One to see corruption." (**Psalms 16:9–10**)

"But this I confess unto thee, that after the way which they call heresy, so worship I the God of my fathers, believing all things which are written in the law and in the prophets: And have hope toward God, which they themselves also allow, that *there shall be a resurrection of the dead, both of the just and unjust.*" (**Acts 24:14–15**)

"And I saw the dead, small and great, stand before God; and the books were opened: and another book was opened, which is the book of life: and the dead were judged out of those things which were written in the books, according to their works. And the sea gave up the dead which were in it; and death and hell delivered up the dead which were in them: and *they were judged every man according to their works.*" (**Revelation 20:12–13**)

"But after thy hardness and impenitent heart treasurest up unto thyself wrath against the day of wrath and revelation of the righteous judgment of God; *Who will render to every man according to his deeds.*" (**Romans 2:5–6**)

"For Christ also hath once suffered for sins, the just for the unjust, that he might bring us to God, being put to death in the flesh, but quickened by the Spirit: By which *he went and preached unto the spirits in prison*: Which sometimes are disobedient, when once the long-suffering of God waited in the days of Noah, while the ark was preparing, wherein few, that is, 8 souls were saved by water." (**1 Peter 3:18–20**)

"*For this cause was the gospel preached also to them that are dead, that they might be judged according to men in the flesh*, but live according to God in the spirit." (**1 Peter 4:6**)

"But *if the wicked will turn from all his sins that he hath committed, and keep all my statutes,* and do that which is lawful and right, *he shall surely live, he shall not die.* All his transgressions that he hath committed, they shall not be mentioned unto him: in his righteousness that he hath done he shall live." **(Ezekiel 18:21–22)**

SALVATION VERSUS EXALTATION

The teachings about grace in the second chapter of Ephesians are perhaps the most quoted by evangelical, Nicean, and protestant Christians. "For by grace are ye saved," Paul taught the Ephesians, "through faith; and that not of yourselves: it is the gift of God: not of works, lest any man should boast" (Ephesians 2:8–9). When reading these two verses, the student of the scriptures must be aware of the meaning of "saved" versus the meaning of "exalted."

Men are thus saved by grace alone, in the sense of being resurrected, as all mankind will be resurrected; they are saved by grace coupled with obedience, in the sense of gaining eternal life.

The gospel plan is to save men into the Celestial Kingdom, and thus Paul teaches salvation by grace through faith, through obedience, through accepting Christ, through keeping the commandments.

Thus, all will be resurrected, saved in that sense, by grace, by the gift of Christ through His death on the cross and His resurrection. And all who desire to be exalted, that is to live again in the presence of God the Father, in the Celestial Kingdom, must be obedient to the laws of the Gospel as given by Jesus Christ, and through His atonement, His suffering in Gethsemane, and on the cross.

Evangelical, Nicean, and protestant Christians do not differentiate between salvation and exaltation; for them there is no such thing as exaltation or degrees of glory as stated in **1 Corinthians 15:40–42**, only salvation, meaning eternal life.

"There are also celestial bodies, and bodies terrestrial: but the *glory of the celestial* is one, and the *glory of the terrestrial* is another. There is one glory of the sun, and another glory of the moon, and another glory of the stars: for one star differeth from another star in glory. *So also is the resurrection of the dead.* It is sown in corruption; it is raised in incorruption." **(1 Corinthians 15:40–42)**

"*I knew a man in Christ* above fourteen years ago, (whether in the body, I cannot tell; or whether out of the body, I cannot tell: God knoweth;) such an one caught up to *the third heaven.*" **(2 Corinthians 12:2)**

Note: 2 Corinthians 12:2 and 1 Corinthians 15:40–42 unmistakably tell us that "salvation" is nothing like the "Protestant" definition of "universal salvation for all" by the "Grace of God." These verses inform us that there are different "degrees of salvation and glory" or exaltation. What does man have to do to achieve salvation to one of these "degrees of glory"?

CHAPTER 46

SALVATION FOR THE DEAD

"For this cause was the gospel preached also to them that are dead, that they might be judged according to men in the flesh, but live according to God in the spirit." **(1 Peter 4:6)**

Almost all Christian churches teach that unless a person believes in Christ and is baptized while in this Earthly life, their soul will spend eternity is Hell, even those unfortunates who may have never heard of Christ.

SALVATION FOR THE DEAD

Scriptures used by some Christian faiths to substantiate their belief and teaching that those who did not hear of Christ and His teachings before death are doomed:

"Now that the dead are raised, even Moses shewed at the bush, when he calleth the Lord the God of Abraham, and the God of Isaac, and the God of Jacob. For he is not a God of the dead, but of the living: for all live unto him." **(Luke 20:37–38)**

"For the living know that they shall die: but the dead know not any thing, neither have they any more a reward; for the memory of them is forgotten." **(Ecclesiastes 9:5)**

NOW THE REST OF THE STORY . . . (scriptures that further explain or clarify the topic)

"For to this end Christ both died, and rose, and revived, that he might be *Lord both of the dead and living.*" **(Romans 14:9)**

"Else what shall they do which are *baptized for the dead*, if the dead rise not at all? Why are they then baptized for the dead?" **(1 Corinthians 15:29)**

"For this cause was the gospel preached to them that are dead, that they might be judged according to men in the flesh, but live according to God in the spirit." **(1 Peter 4:6)**

"For Christ also hath once suffered for sins, the just for the unjust, that he might bring us to God, being put to death in the flesh, but quickened by the Spirit: By which *he went and preached unto the spirits in prison*: Which sometimes are disobedient, when once the long-suffering of God waited in the days of Noah, while the ark was preparing, wherein few, that is, 8 souls were saved by water." **(1 Peter 3:18–20)**

> *Note: Why would Christ, during the three days He was dead and before His Resurrection, go to the "spirits in prison" and preach to them? Answer: because they cannot be judged for something they knew nothing about. They needed to be given knowledge of Christ and taught the gospel.*

"Jesus said unto her, I am the resurrection, and the life: *he that believeth in me, though he were dead, yet shall he live*: And whosoever liveth and believeth in me shall never die. Believest thou this?" **(John 11:25–26)**

"Verily, verily, I say unto you, He that heareth my word, and believeth on him that sent me, hath everlasting life, and shall not come into condemnation; but is passed from death unto life. Verily, verily, I say unto you, The hour is coming, and now is, *when the dead shall hear the voice of the Son of God: and they that hear shall live.*" **(John 5:24–25)**

"Therefore my heart is glad, and my glory rejoiceth: my flesh also shall rest in hope. For *thou wilt not leave my soul in hell*; neither wilt thou suffer thine Holy One to see corruption." **(Psalms 16:9–10)**

"For great is thy mercy toward me: and *thou hast delivered my soul from the lowest hell.*" **(Psalms 86:13)**

> *Note: In Psalms 16:9–10 and 86:13, David is rejoicing because God will not leave his soul in hell.*

"For David speaketh concerning him, I foresaw the Lord always before my face, for he is on my right hand, that I should not be moved: Therefore did my heart rejoice, and my tongue was glad; moreover also my flesh shall rest in hope: *Because thou wilt not leave my soul in hell*, neither wilt thou suffer thine Holy One to see corruption. Thou hast made known to me the ways of life; thou shalt make me full of joy with thy countenance. Men and brethren, let me freely speak unto you of the patriarch David, that he is both dead and buried, and his sepulchre is with us unto this day. Therefore being a prophet, and knowing that God had sworn with an oath to him, that of the fruit of his loins, according to the flesh, he would raise up Christ to sit on his throne; He seeing this before spake of the resurrection of Christ, *that his soul was not left in hell*, neither his flesh did see corruption." **(Acts 2:25–31)**

> *Note: God manifested it to David that he would someday leave hell and return to the Father in Heaven.*

"*And I saw the dead, small and great, stand before God*; and the books were opened: and another book was opened, which is the book of life: and *the dead were judged* out of those things which were written in the books, *according to their works.* And the sea gave up the dead which were in it; and death and hell delivered up the dead which were in them: and *they were judged every man according to their works.*" **(Revelation 20:12–15)**

See chapter 24: **"Heaven — Hell — Degrees of Glory"**
See chapter 40: **"Repentance"**
See chapter 7: **"Baptism for the Dead"**
See chapter 45: **"Salvation for All Mankind"**

CHAPTER 47

SATAN AND JESUS ARE BROTHERS

AND WE ARE THEIR
BROTHERS AND SISTERS

"Now there was a day when the sons of God came to present themselves before the Lord, and Satan came also among them." **(Job 1:6)**

This is a very controversial subject among Christian faiths. While The Church of Jesus Christ of Latter-Day Saints and the Bible teach that all of us, including the Savior and Satan, are the literal children of God the Father, other Christian faiths cannot fathom this concept and reject it.

Satan and Jesus are Brothers

And We Are Their
Brothers and Sisters

The name *Lucifer* means the "Shining One" or "Light-Bearer." He is also known as the "Son of the Morning." Lucifer is a spirit son of Heavenly Father and led the rebellion in the premortal life. The name *Lucifer* appears only once in the Bible in (Isaiah 14:12).

"Now there was a day when *the sons of God* came to present themselves before the Lord, and *Satan came also among them.*" (**Job 1:6**)

"Then the Lord answered Job out of the whirlwind, and said, Who is this that darkeneth counsel by words without knowledge? Gird up now thy loins like a man; for I will demand of thee, and answer thou me. Where wast thou when I laid the foundations of the earth? declare, if thou hast understanding. Who hath laid the measures thereof, if thou knowest? or who hath stretched the line upon it? Whereupon are the foundations thereof fastened? or who laid the corner stone thereof; *When the morning stars sang together,* and *all the sons of God shouted for joy?*" (**Job 38:1–7**)

"*How art thou fallen from heaven, O Lucifer, son of the morning!* how art thou cut down to the ground, which didst weaken the nations! For thou hast said in thine heart, I will ascend into heaven, I will exalt my throne above the stars of God: I will sit also upon the mount of the congregation, in the sides of the north: I will ascend above the heights of the clouds; I will be like the most High." (**Isaiah 14:12–14**)

"And there was war in heaven: Michael and his angels fought against the dragon; and the dragon fought and his angels, And prevailed not; neither was their place found any more in heaven. And the great dragon was cast out, that old serpent, called the Devil, and *Satan,* which deceiveth the whole world: *he was cast out into the earth, and his angels were cast out with him.*" (**Revelation 12:7–9**)

"And he said unto them, I beheld *Satan* as lightning *fall from heaven.*" (**Luke 10:18**)

See chapter 37: **"Premortal Existence of Spirits"**
See chapter 21: **"God — Who Is He?"**

CHAPTER 48

SEXUALITY

CHASTITY AND VIRTUE

ABORTION

HOMOSEXUALITY

& SEXUAL DECEPTION

"Blessed is the man that endureth temptation: for when he is tried, he shall receive the crown of life, which the Lord hath promised to them that love him. Let no man say when he is tempted, I am tempted of God: for God cannot be tempted with evil, neither tempteth he any man: But every man is tempted, when he is drawn away of his own lust, and enticed. Then when lust hath conceived, it bringeth forth sin: and sin, when it is finished, bringeth forth death. Do not err, my beloved brethren." **(James 1:12–16)**

Some Christians and their churches not only condone the homosexual lifestyle (LGBTQ), they ordain them as pastors, priests, and bishops. What does the Bible, which they consider to be holy scripture, say about this?

CHASTITY AND VIRTUE

Scriptures used by some Christian faiths to substantiate their belief and teaching in support of Chastity and Virtue are generally the same as LDS teachings.

NOW THE REST OF THE STORY . . . (scriptures that further explain or clarify the topic)

"This I say then, Walk in the Spirit, and *ye shall not fulfil the lust of the flesh.* For the flesh lusteth against the Spirit, and the Spirit against the flesh: and these are contrary the one to the other: so that ye cannot do the things that ye would. But if ye be led of the Spirit, ye are not under the law. Now *the works of the flesh are manifest, which are these; Adultery, fornication, uncleanness, lasciviousness,* Idolatry, witchcraft, hatred, variance, emulations, wrath, strife, seditions, heresies, Envyings, murders, drunkenness, revellings, and such like: of the which I tell you before, as I have also told you in time past, that *they which do such things shall not inherit the kingdom of God.*" (**Galatians 5:16–21**; see also **Ephesians 5**)

"But I say unto you, That whosoever looketh on a woman to lust after her hath committed adultery with her already in his heart." (**Matthew 5:28**)

"Having therefore these promises, dearly beloved, *let us cleanse ourselves from all filthiness of the flesh and spirit,* perfecting holiness in the fear of God." (**2 Corinthians 7:1**)

"That they may teach the young women to be sober, to love their husbands, to love their children, To be discreet, *chaste,* keepers at home, good, obedient to their own husbands, that the word of God be not blasphemed. Young men likewise exhort to be sober minded." (**Titus 2:4–6**)

"According as his divine power hath given unto us all things that pertain unto life and godliness, through the knowledge of him that hath called us to glory and *virtue:* Whereby are given unto us exceeding great and precious promises: that by these ye might be partakers of the divine nature, having escaped the corruption that is in the world through lust. And beside this, giving all diligence, *add to your faith virtue;* and to virtue knowledge." (**2 Peter 1:3–5**)

"In like manner also, that *women adorn themselves in modest apparel,* with shamefacedness and sobriety; not with broided hair, or gold, or pearls, or costly array; But (which becometh women professing godliness) with good works." (**1 Timothy 2:9–10**)

"Finally, brethren, whatsoever things are true, whatsoever things are honest, whatsoever things are just, *whatsoever things are pure,* whatsoever things are lovely, whatsoever things are of good report; *if there be any virtue,* and if there be any praise, *think on these things.*" (**Philippians 4:8**)

"Dearly beloved, I beseech you as strangers and pilgrims, *abstain from fleshly lusts*, which war against the soul." **(1 Peter 2:11)**

ABORTION

Scriptures used by some Christian faiths to substantiate their belief and teaching in support of Abortion:

"And the Lord God formed man of the dust of the ground, and breathed into his nostrils the breath of life; and man became a living soul." **(Genesis 2:7)**
> *Note: Some claim that life does not begin until the first breath.*

NOW THE REST OF THE STORY . . . (scriptures that further explain or clarify the topic)

"If men strive, and hurt a woman with child, so that her fruit depart from her, and yet no mischief follow: he shall be surely punished, according to the woman's husband and will lay upon him, and he shall pay as the judges determine. And *if any mischief follow, then thou shalt give life for life."* **(Exodus 21:22–23)**
> *Note: If a woman is harmed in any way that causes her to birth the child unnaturally and neither the mother nor the child is harmed there shall be restitution. But if the child does not survive and dies then serious consequences shall follow.*

HOMOSEXUALITY

Scriptures used by some Christian faiths to substantiate their belief and teaching in support of Homosexuality:

"Judge not, that ye be not judged. For with what judgment ye judge, ye shall be judged: and with what measure ye mete, it shall be measured to you again. And why beholdest thou the mote that is in thy brother's eye, but considerest not the beam that is in thine own eye? Or how wilt thou say to thy brother, Let me pull out the mote out of thine eye; and, behold, a beam is in thine own eye? Thou hypocrite, first cast out the beam out of thine own eye; and then shalt thou see clearly to cast out the mote out of thy brother's eye." **(Matthew 7:1–5)**

"There shall be *no whore* of the daughters of Israel, *nor a sodomite* of the sons of Israel. Thou shalt not bring the hire of a whore, or the price of a dog, into the house of the Lord thy God for any vow: for even *both these are abomination unto the Lord thy God.*" **(Deuteronomy 23:17–18)**

"*Thou shalt not lie with mankind, as with womankind*: it is abomination." **(Leviticus 18:22)**

"*If a man also lie with mankind, as he lieth with a woman, both of them have committed an abomination*: they shall surely be put to death; their blood shall be upon them." **(Leviticus 20:13)**

"The shew of their countenance doth witness against them; and they declare their sin as Sodom, they hide it not. *Woe unto their soul!* for they have rewarded evil unto themselves." **(Isaiah 3:9)**

"For this cause God gave them up unto vile affections: for even *their women did change the natural use into that which is against nature: And likewise also the men, leaving the natural use of the woman, burned in their lust one toward another; men with men* working that which is unseemly, and receiving in themselves that recompence of their error which was meet . . . Being filled with all unrighteousness . . . Who knowing the judgment of God, that they which commit such things are worthy of death, not only do the same, but have pleasure in them that do them." **(Romans 1:26–32**; verses 28, 30, and 31 omitted for brevity**)**

"Know ye not that *the unrighteous shall not inherit the kingdom of God?* Be not deceived: neither fornicators, nor idolaters, nor adulterers, nor effeminate, nor abusers of themselves with mankind." **(1 Corinthians 6:9)**

"For whoremongers, for them that *defile themselves with mankind*, for menstealers, for liars, for perjured persons, and if there be any other thing that is contrary to sound doctrine." **(1 Timothy 1:10)**

"Even as Sodom and Gomorrha, and the cities about them in like manner, giving themselves over to fornication, and *going after strange flesh*, are set forth for an example, suffering the vengeance of eternal fire. Likewise also *these filthy dreamers defile the flesh*, despise dominion, *and speak evil of dignities.*" **(Jude 1:7–8)**

"And Enoch also, the seventh from Adam, prophesied of these, saying, Behold, the Lord cometh with ten thousands of his saints, To execute judgment upon all, and to convince all that are ungodly among them of all their ungodly deeds which they have ungodly committed, and of all their hard speeches which ungodly sinners have spoken against him. These are murmurers, complainers, *walking after their own lusts*; and their mouth speaketh great swelling words, having men's persons in admiration because of advantage. But, beloved, remember ye the words which were spoken before of the apostles of our Lord Jesus Christ; How that *they told you there should be mockers in the last time, who should walk after their own ungodly lusts.* These be they *who separate themselves, sensual*, having not the Spirit." **(Jude 1:14–19)**

"Mortify therefore your members which are upon the earth; fornication, uncleanness, *inordinate affection*, evil concupiscence, and covetousness, which is idolatry: *For which things' sake the wrath of God cometh on the children of disobedience.*" (**Colossians 3:5–6**)

"*Blessed is the man that endureth temptation*: for when he is tried, he shall receive the crown of life, which the Lord hath promised to them that love him. Let no man say when he is tempted, I am tempted of God: for God cannot be tempted with evil, neither tempteth he any man: But *every man is tempted, when he is drawn away of his own lust*, and enticed. Then when lust hath conceived, it bringeth forth sin: and sin, when it is finished, bringeth forth death. Do not err, my beloved brethren." (**James 1:12–16**)

SEXUAL DECEPTION

Scriptures used by some Christian faiths to substantiate their belief and teaching in support of Sexual Deception:

"Judge not, that ye be not judged. For with what judgment ye judge, ye shall be judged: and with what measure ye mete, it shall be measured to you again. And why beholdest thou the mote that is in thy brother's eye, but considerest not the beam that is in thine own eye? Or how wilt thou say to thy brother, Let me pull out the mote out of thine eye; and, behold, a beam is in thine own eye? Thou hypocrite, first cast out the beam out of thine own eye; and then shalt thou see clearly to cast out the mote out of thy brother's eye." (**Matthew 7:1–5**)

NOW THE REST OF THE STORY . . . (scriptures that further explain or clarify the topic)

"*The woman shall not wear that which pertaineth unto a man, neither shall a man put on a woman's garment*: for all that do so are abomination unto the Lord thy God." (**Deuteronomy 22:5**)

> *Note: Do not dress in clothing of the opposite sex nor present yourself as a gender of which you are not for the purpose of sexual deception.*

OTHER SCRIPTURES YOU MAY WANT TO READ

2 Peter 2

CHAPTER 49

TEMPLES

"And whoso shall swear by the temple, sweareth by it, and by him that dwelleth therein." **(Matthew 23:21)**

Why don't other Christian faiths build temples, worship, and perform sacred ordinances to the Lord in them?

TEMPLES

Scriptures used by some Christian faiths to substantiate their belief and teaching questioning temples as "The House of the Lord":

"Howbeit the most High dwelleth not in temples made with hands; as saith the prophet, Heaven is my throne, and earth is my footstool: what house will ye build me? saith the Lord: or what is the place of my rest?" **(Acts 7:48–49)**

"God that made the world and all things therein, seeing that he is Lord of heaven and earth, dwelleth not in temples made with hands." **(Acts 17:24)**

"Know ye not that ye are the temple of God, and that the Spirit of God dwelleth in you? If any man defile the temple of God, him shall God destroy; for the temple of God is holy, which temple ye are." **(1 Corinthians 3:16–17)**

NOW THE REST OF THE STORY . . . (scriptures that further explain or clarify the topic)

"Go and tell my servant David, Thus saith the Lord, *Shalt thou build me an house for me to dwell in?*" **(2 Samuel 7:5)**

"And *let them make me a sanctuary; that I may dwell among them.*" **(Exodus 25:8)**

"Therefore thus saith the Lord; I am returned to Jerusalem with mercies: *my house shall be built in it,* saith the Lord of hosts, and a line shall be stretched forth upon Jerusalem." **(Zechariah 1:16)**

"Even *he shall build the temple of the Lord*; and he shall bear the glory, and shall sit and rule upon his throne; and he shall be a priest upon his throne: and the counsel of peace shall be between them both." **(Zechariah 6:13)**

"And he said unto me, Solomon thy son, *he shall build my house and my courts*: for I have chosen him to be my son, and I will be his father." **(1 Chronicles 28:6)**

"Moreover I will make a covenant of peace with them; it shall be an everlasting covenant with them: and I will place them, and multiply them, and *will set my sanctuary in the midst of them for evermore. My tabernacle also shall be with them*: yea, I will be their God, and they shall be my people." **(Ezekiel 37:26–27)**

"Afterward I came unto the house of Shemaiah the son of Delaiah the son of Mehetabeel, who was shut up; and he said, *Let us meet together in the house of God, within the temple,* and let us shut the doors of the temple: for they will come to slay thee; yea, in the night will they come to slay thee." **(Nehemiah 6:10)**

"One thing have I desired of the Lord, that will I seek after; that *I may dwell in the house of the Lord all the days of my life,* to behold the beauty of the Lord, and to inquire in his temple." **(Psalms 27:4)**

"And whoso shall swear by the temple, sweareth by it, *and by him that dwelleth therein.*" (**Matthew 23:21**)

"Do ye not know that they which minister about holy things *live of the things of the temple?* and they which wait at the altar are partakers with the altar?" (**1 Corinthians 9:13**)

"And what agreement hath the temple of God with idols? for ye are the temple of the living God; as God hath said, *I will dwell in them, and walk in them*; and I will be their God, and they shall be my people." (**2 Corinthians 6:16**)

"And *daily in the temple*, and in every house, they ceased not *to teach and preach Jesus Christ.*" (**Acts 5:42**)

"And they, *continuing daily with one accord in the temple*, and breaking bread from house to house, did eat their meat with gladness and singleness of heart, Praising God, and having favour with all the people. And the Lord added to the church daily such as should be saved." (**Acts 2:46–47**)

"And he led them out as far as to Bethany, and he lifted up his hands, and blessed them. And it came to pass, while he blessed them, he was parted from them, and carried up into heaven. And they worshipped him, and returned to Jerusalem with great joy: And were *continually in the temple*, praising and blessing God. Amen." (**Luke 24:50–53**)

> *Note: These were Christ's Apostles who were <u>continually</u> in the temple worshiping God.*

The following websites will help you to explain why Mormons build temples and what Mormons do in temples.

Why Mormons Build Temples

https://www.lds.org/church/temples/why-mormons-build-temples

What Mormons Do in Temples

http://www.ldsliving.com/Church-Video-Explains-Temple-in-2-Minutes/s/82804

CHAPTER 50

TITHING AND OFFERINGS

"Will a man rob God? Yet ye have robbed me. But ye say, Wherein have we robbed thee? In tithes and offerings. Ye are cursed with a curse: for ye have robbed me, even this whole nation. Bring ye all the tithes into the storehouse, that there may be meat in mine house, and prove me now herewith, saith the LORD of hosts, if I will not open you the windows of heaven, and pour you out a blessing, that there shall not be room enough to receive it." **(Malachi 3:8–10)**

Tithing to most Christian faiths is to "just drop in the collection plate" whatever you want. They do not follow the Biblical teaching that the word Tithe means 10% of your income.

Tithing & Offerings

"Will a man rob God? Yet ye have robbed me. But ye say, Wherein have we robbed thee? *In tithes and offerings.* Ye are cursed with a curse: for ye have robbed me, even this whole nation. Bring ye all the tithes into the storehouse, that there may be meat in mine house, and prove me now herewith, saith the Lord of hosts, if *I will not open you the windows of heaven, and pour you out a blessing, that there shall not be room enough to receive it."* **(Malachi 3:8–10)**

Now See the Further Blessings Promised . . .

"And I will *rebuke the devourer for your sakes,* and *he shall not destroy the fruits of your ground;* neither shall your vine cast her fruit before the time in the field, saith the Lord of hosts." **(Malachi 3:11)**

"And Melchizedek king of Salem brought forth bread and wine: and he was the priest of the most high God. And he blessed him, and said, Blessed be Abram of the most high God, possessor of heaven and earth: And blessed be the most high God, which hath delivered thine enemies into thy hand. *And he gave him tithes of all."* **(Genesis 14:18–20)**

"And Jacob vowed a vow, saying, If God will be with me, and will keep me in this way that I go, and will give me bread to eat, and raiment to put on, So that I come again to my father's house in peace; then shall the Lord be my God: And this stone, which I have set for a pillar, shall be God's house: and of all that thou shalt give me *I will surely give the tenth unto thee."* **(Genesis 28:20–22)**

"And all the tithe of the land, whether of the seed of the land, or of the fruit of the tree, *is the Lord's:* it is holy unto the Lord. And if a man will at all redeem ought of his tithes, he shall add thereto the fifth part thereof. And concerning the tithe of the herd, or of the flock, even of whatsoever passeth under the rod, *the tenth shall be holy unto the Lord.* He shall not search whether it be good or bad, neither shall he change it: and if he change it at all, then both it and the change thereof shall be holy; it shall not be redeemed. *These are the commandments,* which the Lord commanded Moses for the children of Israel in mount Sinai." **(Leviticus 27:30–34)**

"Thou shalt truly tithe all the increase of thy seed, that the field bringeth forth year by year. And thou shalt eat before the Lord thy God, in the place which he shall choose to place his name there, the tithe of thy corn, of thy wine, and of thine oil, and the firstlings of thy herds and of thy flocks; that thou mayest learn to fear the Lord thy God always." **(Deuteronomy 14:22–23)**

"Honour the Lord with thy substance, and with the firstfruits *of all thine increase:* So shall thy barns be filled with plenty, and thy presses shall burst out with new wine." **(Proverbs 3:9–10)**

"And the Lord spake unto Moses, saying, Thus speak unto the Levites, and say unto them, When ye take of the children of Israel the tithes which I have given you from them for your inheritance, then ye shall offer up an heave offering of it for the Lord, *even a tenth part* of the tithe." **(Numbers 18:25–26)**

"But woe unto you, Pharisees! *for ye tithe* mint and rue and all manner of herbs, and pass over judgment and the love of God: these ought ye to have done, and not to leave the other undone." **(Luke 11:42)**

"For this Melchisedec, king of Salem, priest of the most high God,.... To whom also Abraham gave a tenth part of all; . . . Now consider how great this man was, unto whom even the patriarch Abraham gave the tenth of the spoils. . . . *And verily they that are of the sons of Levi, who receive the office of the priesthood, have a commandment to take tithes of the people according to the law,* . . . And as I may so say, Levi also, who receiveth tithes, payed tithes in Abraham." **(Hebrews 7:1–9**; verses 3, 6, 7, and 8 omitted for brevity**)**

"And *as soon as the commandment came* abroad, the children of Israel brought in abundance the firstfruits of corn, wine, and oil, and honey, and of all the increase of the field; and *the tithe of all things brought they in abundantly."* **(2 Chronicles 31:5)**

CHAPTER 51

WHAT IS A SAINT?

"To all that be in Rome, beloved of God, called to be saints: Grace to you and peace from God our Father, and the Lord Jesus Christ." (**Romans 1:7**)

To most Christian faiths, a saint is an exalted person, one who has performed miracles, a person who because of these miracles has been canonized a saint by the church. The Bible teaches us that "saints" is the term used in the Bible describing those who belong to the Church of Christ.

WHAT IS A SAINT?

Many Christian faiths believe and teach that "saints" are God's elect on the earth, men and women who have lived exemplary, virtuous, and holy lives. Some Christian faiths venerate and pray to these "saints," asking them to intercede on their behalf with God.

NOW THE REST OF THE STORY . . . (scriptures that further explain or clarify the topic)

"Paul, an apostle of Jesus Christ by the will of God, to the *saints* which are at Ephesus, and to the faithful in Christ Jesus." **(Ephesians 1:1)**

"Unto the church of God which is at Corinth, to them that are sanctified in Christ Jesus, *called to be saints*, with all that in every place call upon the name of Jesus Christ our Lord, both theirs and ours." **(1 Corinthians 1:2)**

"For God is not the author of confusion, but of peace, as in all churches *of the saints*." **(1 Corinthians 14:33)**

"To all that be in Rome, beloved of God, *called to be saints*: Grace to you and peace from God our Father, and the Lord Jesus Christ." **(Romans 1:7)**

"Paul, an apostle of Jesus Christ by the will of God, and Timothy our brother, unto the church of God which is at Corinth, with all *the saints* which are in all Achaia." **(2 Corinthians 1:1)**

"Paul and Timotheus, the servants of Jesus Christ, to all *the saints* in Christ Jesus which are at Philippi, with the bishops and deacons." **(Philippians 1:1)**

"To the *saints* and faithful brethren in Christ which are at Colosse: Grace be unto you, and peace, from God our Father and the Lord Jesus Christ." **(Colossians 1:2)**

"Salute all them that have the rule over you, and all *the saints*. They of Italy salute you." **(Hebrews 13:24)**

Scripturally, the "saints" are the members of Christ's Church, nothing more and nothing less.

OTHER SCRIPTURES YOU MAY WANT TO LOOK AT

Revelations 13:7	Revelation 17:6	Acts 9:13
Revelations 15:3	Revelation 18:24	Romans 15:26
Revelation 16:6	Revelation 20:9	Ephesians 4:11–12

Appendix A

WHY MOST CHRISTIANS BELIEVE THE BIBLE

As Far as It Is Translated Correctly!

By Mark J. Stoddard
Meridian Magazine, January 19, 2016
[Included by permission from the author Mark J. Stoddard, January 6, 2017]

Bible believers are famous for their narrow views—"my interpretation of the Bible is right and you're wrong, and so you are not a Christian." But one thing they all seem to agree on is that the Bible is the Word of God **as far as it is translated correctly**.

Mormons quote Joseph Smith in the Wentworth Letter that, "We believe the Bible to be the word of God as far as it is translated correctly."

Why this is objectionable to other Bible believers is beyond me. The self-proclaimed protectors of the Bible think this demeans the Bible. But hold on. Mormons love the Bible despite translation problems so let's examine that Mormon idea and see if Mormons are unique in this belief.

While Jesus was hanging upon the cross a thief hanging next to him pled for divine recognition, to which Christ replied in the King James authorized translation of Luke 23:43, "Verily I say unto thee, Today shalt thou be with me in paradise."

Christ seemed to be saying that the thief would be with Jesus in a place called paradise this very day after their deaths.

But, what seems like a clear statement is controversial to some religions that don't believe in an afterlife paradise where souls go after death to await the judgments. Those religions point to a different translation of that verse that reads, "Verily I say unto thee today, *Thou shalt be with me in paradise.*" (Italics added.) Notice here that the *comma* is after the word "*today*" instead of before the word "today." That translation allows some religions to say that only after the final judgment will people be in paradise; that there is nothing in between; no purgatory or spirit prison; nothing.

But what this really shows is that a translation from Greek and other languages is subject to some ambiguities or differences of subtle opinion in how the translation should be. Or, stated rather obviously, they believe in their own translation. They claim the other translations are wrong.

Recently the Oxford Press released a massive rewrite or new translation of the Bible that is gender neutral. God is not male, in the Oxford, nor is there any patriarchal imagery or language. If one considers the *Oxford Press rewrite of the Bible* a proper translation, then one must reject the King James translation as well as many other versions, too. If you don't consider that gender neutral translation proper, then you consider it an improper translation. Uh oh.

Just as with the people who reject the translation of Christ's word by the translators of King James Version, then BOTH those who accept and reject the *Oxford Press* gender neutral version, believe the Bible to be the word of God as far as it is translated correctly. Whoops!

NonCatholic Christians believe the Catholic scholars erred by adding the Apocrypha (those writings of the Maccabees and others). Catholic scholars believe they were right in including the Apocrypha but omitting many other gospels used until the 5th century CE including the Infancy Gospels, Jewish Christian, Sayings, Passion and many more.

So all of the above religions, and scholars, believe the Bible is true provided the compilers were correct in which books/scrolls they included in The Book.

Which leads to another minor matter. Translating the sacred book's popular title, "The Bible," into "The Book" is either a renaming of the Bible, or a mistranslation of the Greek word for "Bible" which means "books." So a correct translation should be The Books. Picky, picky; so much so that the great Catholic scholar Thomas Acquinas who wrote Summa Theologica, (where he discusses how many angels could dance on the head of a pin) must be smiling at my pickiness.

Since virtually every Christian and Jew only believe the Old and or New Testaments to be the word of God as far as they are translated correctly, why are the Mormons singled out as the only ones who believe this concept? I think I know.

Simply put, they said the Bible is true where translated correctly first and don't like Joseph Smith getting the credit. Joseph Smith's declaration was not derogatory to the holy writ, but realistic and prophetic, for he knew that the Bible had not only undergone attempts by clerics to translate the Bible to fit their agenda, but that in the future—yes, Joseph was a Seer—Oxford and others would continue to retranslate, so he was warning us. The Mormons simply refuse to allow the multitude of translators to hem them into their agenda.

But to all of that—so what? It is a minor point and one every Christian should be able to agree upon.

More importantly, reading ANY translation of the Bible and then following it religiously, judiciously, and adamantly, would take a huge bite out of crime, poverty, intolerance and it would mean we would have to start loving our neighbors as our selves—although I'm not sure our neighbors could stand that much affection.

APPENDIX B

TWO PROTESTANT MINISTERS

The full-time missionaries for our ward called me in a panic. They had just knocked on the door of a Protestant minister and his wife. They were very friendly and told the missionaries that they would love to talk with them but that right now was not a good time. "Could you come back next Tuesday around 7 p.m.?" they asked. "We are both ministers and have a list of things that we would like to you about."

Both of these missionaries had been on their mission for about a year now and had stopped by my home many times asking me for help after they had been talking to someone on the street who had presented them with a scripture from the Bible supporting their churches belief; the missionaries did not know of a Bible scripture to support the LDS teaching regarding the doctrine they were discussing.

The question and fear on the missionaries' minds was, "How was this meeting going to go?" Was this couple really interested in learning about the LDS faith? Or were they setting up the missionaries for a full-frontal attack? "What will we do if they start attacking us? Neither one of us knows the Bible that well."

I promised the missionaries that I would be happy to go with them to talk to this couple. "Don't worry" I said, "I will not allow this to be anything but a friendly educational experience lesson for all."

On our way over to their home that Tuesday, the missionaries and I agreed that we would not use this meeting to try to teach a lesson to this couple; we would let them ask us their questions and do our best to answer them. If the missionaries did not feel comfortable with their Bible knowledge to answer a question, then I would help them.

We arrived and were welcomed into their home. When we sat down they had their Bibles out and a long list of items they wanted to discuss. We opened with a prayer, and a short get-to-know-each-other discussion. Both the husband and his wife had been searching for a church they felt comfortable attending, a church that taught what they believed. They had investigated five or six different Protestant churches over the years trying to find one that they felt comfortable with.

They told us that they had finally found one about a year ago, and as luck would have it for them, this church was looking for a full-time pastor. This was more than they could hope for, as being full-time ministers had long been a desire of theirs.

Immediately the questions started coming about LDS doctrine. Each question was followed with a scripture from the Bible supporting what they had been taught by their churches and their Protestant belief. Was the "attack the Mormons" Bible bash about to begin? The missionaries immediately gave me that look of "Help."

My answer to their first question and Bible scripture was, "You know, that is one of my favorite scriptures too." Big smiles on the husband and wife's part. I then gave them another scripture from the Bible and asked, "Have you ever thought about this scripture?" I then asked them to read the scripture aloud from their Bible. After they finished reading the scripture I then asked them, "What does this scripture mean to you?"

Silence for a little while . . . a little explanation . . . and then they answered with another Bible scripture on that subject. Again I said to them, "I like that scripture also." More big smiles. "What are your thoughts about this scripture?" I asked. And again, I let them read the scripture aloud and ponder it for a while. We then discussed what this scripture meant to them. The big smiles began to turn into looks of "this isn't going the way we planned."

This went on for an hour and a half of their asking questions, followed with scriptures presented by the minister couple to justify their belief and teachings, followed by Bible scriptures presented by the missionaries and me, that showed them what I call the "Rest of the Story" or "scriptures that correctly explained the doctrine and/or teaching." At no point did anyone Bible bash or attack the other. Each time when the husband or his wife would present a scripture from the Bible in an attempt to show us that their belief and their church's teaching was correct, and the LDS teaching or doctrine was wrong, we, in a friendly and non-confrontational manner, responded to them that we liked the scripture(s) they were showing us also, and then presented them with another scripture that further explained the teaching or doctrine and asked them what they thought about the scripture. Their response each and every time was wide-eyed amazement on their part, accompanied by that look of "this isn't going the way we planned."

That is, until the husband raised his voice and said, "This isn't fair!"

I answered, "I'm sorry, I don't understand."

Again he said, "This isn't fair! You have spent the last hour and a half showing us scriptures that clearly and fully explain every question we have presented to you; and none of the churches we have belonged to have ever shown us these scriptures or taught them to us." Then he said, "We definitely have to talk some more."

An appointment was made for the next week to come and visit with them again.

It became very obvious to the missionaries that if I had not been with them, or at least someone with a good understanding of Bible scripture, that this minister couple would have chewed them up and spit them out. This couple had a goal and a plan of attack, and it was to show these missionaries that they did not know what they were talking about, and hopefully shake up the testimony of the missionaries. The missionaries would have walked out of that meeting with their tails between their legs. Instead, we were able to participate in a calm and educational experience for all. It was the minister couple who were questioning their testimony of what they had been taught and what they were teaching others.

I want to make one thing clear: I am not a master of the Bible. I know concepts, I remember scriptures vaguely. But to quote them word for word or give you book, chapter and verse, it probably isn't going to happen. I just don't have the memory for it. During the time of this visit with this minister couple, I was in the process of writing this book. I had it on my iPad, listed by chapter and topic. I could quickly look up the chapter with the scriptures for the topic we were discussing. I had the tools I needed to do the task requested of me by the missionaries and passed on to me by the Holy Ghost. I take this book with me everywhere I go because I don't want to fail the Savior, nor do I want to fail the person(s) I am talking with and teaching. I don't want to have to explain to the Lord why I showed up unprepared for the task he had given to me.

Many missionaries are now using this book. Those who I have been fortunate enough to keep in contact with have all told me how much this book has helped them on their mission. How much it has helped them with their Bible knowledge. Our stake Mission Prep Class is using it to prepare our young adults for their mission. Our mission president has approved this book to be used by those missionaries he oversees.

This is why I wrote this book. To help our missionaries on their mission, to help those you will be teaching, and to help you to bring more of Heavenly Father's children back home to Him. Your mission will be successful, your mission experience will bring you and others much happiness. But only if you properly prepare yourself, work hard, and avail yourself with the tools that will grow your skills and testimony.

APPENDIX C

A NEW APPROACH TO TEACHING

This work is meant for educational and teaching purposes only. Please do not use it for the purpose of "Bible Bashing" or attacking any person's faith, convictions, or church. Use it only for teaching with the spirit.

When an investigator presents you with a Bible scripture, please, don't dispute or attack him or her with another, and by all means, do not argue. No one will learn in a hostile environment, it will only chase away the spirit.

Instead, politely acknowledge the scripture by telling them how much you like it also, and then present another scripture from the Bible and ask, "Have you thought about this scripture?" Hand them your Bible and let them read the scripture out loud to you; then ask them what the scripture means to them. Then if necessary, explain the scripture to them.

All discussions should always be with love, compassion, and understanding.

EXAMPLE #1

When someone starts attacking the church, our doctrines, etc., or just says "I don't believe what you Mormons believe," DON'T be combative. Instead ask them why they feel that way.

1. Politely ask them to help you to understand what it is they don't believe, what they don't like, or agree with about Mormon teachings.
2. Explain to them that you sincerely want to know (understand) what they believe and why.
3. Again, DON'T Attack. LISTEN to what they have to say.
4. Make note of what they have to say and any scriptures they may present to you.
5. If they do not give you scripture support for their position, ask for one, "Can you show me a scripture we could read?"

6. When presented with a scripture substantiating what they believe, be polite and agree with them. Say something like, "That's a great scripture—I like that one too."

7. Now present them with a scripture supporting LDS doctrine by asking, "Have you thought about this scripture (name the scripture)?"

8. Hand them your Bible and ask them to read it out loud to you.

9. Ask them, "What does this scripture mean to you?"

10. Ask them for their thoughts about the scripture they just read to you.

11. You could even say something like, "You know, I thought just like you, until someone showed me this scripture, and a few others."

12. At this point you could ask them to read another scripture or two on the topic.

13. Agree with them excitedly when their comments are positive and favor LDS doctrine.

14. Do this for every LDS topic of faith that they believe is different from what we believe.

15. If things are going smoothly and they are willing to continue talking with you, great.

16. If they don't have the time at the moment to continue talking with you, ask them if you could meet with them at a later time so that they could continue helping you to understand their faith, church, or what they believe.

17. Before leaving them say something like . . . "Thank you for sharing your thoughts with me/us. It's so interesting to understand what others believe and why they believe it. I/we look forward to learning more from you."

What you have just done here is . . .

1. Shown the person you are talking to that you are interested in what they have to say.

2. Shown the person you are talking to that you are not a threat.

3. Shown the person that you are not here to tell them that they are wrong.

4. Shown the person that you are sincerely interested in what they believe and why they believe it.

5. Given them something scripturally to think about.

EXAMPLE #2

You and your companion are tracting; you see someone and introduce yourselves. The person or persons immediately say to you, "I already belong to a church. I'm really not interested."

1. Don't just say "nice meeting you," and then walk away.

2. Say something like . . . "That's wonderful, what church do you belong to?"

When they tell you, say something like . . .

3. "I have always wanted to know what (the name of their church) believe. Do you have a few minutes to tell or teach me?"
4. "Do you have a few minutes to talk to me about the (name) church?"

Now go to "Example #1, Step 3 above and continue through Step 17.

EXAMPLE #3

You and your companion are tracting and someone you are talking to says, "You Mormons don't believe in the same God or the same Jesus we Christians believe in."

1. You then politely say, "I don't understand. Would you mind explaining what is different about the God / Jesus you believe in and the God / Jesus we believe in?"
2. They will probably say something like, "You Mormons believe in a God and Jesus that are two separate and distinct persons and not one essence and being as taught in the Trinity."
3. You now politely ask them, "Would you help me understand by showing me some Bible scriptures that say God and Jesus are one being and not separate individuals?"
4. After they show you or give you some scriptures stating that God and Jesus are one and the same being, you say, "I like that (those) scripture(s) too. Have you thought (or What do you think) about [the name of the scripture]?"
5. Now show them a scripture from the chapter "Godhead — Trinity — Three Separate Beings." Let them read it to you, and then ask them what the scripture means to them.
6. Listen to what they have to say.
7. If they disagree with the scripture you showed them, you may need to show them more scriptures.
8. Let them read the scriptures to you.
9. Again, ask them what the scripture means to them.
10. At some point, you may need to explain the scripture to them if they don't understand it.

Hopefully after you have shown them one or more scriptures, they will understand, accept the scripture(s) and agree you. If so, be excited for them. If needed show them some more scriptures.

Now would be a good time to explain to them when and how the concept of the Trinity came about.

EXAMPLE #4

You and your companion are tracting and someone you are talking to says, "You Mormons aren't Christians."

1. You then politely say, "I don't understand.... Would you mind explaining why you believe Mormons aren't Christians"?
2. You will probably be given an answer similar to Example #3 above.
3. You now politely ask them, "Would help me understand by showing me some Bible scriptures that demonstrate what you are talking about?"

EXAMPLE #5

You and your companion are tracting and you see someone unloading their car, or working in their yard. Maybe they could use a little help....

1. Politely and caringly ask them if they could use some help.
2. If so help them and when finished, introduce yourselves.
3. Do not use this approach unless the person(s) appear to really need some help.

EXAMPLE #6

And don't forget the straight forward and honest "Hi we are missionaries form the Church of Jesus Christ of Latter-Day Saints, I'm (your name) and this is my companion (his/her name).

1. Okay, Panic City, Now What Do I Do?! . . . Just kidding.

Now it is time to ask some questions. For example . . .

2. What do you know about the Church of Jesus Christ of Latter-Day Saints?
3. Would you be interested in learning about the LDS church?
4. If the answer is "yes," you know what to do.
5. If the answer is "no," ask them why.
6. Do you belong to a church? If so which one.
7. Do you go to church regularly?
8. Do you believe in God?
9. If the answer is "no," ask them why.
10. If the answer is "yes," ask them what they believe about God.
11. Do you believe or does your church teach that you are literally "a child of God"?
12. Do you know that the Bible actually teaches this?
13. Do you believe or does your church teach that you and your family can be together in Heaven forever? Would you like to know more?
14. Do you know that the Bible actually teaches this?

Think about other questions that you could ask. Write them down.

Other Phrases You Can Use . . .

"As missionaries, we are not here to convert you to our church. We are here to talk to you about what you believe and why you believe it, and if you are interested, we are here to talk to you about what we believe and why we believe it. In other words, we are here to learn from each other."

"Do you know that there are over 30,000 Christian faiths around the world? All teaching something different about the same God. Which one is correct? If they are all teaching something different, they can't all be correct."

"Do you know that there are over 50 English language versions of the Bible alone? And they all translate verses differently, changing the verse's meaning and doctrine."

CHAPTER NOTES

A Question of Faith

1. J. K. Rowling, *Harry Potter and the Goblet of Fire* (New York: Scholastic, 2002).

Introduction—Who — What — When — Where — Why — and How?

1. Hartman Rector Jr., "You Shall Receive the Spirit," *Ensign,* January 1974.

Chapter 4

1. Wikipedia, s.v. "Saint Timothy," last modified January 30, 2018, 18:43, https://en.wikipedia.org/wiki/Saint_Timothy.

Chapter 6

1. "Doctrine of Baptism," *St. John Cantius Parish,* accessed April 17, 2018, http://www.cantius.org/go/sacraments/baptism/doctrine_of_baptism.

Chapter 10

1. Wikipedia, s.v. "Development of the New Testament Canon," last modified March 26, 2018, 5:28, https://en.wikipedia.org/wiki/Development_of_the_New_Testament_canon.

Chapter 11

1. "What Is Sola Scriptura?" *Got Questions,* accessed April 17, 2018, https://www.gotquestions.org/sola-scriptura.html.

Chapter 18

1. Clayton Kraby, "CH Spurgeon and the FIve Solas of the Reformation," *Reasonable Theology,* accessed April 17, 2018, https://reasonabletheology.org/ch-spurgeon-and-the-five-solas-of-the-reformation.
2. Fr. Theodore Stylianopoulos, "How Are We Saved?" *Greek Orthodox Archdiocese of America,* November 2, 2012, www.goarch.org/-/how-are-we-saved-.
3. Dietrich Bonhoeffer, *The Cost of Discipleship,* Touchstone, 1st edition, September 1,1995
4. Wikipedia, s.v. "Sola Fide," last modified April 17, 2018, 16:08, https://en.wikipedia.org/wiki/Sola_fide.
5. Matt Slick, "The Didache," *Christian Apologetics & Research Ministry,* accessed April 17, 2018, https://carm.org/didache; Wikipedia, s.v. "First Epistle of Clement," last modified February 13, 2018, 4:27, https://en.wikipedia.org/wiki/First_Epistle_of_Clement

Chapter 20

1. Jeffrey R. Holland, "The Only True God and Jesus Christ Whom He Hath Sent," *Ensign,* November 2007.

Chapter 22

1. James E. Talmage, *Jesus the Christ,* (1916), 500.
2. Tim Dowley, ed., *Eerdman's Handbook to the History of Christianity* (Grand Rapids, MI: Eerdmans Publishing, 1977); J. N. D. Kelly, *Early Christian Doctrines,* rev. ed. (New York: HarperOne, 1978); Eugene Seaich, *Mormonism, the Dead Sea Scrolls, and the Nag Hammadi Texts* (Sounds of Zion, 1980).
3. Kelly, *Early Christian Doctrines.*
4. Ibid.

Chapter 25

1. John Trigilio Jr., *Catholicism for Dummies*, 2nd ed. (Hoboken, NJ: John Wiley & Sons, 2011).

Chapter 33

1. Alfred T. Overstreet, *Are Men Born Sinners? The Myth of Original Sin*, (Medford, OR: Evangel Books, 1995).

Chapter 37

1. Everett Ferguson, *Encyclopedia of Early Christianity*, 1st ed. (London: Routledge, 1990), 285.

Chapter 38

1. Wikipedia, s.v. "Universal Priesthood," last modified March 21, 2018, 1:18, https://en.wikipedia.org/wiki/Universal_priesthood.
2. Ibid.
3. Ibid.

Chapter 43

1. Keith A. Mathison, *The Shape of Sola Scriptura* (Moscow, ID: Canon Press, 2001), 161.

ACKNOWLEDGMENTS

Many have helped with this work and I wish to thank them all. None is more appreciated than my dear wife, Sandra. Without her encouragement, insight, and editing skills, this book may not have come to fruition.

I need to thank the many returned and active missionaries who contributed their requests, experiences, and knowledge. It is because of them that this book has been written.

I must thank John Burgon, first counselor in the Carlsbad California Mission Presidency, whom I have worked with for the past seven years in the San Diego Temple, who has spent countless hours reviewing this book as I have written and rewritten chapters. He has encouraged and motivated me to complete this work and to get it published.

I wish to thank the San Diego Temple workers who have helped in reviewing and making suggestions for the betterment of this effort.

I would also like to thank those at Cedar Fort who have contributed their skills to this work: Vikki Downs, for her help with marketing; Shawnda Craig, for her design work on the cover; Carolyn Nelson, for designing my website; Kathryn Watkins, for helping my book get accepted in the first place; and Kaitlin Barwick, for coordinating the editing of the manuscript.

There are three others that I am the most thankful for, for Their influence and guidance in writing this book. Without Their help, this book would never have come to pass: our Heavenly Father, His Son Jesus Christ, and the Holy Spirit.

Thank You.
Michael W. Grant

ABOUT THE AUTHOR

Michael Grant was preparing to become a Catholic priest when he was introduced to the Church of Jesus Christ of Latter-day Saints and the Book of Mormon. Initially, the Mormon missionaries got nowhere with him because they did not know the Bible scriptures that substantiated their doctrine. Once the missionaries found a member who knew the Bible, Michael learned that their doctrine was true.

On September 17, 1966, Michael was baptized and confirmed a member of The Church of Jesus Christ of Latter-Day Saints.

He served a two-year stake mission, taught Gospel Principles and Gospel Doctrine classes, served in the stake Sunday School presidency and high priest group leadership, and since 2009 has served as an ordinance worker in the San Diego California Temple.

Since his conversion to the LDS Church, Michael has regularly taught with the full-time missionaries and witnessed the same pattern over and over—investigators wanting support from the Bible and missionaries that only knew the Book of Mormon. It has since been Michael's goal to help the missionaries learn and teach LDS doctrine from the Bible.

Michael's professional life has been one of an entrepreneur and business owner. He has started and owned five businesses in the fields of aviation, electronics, and finance.

Michael and his wife live in Murrieta, California. They have six children and eleven grandchildren.

Scan to visit

booksbymichaelgrant.com

REGISTER YOUR BOOK!

Register your purchase on our website for FREE chapter updates,
teaching aids, and suggestions from missionaries and gospel teachers.